After the Revolution

After the Revolution

Profiles of Early American Culture

—

Joseph J. Ellis

—

W·W·Norton & Company

New York / London

The text of this book is composed in Linotype Caledonia with American
Type Founders Deepdene display type.
Composition by the Maple-Vail Book Manufacturing Group.
Manufacturing by the Haddon Craftsmen, Inc.
Book design by Cynthia Krupat.

For information about permission to reproduce selections from
this book, write to Permissions, W. W. Norton & Company, Inc.,
500 Fifth Avenue, New York, NY 10110

Library of Congress Cataloging-in-Publication Data
Ellis, Joseph J.
    After the revolution.
    Includes bibliographical references and index.
    1. United States—Civilization—1783–18.65. 2. Intellectuals—
United States—Biography. I. Title.
E164.E4   1979   920'.073   79–16771

ISBN 0-393-32233-5

W. W. Norton & Company, Inc.
500 Fifth Avenue, New York, N.Y. 10110
www.wwnorton.com

W. W. Norton & Company Ltd.
Castle House, 75/76 Wells Street, London W1T 3QT

2 3 4 5 6 7 8 9 0

For Toni and Peter

Contents

Preface

The pages that follow are concerned with the American Revolution, with the generation of Americans that came of age during the revolutionary crisis, with the expectations they harbored for the future of American culture, and with their responses when that future failed to materialize. After attempting to identify the rapidly changing social conditions and values of revolutionary America, I try to tell the story of four men whose lives grew out of that social context: Charles Willson Peale, an artist; Hugh Henry Brackenridge, a novelist; William Dunlap, a dramatist and theater manager; and Noah Webster, an educator, linguist, and all-purpose polemicist. Each of these men believed that the American Revolution was more than a war for colonial independence. Each expected the Revolution to alter American society in fundamental ways. Each thought that the Revolution would remove long-standing constraints to national development and thereby unleash vast reservoirs of untapped energy within American society and within individual personalities. Each believed that postrevolutionary America would become the cultural as well as the political capital of the world. As incongruous as it may sound to us, who know about Hollywood, best-sellers, television ratings, and popular taste, each of these eighteenth-century Americans assumed that the people-at-large would eagerly support American artists, poets, and playwrights who would soon rival Rembrandt, Milton, and Shakespeare.

Expectations this excessive, you might say, are doomed from the start. But the belief that revolutionary America was on the verge of a cultural explosion appears nonsensical to us mainly because we know it did not happen. Eighteenth-century Americans not only lacked the advantage of such hindsight but also operated from a set of assumptions that made the vision of American cultural ascendancy seem quite plausible. The critical assumption, which gained widespread currency in the middle of the eighteenth century and then grew in acceptance during and after the Revolution, concerned the vitalizing, almost miraculous power of individual freedom. The position in which the American colonists found themselves when Parliament began to impose taxes in 1764 heightened this concern by encouraging a stark contrast between the debilitating impact of arbitrary power and the liberating effect of free choice. As David Ramsay put it in 1789, the conflict with England "gave a spring to the active powers of the inhabitants, and set them on thinking, speaking and acting far beyond that to which they had been accustomed."[1] American colonists began to envision severance from the empire as the splitting of an atom, initiating a chain reaction with unprecedented consequences for politics, trade, and the arts. The Abbé Raynal, a French *philosophe* who a few years earlier had described North America as a cultural desert, confessed that the American Revolution released pent-up national energies that required him to alter his analysis. "A new Olympus, a new Arcady, a new Athens, a new Greece will perhaps give birth on the continent . . . to new Homers," he predicted in 1778. "Perhaps there will be another Newton in New England. It is in British America, let there be no doubt," Raynal proclaimed, "that the first rays of knowledge are to shine. . . ."[2]

By the 1830s there was no doubt that Raynal's prediction had not come true. Virtually every contemporary commentator felt obliged to note that, whatever else America had contributed to the world, as a cultural capital she was a miserable disappointment. In Scotland the caustic wit of Sydney Smith mocked American pretensions with a series of rhetorical questions that have continued to echo through the ages. "In the four quarters of the globe," asked Smith, "who reads an American book? or goes to an American play? or looks at an American picture or statue?"[3] The answer, of course, was "Nobody." Frances Trollope explained why in her *Domestic Manners of the Americans* (1832) when she described American art and literature as "trash" and a "mass of slip-slop."[4]

Although both Smith and Trollope could be—and often were —dismissed as prejudiced witnesses, their negative judgment was confirmed by some of America's staunchest supporters. "It must be acknowledged," wrote Alexis de Tocqueville, "that in few of the civilized nations of our time have the higher sciences made less progress than in the United States; and in few have great artists, distinguished poets, or celebrated writers been more rare."[5] Ralph Waldo Emerson faced the issue with accustomed candor and with unaccustomed clarity. "This country has not fulfilled what seemed the reasonable expectation of mankind," he told a Dartmouth audience in 1838. "Men looked, when all feudal straps and bandages were snapped asunder, that nature, too long the mother of dwarfs, should reimburse itself by a brood of Titans, who should laugh and leap in the continent and run up the mountains. . . . But the mark of American merit in painting, in sculpture, in poetry, in fiction, in eloquence, seems to be a certain grace without grandeur, and itself not new but derivative, a vase of fair outline, but empty. . . ."[6]

The chapters that follow do not constitute an extended quarrel with this verdict. I did not set out to discover any long-lost American masterpieces, and, to the best of my knowledge, I have not stumbled across any in the course of my research. The book does try to identify the obstacles that aspiring artists and writers faced, thereby suggesting some of the reasons why few works of high culture from that era compel the admiration of critics today. But my central concern has been historical rather than aesthetic. I do not mean to juxtapose these two concerns, for I consider them inseparable. But I do believe that our ability to appreciate a poem or play or painting depends heavily on our understanding of its time and place—which is to say that I am most interested in understanding these men and their works within the historical context of postrevolutionary America.

Even that limited goal establishes a rather imposing set of dual obligations. On the one hand, the generation of Americans who came of age during the American Revolution found themselves growing old in a world drastically different from the one they had entered. The political differences, all a consequence of the successful Revolution, are obvious: America had changed from a dependent colony ruled by an English monarch and Parliament to an independent nation with its own republican government. But the American Revolution also accelerated a long train of social and attitudinal changes that had their origins in the decades before American separation from the empire. A complex constellation of traditional assumptions about the limits required on personal freedom, the dangers of excessive wealth, the need for self-control, and the primacy of communal responsibility were eroding in the face of demographic and economic expansion. In its place emerged a new network of convictions that have since been enshrined as articles of faith in the liberal creed: these include the belief in individual autonomy and self-expression, a commitment to equality of opportunity and a fond hope that it will lead to social equality, homage to the principles of popular sovereignty and social mobility, and the presumption that there is a rough correlation between talent and the possession of material wealth. All Americans, artists and authors as well as farmers, merchants, and politicians, were affected by this major transformation. In fact, the extravagant cultural expectations and the corresponding disappointments and self-proclaimed cultural failures of the revolutionary generation are incomprehensible unless rooted firmly in this social context. The first two chapters of the book represent my effort to explain that context.

On the other hand, every member of the revolutionary generation is an intricate microcosm with a story all its own, fully as complicated as the history of a nation or society. A personality is invariably comprised of innumerable strands, hues, shadings, and textures, which converge to form a pattern of behavior that is more than a mere reflection of prevailing social conditions, more than an incidental piece of datum conjured up to support a generalization. One must certainly be cognizant of the broad, long-range social currents that sweep a life along, but simultaneously recognize that the rich particularities of a specific life must not be shoved gracelessly into grandiose categories that obliterate its idiosyncracies and therefore its humanity. Isaiah Berlin's celebrated distinction accurately describes my own temperamental leanings here: the historian must be part hedgehog and part fox; that is, he must know "one big thing" and several "little things," must pursue a unifying vision while remaining sensitive to the peculiarities and the bedeviling varieties of his subject.[7] The four biographical chapters represent my effort to illustrate the central intellectual problem of the era and to do so in a way that does justice to the complexity and human charm of each distinctive personality.

Each of my profiles describes men who were also torn by dual allegiances, though not the same ones that afflict contemporary historians. In the specialized language of the social sciences, they were "premodern" men, meaning that their lives coincided with the emergence of modern social conditions—democratic politics, a capitalistic economy on the verge of industrialization, an individualistic psychology, a society committed to growth rather than to stability. But these categories and labels have an abstract quality; they hover over the era like Platonic forms or Emersonian oversouls. Unless clothed in the flesh and blood of real human beings, they remain lifeless forces lacking the capacity to advance understanding. Each of the personalities encountered in subsequent pages reveals how complicated and paradoxical the adjustment to modern institutions and values really was. Like most men, as they moved one foot forward into the future they left the other firmly planted in the past. This left them straddling a great divide, a somewhat awkward posture in theory but one that in practice possessed a grace and integrity all its own. If the historians of modernization often make social change seem like a streamlined express that glides effortlessly from one station in time to another, I hope these profiles convey a fuller sense of the journey itself, with all the bumps, emergency stops, backward glances, and apprehensions about the final destination. In their ambivalence, their inconsistency, their capacity for irony, and their expressions of fear and hope toward the idea of progress, they might even look familiar to our age.

Yet, in the end, they were creatures of their own time. No member of the revolutionary generation, for example, would have understood our modern definition of "culture." Noah Webster defined the term for his age without even hinting at our modern notion of culture as a distinctive region of insight or sensibility segregated from the mundane activities of everyday life. For Webster, culture referred to farming; it was "the act of tilling and preparing the earth for crops; cultivation; the application of labor or other means of improvement."[8] As Raymond Williams has shown, the history of the word "culture" is a fascinating record of verbal and intellectual adaptation to the social and economic changes of the modern world.[9] No late-eighteenth-century American had the need for a word referring to a separate sphere of refined human activity, because it was presumed that the arts would flourish in the free and open air of the marketplace alongside all other human activities. Artistic, political, social, and economic development were not conceived of as autonomous spheres or disciplines; they were all interrelated. The absence of established disciplinary boundaries allowed men and women to speculate freely about the relationship between civil liberty and literature, the arts and economic growth, social equality and language. There was no presumed tension between artistic values on the one hand and public opinion or the values of the marketplace on the other. The market, in fact, was regarded as the benign environment in which the unrestricted movement of men and ideas would create exciting new cultural possibilities. These Americans had not yet learned to think in the same categories that we do.

•

Specialization and the acceptance of discreet disciplinary borders are now established ways of approaching knowledge. In the course of my research and writing I have crossed over several of these borders and have tried to learn as much as possible about the local terrain. Permanent residents of the various regions have frequently provided aid, comfort, and maps of the territory. With their assistance I have tried to roam widely, exploring art, fiction, drama, political and educational philosophy, as well as the scholarly literature generated by social and intellectual historians of the era. If I have unknowingly overlooked a major landmark, taken a wrong turn, or stumbled clumsily into a well-known pitfall, it is probably because I have often used the excellent directions of others in order to go my own way. In my defense, I did try to keep my eyes open as I traveled and to spend enough time in each place to qualify as something more than a tourist.

I began working on this project in 1971, then put my notes aside for three years in order to write a book on the United States Military Academy and the problems of the American army after Vietnam. As it turned out, the two topics were not as dissimilar as they first seemed. Contemporary concerns and historical interests are seldom separable, and in my case the disillusionment that followed the Vietnam War, the waning of political activism, the decline of enthusiasm for social reform, and, more generally, the increased pessimism concerning the viability of liberal institutions and ideals—all these developments affected my perception of the revolutionary generation. Whether my preoccupation with disillusionment and my fascination with irony and paradox are present-minded distortions or insights into the eighteenth century rendered possible by our recent history, I must leave for the reader to judge. I admit to feeling a special kinship with each of the personalities described in the following pages. Although it is now a cliché of modern psychology to observe that we are all bundles of contradictions, the special pattern of irreconcilable polarities I discern in these late-eighteenth-century characters is both distinctive and, at least to me, familiar. I hope that I have written a book in which these personalities come alive for others too, not only as illustrations of postrevolutionary American culture but also as recognizable human beings with a vitality and immediacy possible only in a life being lived.

My own life was made considerably easier when the National Endowment for the Humanities provided financial support in the form of a summer stipend and then a fellowship that allowed me to take a year off from teaching duties in 1975–76. It often occurred to me that this was just the kind of federal assistance that Peale and Dunlap kept pleading for. A grant from Mount Holyoke College helped defray duplication and typing expenses. Sibley Hoobler made his marvelous accommodations in northern Michigan available for two summers, so that I could write a paragraph in the morning and cast to a rising trout that evening. Thanks are also due the librarians and staff of the following institutions: the American Philosophical Society, the Library of Congress, the Hampshire Inter-Library Consortium, The New-York Historical Society, the New York Public Library, the William Allan Neilson Library at Smith College, the Western Pennsylvania Historical Society, the United States Military Academy Library, and the Yale University Library. A special debt of gratitude is owed to Anne Edmonds and Nancy Devine of the Williston Library at Mount Holyoke College.

The book benefited from the criticism of many colleagues and friends. The Five-College Faculty Seminar in American Studies offered many suggestions about how to handle Noah Webster. Three members of my seminar in early American culture at Mount

Holyoke—De Dee Dillworth, Elizabeth Fisher, and Tara Fitz-patrick—provided especially insightful comments on the early sections of the book. Chapters or chapter-sized segments of the manuscript were read by Susanna Barrows, Richard Buel, Stephen Ellenburg, James Ellis, Everett Emerson, Ann Foley, Robert Gross, Grant Holcomb, Linda Kerber, Bruce Kuklick, Ben Reid, Mary Rountree, Robert Schwartz, Charles and Margot Trout, David Truman, and Gordon Wood. All or most of the manuscript was read, in some cases several times, by Richard Johnson, William McFeely, Edmund Morgan, Stephen Nissenbaum, and Jack Wilson, good friends as well as exacting scholars who did me the service of blending candid criticism with personal encour-agement. As far as I can tell, not a single one of my critical readers agreed with all that I said or my way of saying it. While others deserve part of the credit for whatever is good in the book, I am responsible for the rest.

Catharine LaRose and Kathleen Heath were responsible for reading my scrawl—I can't type—and typing the several drafts. James Mairs ushered the manuscript through W. W. Norton with dispatch and grace; Judith Sonntag at Norton caught most of my stylistic gaffes and had the courage to tell me what she thought of the whole thing. Antonia Woods Ellis read each draft and made editorial suggestions at crucial stages of the revisions. More important, she helped me to fit the writing into a comfortable rhythm of work and play that kept me and the book in daily con-tact with common sense. Peter Woods Ellis, born while the book was being wrirtten, sits beside me at this moment, drawing and coloring on my scrap paper and serving as a model of scholarly concentration.

J.J.E.

South Hadley, Massachusetts

Part One

Premonitions and Paradoxes in the Revolutionary Era

❧✦

If there is any period one would desire to be born in, is it not the age of Revolution; when the old and the new stand side by side and admit of being compared; when the energies of all men are searched by fear and by hope; when the historic glories of the old can be compensated by the rich possibilities of the new era? This time, like all times, is a very good one, if we but know what to do with it.

Ralph Waldo Emerson, *The American Scholar* (1837)

Chapter One

Premonitions:

An American Athens

❧❦

When a great question is first started, there are very few,
even of the greatest minds, which suddenly and intu-
itively comprehend it, in all its consequences.

John Adams, *Novanglus* (1774)

During the middle decades of the eighteenth century there began
to appear, for the first time, published prophecies of imminent
American cultural greatness. The word "culture" was never used.
Writers referred instead to the fine arts, the arts and sciences,
belles lettres, or the muses. Nor was the total number of pamphlet and essays devoted primarily to cultural questions very
large. Religion remained the most written about subject in prerevolutionary America, and even after the passage of the Stamp
Act in 1765, when political and constitutional issues began to
claim a greater share of readers' attention, theological and ecclesiastical publications still dominated the lists. What merits attention, however, is not the relatively small number of writings on
cultural subjects but the extremely optimistic character of the
comments that were made.

The initial celebration of America's cultural prospects seems
to have accompanied, or at least coincided with, the end of the
French and Indian War. In 1758, for example, an elderly Connecticut woman named Martha Brewster, who described herself

as "a humble widow," published a collection she called *Poems on Diverse Subjects*. One of them, entitled "A Dream," described her vision of a future in which Americans dominated the world in philosophy, literature, and the arts; her grandsons, she predicted, would come of age in an America bursting with creative genius. There were "Four Ages of Man," she observed, the "budding, blooming, ripening, withering States," and the English colonies in North America were moving rapidly toward their age of bloom.[1] The following year the *New American Magazine* appeared in Woodbridge, New Jersey; its editor, who wrote under the pseudonym "Sylvanus Americanus," described himself as a combination of Virgil and Cicero. He foresaw the emergence of an Augustan Age "this side the Atlantic" now that the French had been defeated and the continent was safely under the aegis of English influence.[2] In Boston that same year Jonathan Mayhew, the leading liberal minister of the day, proclaimed that providence had vanquished the French menace and thereby paved the way for "a mighty empire . . . in numbers little inferior perhaps to the greatest in Europe, and in felicity to none." Mayhew saw a bucolic empire of "happy fields and villages," but he also conjured up the image of a "spacious kingdom of learning" where poetry and philosophy would coexist with "the purest religion since the time of the apostles."[3]

When news of the total defeat of the French armies in Canada reached the colonies in 1760, it touched off another round of effusive declarations. Ezra Stiles delivered a thanks-giving sermon to his congregation in Newport, Rhode Island, and focused on the propitious signs that "this Land may be renowned for Science and Arts." Stiles did not specify the time when cultural greatness would arrive, but he did indicate that it was both imminent and inevitable. "Not only science, but the elegant Arts are introducing apace," he noted, "and in a few years we shall have . . . Painting, Sculpture, Statuary, but first of all the greek Architecture in considerable Perfection among us."[4] In Philadelphia a young graduate of the Pennsylvania Academy by the name of Francis Hopkinson put the same vision to verse:

> *Fair Science softning, with reforming Hand,*
> *The native Rudeness of a barbarous Land*

It must be so, prophetic Fancy cries,
See other Popes, *and other* Shakespeares *rise.*[5]

Hopkinson not only wrote poems; he also composed songs, played musical instruments, and painted portraits, as if he were anticipating that several of the muses would pay him a personal visitation. His friend and classmate, Nathaniel Evans, predicted that Philadelphia was the worthy successor to London and Rome as the cultural capital of the world:

> *O would the Muses, sweet celestial Maids!*
> *In this fair Land vouchsafe to fix their Seat,*
>
> .   .   .
>
> *Much do we need their Aid, and sacred Lore,*
> *To virtuous Acts to animate the Soul.*[6]

Meanwhile, Philadelphia's most prominent resident wondered why America had not already surpassed England in the arts. "Why should that petty Island," asked Benjamin Franklin, "which compar'd to America is but like a stepping Stone in a Brook, scarce enough of it above Water to keep one's Shoes dry; why, I say, should that little Island, enjoy in almost every Neighbourhood, more sensible, virtuous and elegant Minds, than we can collect in ranging 100 Leagues of our vast Forests?" Although Franklin did not answer his own question, he expressed confidence that the passage of time would work to America's advantage: " 'Tis said," he coyly observed, "the Arts delight to travel Westward."[7]

Franklin was merely reiterating an old and venerable idea, which had its roots in classical Greece and Rome, had been reasserted by European historians and scholars during the Renaissance, and had been advocated sporadically by a few American colonists in the seventeenth and early eighteenth centuries. Known as the *translatio studii* or the *translatio imperii*, the idea was simple: namely, that civilization, like the sun, moved from east to west and that the North American continent was therefore destined to become the habitat for the arts and sciences at some unspecified time in the future. John Winthrop borrowed from this theme in his *Modell of Christian Charity* (1630) when he described the Puritan settlements in New England as the providential locus of the kingdom of God on earth. Winthrop's vision was religious rather than cultural, but it depicted the New World as a favored environment in which cherished values that were dead or dying in England and Europe would flourish once again. In 1725 Jeremiah Dummer, another New Englander who defended the providential character of the region, observed that "religion & polite learning have bin travelling westward ever since their first appearance in the World" and predicted that "they won't rest until they have fixt their chief Residence in Our part of the World."[8]

The most eloquent and popular expression of this idea was written in 1726 by the Anglican divine George Berkeley. In his "Verses on the Prospect of Planting Arts and Learning in America," Berkeley had described the New World as the ideal environment for the flowering of the arts and sciences, the worthy heir of the cultural traditions established by the Greeks, continued by the Romans during the reign of Augustus, and most recently nourished in England from the late sixteenth to the early eighteenth centuries. In the grand cyclical pattern of civilization, Berkeley asserted, there was a continual rising and falling of empires and a discernible westward drift to the movement of history. This boded well for the American colonies:

> *There shall be sung another golden age,*
> *The rise of empire and of arts,*
> *The good and great inspiring epic rage,*
> *The wisest heads and noblest hearts.*
>
> *Not such as Europe breeds in her decay;*
> *Such as she bred when fresh and young,*
> *When heavenly flame did animate her clay,*
> *By future poets shall be sung.*
>
> *Westward the course of empire takes its sway;*
> *The first four acts already past,*
> *A fifth shall close the drama with the day;*
> *Time's noblest offspring is the last.*[9]

Berkeley's imagery rested on several key assumptions worthy of notice because they were shared by prominent American commentators like Franklin and Stiles. First, Berkeley presupposed a close connection between what he called "the rise of empire and of arts." In other words, he assumed an unbreakable association between political and economic development and the development of high culture. Only a society with burgeoning political, economic, and military power could be expected to product first-rate art and literature in great abundance. Second, he posited a kind of global conservation-of-cultural-energy principle: namely, only one nation could possess the requisite ingredients for artistic greatness at any one moment in history. The muses traveled in a flock; they left one country *en masse* when it began to decline, flew west, then landed in a rising nation-state. Third, Berkeley described the movement of civilization toward America in terms that were at once optimistic and fatalistic. The imminent migration of the arts and learning across the Atlantic was part of a grand historical design outside of human control. Americans were destined to be its beneficiaries whether they liked it or not.

Although it was written in 1726 and published in 1752, Berkeley's poem did not receive widespread circulation in the colonial press until the late 1750s and early 1760s. Its popularity, in short, was part of the upsurge of interest in America's cultural prospects that surfaced in the years immediately preceding the constitutional crisis with England. Berkeley's verses did not *cause* this upsurge of interest; as the most graceful expression of the belief in American cultural ascendancy, it was simply the best remembered and most frequently cited version of an increasingly popular theme. Andrew Burnaby, who traveled through the middle colonies in 1759, reported that "an idea strange as it is visionary, has entered into the minds of the generality of mankind, that empire is travelling westward; and everyone is looking forward with eager and impatient expectation to that destined moment. . . ." John Adams recalled that "the observation that arts, sciences, and empire had travelled westard" was a commonplace when he was a young lawyer in Massachusetts, "and in conversation it was always added since I was a child, that the next leap would be over the Atlantic into America."[10]

In the years between the Peace of Paris (1763) and the Declaration of Independence, the assertion that America was predestined to burst forth in a sudden frenzy of artistic and literary creativity appeared in several different guises. Berkeley's poem, often accompanied by editorials endorsing its uplifting message, cropped up sporadically in colonial newspapers and magazines. Traveling actors recited addresses on the theme before the start of plays in makeshift theaters. Ministers committed to a millennial view of history periodically made reference to the prominence of the arts under Christ's thousand-year reign. Whig political pamphlets occasionally included the claim that imperial taxation policies were but another sign of English degeneration and decline that would drive the muses toward America. Even English commentators referred to the inevitable rise of American culture. In 1774 *Lloyd's Evening Post* of London printed an account of two Americans who visited the city two hundred years later and found it in ruins, much like Rome. "The next Augustan age will dawn on the other side of the Atlantic," wrote Horace Walpole. "There will, perhaps, be a Thucydides at Boston, a Xenophon at New York, and, in time, a Virgil at Mexico." But most published discussions of high culture in America, it should be noted, were brief asides made in passing, part of an essay or sermon devoted to another topic.[11]

There were two prominent exceptions. In September of 1770 John Trumbull read *An Essay on the Use and Advantages of the Fine Arts* to the graduating class at Yale. Trumbull's version of cultural history followed the conventional formula: he located the source of the arts in classical Greece; then the muses appeared in Rome with Augustus, Cicero, and Horace; then they emerged in Renaissance Italy; and then the arts blossomed again in Elizabethan England with the appearance of Spenser and Shakespeare. There was "a short eclipse [during] the luxurious reign of Charles II," but the emergence of Pope and Addison signaled that English culture had revived and "shone forth with superior brightness in the prosperous days of William and Anne."

Trumbull placed a great deal of emphasis on the connection between high culture and what he called "the unconquered spirit of freedom." Under oppressive regimes and arbitrary rulers like Charles II, the arts tended to atrophy. But when governments adopted liberal policies "the fine Arts have been studiously cultivated and hath shined forth with peculiar lustre." He claimed, for example, that the American opposition to the Stamp Act and to

English imperial policies "have awakened the spirit of freedom" and thereby demonstrated that America was fertile ground for creative artists. He concluded with a rapturous poetic vision *à la* Berkeley:

> *In mighty pomp America shall rise;*
> *Her glories spreading to the boundless skies;*
> *Of ev'ry fair, she boasts the assembled charms;*
> *The Queen of Empires and the Nurse of Arms.*

> *See bolder Genius quit the narrow shore,*
> *And unknown realms of science dare t'explore;*
> *Hiding in the brightness of superior day*
> *The fainting gleam of Britain's setting ray.*

> *This land her Steele and Addison shall view,*
> *The former glories equal'd by the new;*
> *Some future Shakespeare charm the rising age*
> *And hold in magic chains the listning stage.*[12]

The other full-scale exploration of the role of the arts in America was also a commencement address, this one delivered at Princeton in 1771 and published in Philadelphia the following year. Written by two graduating seniors, Hugh Henry Bracken-ridge and Philip Freneau, *A Poem on the Rising Glory of America* neatly summarized the arguments offered by various champions of American cultural ascendancy during the preceding decade. Brackenridge and Freneau also traced the transit of culture from Athens to Rome to England; they too proclaimed that the inevitable next stop was America:

> *we too shall boast*
> *Our Alexanders, Pompeys, heroes, kings*
> *That in the womb of time yet dormant lye*
> *Waiting the joyful hour for life and light.*

The time was rapidly approaching, they assured their listeners, when there would be a new Pope writing classical verse by the Schuylkill River and a new Hampden by the Susquehanna. More-over, the young prophets sounded like millennialists when they claimed that America's reign of cultural supremacy would last exactly one thousand years. And when it ended, human history would also cease: America was "the final stage . . . of high invention and wond'rous art,/Which not the ravages of time shall waste."[13]

Like Trumbull, Brackenridge and Freneau exalted the miraculous influence of freedom. The muses could only sing, they claimed, "where freedom holds the sacred standard high." History was like a westward-moving caravan, a wagon train in which political, military, and cultural greatness were linked together and freedom provided the fuel. Brackenridge and Freneau were even more specific: the particular kind of freedom most efficacious was commercial freedom, the freedom to trade. Each and every cultural accomplishment, they wrote,

> *Derives her grandeur from the pow'r of trade.*
>
> .   .   .
>
> *For commerce is the mighty reservoir*
> *From whence all nations draw the streams of gain.*
> *'Tis commerce joins discover'd worlds in one.*[14]

It was an unwieldy and implausible combination. Providence, the millennium, freedom, commerce, culture—all quite large and intractable concepts—were fused together in *Rising Glory* and molded into yet another exuberant forecast of American leadership in the arts. Where, one might reasonably ask, were all these ideas coming from? How and why did such optimism originate in prerevolutionary America? Given the paucity of the previous colonial contribution to the arts and sciences, how could such extravagant expectations achieve credibility?

·

One conclusion seems incontrovertible: American cultural expectations were *not* based on a mounting list of past literary and artistic accomplishments. Even the most enthusiastic prophets of the coming cultural apotheosis recognized that colonial America had made few, if any, major contributions to learning and the arts during the first century and a half of settlement. Greatness lay ahead, in the future and not in the past. In fact, the past looked almost completely barren.

In poetry, the verse of Edward Taylor, the most talented poet of colonial America, was buried in trunks awaiting discovery by twentieth-century historians. In painting, the emergence of Benjamin West and John Singleton Copley in the 1750s created considerable excitement that America might at last produce an artist of recognized genius. But first West and then Copley felt obliged to leave America in order to develop their talents. Once they had settled in London, neither artist ever returned, primarily because, as Copley put it, "in comparison with the people [of England]. . . , we Americans are not half-removed from a state of nature." In literature as in painting, Americans looked to England for models, inspiration, and approval. Benjamin Franklin's essays were conscious attempts to duplicate the urbanity of Addison and Steele. And William Byrd's *History of the Dividing Line,* another important American work not published in the eighteenth century and therefore unknown, represented Byrd's effort to show that he was a London gentleman frolicking in the Virginia woods. The one enduring and original philosopher in colonial America, Jonathan Edwards, was a cult hero to a small number of New Light ministers in New England, but Edwards's treatise on free will remained an intellectual weapon in local theological wars between competing sects. Edwards himself was dismissed by his parishioners and spent his latter years ministering to Indians in western Massachusetts, isolated and unappreciated.[15]

Soon after the start of the American Revolution, it is true, Americans would begin to ransack their past for cultural accomplishments in a patriotic effort to provide the new nation with a respectable legacy in the arts and sciences. Then men like Franklin and Edwards would loom large. But in prerevolutionary America, most especially during the middle decades of the eighteenth century, those colonists who gave any thought to the matter at all actually undervalued native writers, artists, and thinkers and felt obliged to apologize for their crudeness. "All things have their season," explained Franklin, "and with young countries as with young men, you must curb their fancy to strengthen their judgment. . . . To America, one schoolmaster is worth a dozen poets, and the invention of a machine or the improvement of an implement is of more importance than a masterpiece of Raphael. . . ."[16] Franklin's explanation made America's cultural poverty a transitory stage like adolescence, to be followed, presumably, by mature and civilized behavior. The Abbé Raynal, a prominent French *philosophe,* was more pessimistic: "Through the whole extent of America," he claimed in 1770, "there has never appeared a philosopher, an artist, a man of learning, whose name has found a place in the history of science or whose talents have been of any use to others."[17] Raynal and his countryman the Abbé de Pauw based their negative evaluations on the scientific theories of the Count de Buffon, whose pioneering *Histoire Naturelle* described the continent of North America as an inherently deficient environment where plants and animals imported from Europe degenerated. De Pauw, who wrote the entry for America in the 1776 edition of the *Encylopédie,* argued that the inhabitants of the New World were permanently condemned to live as diseased semisavages incapable of refinement.[18]

This was too much for even the most deferential and apologetic American. But the semiscientific pronouncements of Raynal and De Pauw were exaggerated versions of a familiar and widely shared belief in America's cultural inferiority. Colonial Americans were profoundly aware that they lived on the periphery of a civilization whose center was London. Prerevolutionary America was a provincial society whose leading members aped the manners of the English aristocracy and whose past accomplishments in the arts were derivative gestures, copies rather than originals. This, at least, was the dominant attitude of most aspiring artists and intellectuals by the middle ages of the eighteenth century.

All this makes it even more remarkable to see incredibly optimistic assertions of national ascendancy in the arts. These predictions, we have seen, predated the outbreak of hostilities over Parliament's right to tax the colonies and therefore cannot be attributed solely to the political crisis of the 1760s and 1770s. Nor did the optimistic estimates depend upon protonationalistic pride in the cultural achievements of preceding generations. If one takes the rhetoric of these cultural projections seriously, it seems to suggest a sudden, almost explosive flowering of the arts in an environment that had previously produced shriveled, unimpressive vegetation. The questions posed earlier thus seem even more vexing and perplexing: how could such buoyant and unprecedented expectations develop in provincial America?

Clues pointing toward an answer can be found in the body of literature devoted to America's expanding role in the British Empire that began to appear on both sides of the Atlantic in the 1750s, at the same time as intimations of cultural greatness first appeared. Although few of these pamphlets and essays contained any mention of the arts, they did reveal a newfound preoccupation with the latent economic power of the English colonies in North America and a heightened awareness of their capacity for growth. The dominant metaphor running through this literature was familial: England, the mother country, was the parent, and the colonies were her children. The parent-child metaphor had long been a fixture in discussions of imperial affairs, primarily because it afforded all commentators the flexible literary device necessary to described an ambiguous, even contradictory relationship. Politically, the colonists were supposedly equal members of the imperial family possessing the same rights and privileges as Englishmen. Economically, the colonies were subordinate client states whose sole function was to increase the wealth of the mother country. The parent-child metaphor performed the important service of masking the conflict between Whig political assumptions and mercantile theory by transforming discussions of sovereignty into discussions of duty, deference, and mutual obligation. In the 1750s, however, writers began to emphasize a new feature of the old metaphor: namely, the natural propensity of all children to grow up. Logically and chronologically, prophecies of an American Athens were linked to prophecies of American economic development and maturity.[19]

Again, Benjamin Franklin was one of the earliest and most enthusiastic champions of America's prospects. His *Observations on the Increase of Mankind,* written in 1751 and first published in 1755, noted that the American population was growing at an unprecedented rate. He estimated, correctly, it turned out, that the overall population of the colonies was doubling every twenty to twenty-five years and that the chief cause of the increase was not immigration but natural fecundity. At this rate, he reasoned, the people in America "will, in another Century be more than the People of England, and the greatest Number of Englishmen will be on this Side the Water." Franklin did not suggest that these demographic facts would lead to a rupture in the empire;

on the contrary, he claimed that the wealth generated by the burgeoning American population would enrich England as well as the colonies. But he did warn that any imperial policy that failed to reckon with the growth of the American populace was courting catastrophe.[20]

Throughtout the 1750s Ezra Stiles had been amassing statistical evidence on New England that confirmed Franklin's estimates. In 1761 Stiles published his results in *A Discourse on the Christian Union*. Like Franklin, he calculated that the total population was doubling every twenty-five years, a development which indicated that "God has great things in design and . . . purposes to make of us a great people." In addition to celebrating the implications of American growth, Stiles also identified some of what he regarded as the underlying reasons for the explosive rate of that growth. "*Free polity, free religion, free property,* and *matrimony,* will soon populate a fertile country," he observed. "These have been the basis of our increase." Just as America's cultural visionaries associated artistic creativity with freedom and liberal government, Stiles linked the development of New England's population with the absence of political, religious, and economic constraints.[21]

Recent studies of the colonial population have tended to confirm the chief conclusions reached in the pioneering demographic work of Franklin and Stiles. We now know, for example, that the American population grew at a relatively steady rate of 3 percent a year during the first three quarters of the eighteenth century, which averages out to a doubling of the population about every twenty-five years. This rate of increase, which exceeded the modern definition of an "exploding population" (i.e., 2.6 percent per year), was primarily the result of a higher annual birth rate (55 births per 1,000 inhabitants) than the anuual death rate (27 per 1,000). Immigration from Europe accounted for approximately 20 percent of the overall increase in the white population during the half-century before the Revolution. America's overall growth rate was five to six times greater that England's: in 1700 there were twenty Englishmen to each American colonist; by 1775 the ratio was three to one. The American population was also unusually young; in 1775 between 45 and 50 percent of the whites were under the age of sixteen. At that same moment the black population was cresting at 20 percent of the total, the largest proportion it has ever achieved.[22]

Modern scholarship on the economic growth of the colonies allows for less precise conclusions, primarily because of important regional differences, the incomplete character of the data available, and disagreements among economic historians over the meaning of the evidence that does exist. Nevertheless, it is clear that the total output of the American colonies increased dramatically during the eighteenth century, most probably at a rate slightly slower than the rate of population increase. Between 1730 and 1750, for example, the population of Pennsylvania rose by about 130 percent, and the amount of bread, wheat, and flour exported from Philadelphia went up approximately 120 percent. The major cause of the rapid growth in total output was the increasing size of the population, although there is some evidence for an increase in per capita production of about .5 percent annually between 1720 and 1775. Despite periodic depressions, an unfavorable balance of trade with England, credit problems, and a persistent shortage of currency, the total wealth of the American colonies rose steadily throughout the eighteenth century, so that by the eve of the Revolution the American population as a whole had a higher standard of living than any European country and, according to the most recent and exhaustive analysis, "the highest achieved for the bulk of the population in any country up to that time." This rise in total wealth helped to mask, or at least mute, a parallel development: the widening gap between rich and poor. Several local studies of the distribution of wealth in prerevolutionary America show that, as the colonial economy became more commercial and capitalistic, the resulting wealth was distributed more unevenly. But the dramatic increase in the total wealth meant that even the poorer half of the population enjoyed a higher standard of living than had their parents or grandparents.[23]

The policymakers at Whitehall did not need modern demographers to tell them of the rapid rise of America's population and productivity. From its inception in 1696, the Board of Trade had insisted upon statistical measurements of colonial demographic and economic developments. Although reports from the colonial governors and customs agents were often incomplete and inaccurate, the major outlines of America's phenomenal growth were known to British officials. The total population of the mainland colonies had increased· from about 240,000 to about 1,200,000 during the first half of the eighteenth century. Between 1700 and 1760 goods imported from the American colonies rose 165 percent. During the same period English exports to America went up over twice as fast, an overall growth rate of almost 400 percent.[24]

For over half a century British officials had interpreted these figures as evidence of the empire's health. In the 1750s, however, questions began to be raised about the long-range implications of such dramatic growth. Self-styled imperial reformers addressed a host of topics: the appropriate American military role against the French; the desirability of political and military alliances among the northern colonies; the best way to fortify royal governors against the challenges of the local assemblies; the wisdom of imitating French administrative models in the colonies; whether or not to allow manufacturing in America. But throughout the scores of pamphlets ran the common recognition that the increasing size and economic importance of the mainland colonies created new problems and exerted new pressures on the old, and inherently ambiguous, imperial relationship. The debate over Anglo-American affairs peaked between 1759 and 1761, when, according to its most recent historian, over 130 pamphlets appeared.[25]

The most important American contribution to this debate was Franklin's *The Interest of Great Britain Considered,* which synthesized the arguments of several competing points of view and provided the clearest statement of the colonial perspective on America's expanding role in the empire. The explicit question facing the English policymakers, wrote Franklin, was what terms to impose on the French now that the French and Indian War had ended. Some officials called for the annexation of Canada; others preferred to leave Canada under French control and annex the island of Guadeloupe. But the implicit question underlying all preferences and disagreements was whether or not to retard the development of the American colonies. "It is true," Franklin admitted, "the accession of the large territory claimed before the war began, especially . . . the possession of Canada, will tend to the increase of the British subjects [in America] faster than if they had been confined within the [Allegheny] mountains."[26] But those British officials who recommended that Canada be left in French hands in order to restrict American expansion, observed Franklin, should realize that American growth was unstoppable. Franklin appended his earlier pamphlet, *Observations on the Increase of Mankind*, as evidence of the inexorable march of the American population. Anyone committed to blocking the advance of these demographic facts, he noted satirically, had only two options: the first was genocide, the wholesale slaughter of all colonists; the second Franklin called "the Egyptian policy," the enactment by Parliament of a law "enjoying the colony midwives to stifle in the birth every third or fourth child." If the colonists had a choice, Franklin thought, "they would prefer the latter" policy, but officials should recognize that these two options afforded the "only means you may keep the colonies to the present size."[27]

Franklin reassured his English readers that, for the short run at least, American growth need not lead toward independence. As long as the colonial population remained spread out over large territory, it would remain agrarian. This meant that the colonies would continue to produce raw materials and consume English manufactured goods, just as they were supposed to do according to mercantile theory. Moreover, much of the worry that English officials exhibited toward American maturation, Franklin claimed, was based on a misapplication of the parent-child metaphor:

The human body and the political differ in this, that the first is limited by nature to a certain stature, which, when attain'd, it cannot, ordinarily, exceed; the other by better government and more prudent police . . . often takes fresh starts of growth, after being long at a stand. . . . The mother being of full stature, is in a few years equal'd by a growing daughter; but in the case of a mother country and her colonies, it is quite different. The growth of the children tends to increase the growth of the mother, and so the difference and superiority is longer preserv'd.[28]

Despite his characteristic knack for accenting the positive, the whole thrust of Franklin's analysis of Anglo-American affairs pointed toward the emergence of a gigantic American empire that must eventually outstrip England. As several British pamphleteers noticed, the only hope he offered imperial officials was temporary: if they were shrewd and prudent, British supremacy might be "longer preserved." But in the long run, no matter how skilled the statesmen in London and Whitehall, the ever increasing pressure produced by American demographic and economic development would prove uncontainable within the British Empire.

One can discover similar arguments in behalf of American destiny at other times in our history. The seventeenth-century Puritan insistence on the providential fate of New England comes to mind. And in the nineteenth century the battery of arguments for westward expansion labeled "Manifest Destiny" also emphasized the irrepressible unfolding of God's will as revealed in American growth. In part because of these similarities, it is worth noting that Franklin's mode of analysis was distinctive in that it depended exclusively on natural, secular causes. Franklin saw no need to attribute the rise of American power to supernatural intervention or divine grace. It was solely a product of discernible trends in history with a momentum of their own. Franklin was not a theologian of national development; he was a social scientist whose optimistic projections had all the prestige of the Enlightenment's approach to social change behind them. Although one could—and many Americans did—envision the cultural flowering of America as a work of divine providence, Franklin's analytical method demonstrated that prophets of America's rising glory need not rely on miracles for their optimistic predictions. Once the connection between socioeconomic progress and the arts was established, it was possible to speak sensibly of a cultural millennium in America and describe it not as an unfathomable act of God but as a natural consequence of human history.

Nevertheless, the kind of demographic argument formulated by Franklin and Stiles in the 1750s and early 1760s did not play a major role in the initial stages of the Anglo-American debate over Parliament's authority in the colonies. American opposition to the Sugar Act (1763), the Stamp Act (1765), and the Townshend Acts (1767) tended to focus on the illegality and immorality of Parliament's policies. At first, colonial pamphleteers did not emphasize the growth and maturity of the American colonies; they accepted the status of children but distinguished between the rights of children and the rights of slaves. And even children, argued writers like John Dickinson and John Adams, possessed natural rights that no self-respecting parent could violate. During the 1760s and early 1770s the American patriots staked out an ideological position based on a denunciation of arbitrary power, commitment to the natural-rights philosophy, and a growing suspicion of British motive and morality.[29]

As the war drew nearer, however, assertions of America's growth and destiny surfaced again. In his *Novanglus* essays of 1773–74 John Adams cited James Harrington's observation in *Oceana* that all colonies, like children, eventually come of age and "wean themselves," adding that "the colonies are now nearer manhood than ever Harrington foresaw...." The following year Sam Adams also predicted that American growth made independence inevitable: "It requires but a small portion of the gift of discernment for anyone to foresee, that providence will erect a mighty empire in America," Adams wrote, "and our posterity will have it recorded in history...." In the parliamentary debates of 1775 Lord Camden struck the same note that Franklin had sounded fifteen years earlier: "It is impossible that this petty island," warned Camden, "can continue in dependence that mighty continent, increasing daily in numbers and in strength. To protract the time of separation to a distant day is all that can be hoped." Edmund Burke also warned his colleagues in the House of Commons that they were swimming against the currents of history: "Whilst we spend our time in deliberating on the mode of governing two millions," said Burke in 1775, "we shall find we have millions more to manage ... you ought not ... to trifle with so large a mass.... You could at no time do so without guilt; and be assured you will not be able to do it long with impunity."[30]

But the most extensive, and by far the most influential, version of this theme was Tom Paine's *Common Sense* (1776). Paine fused together Berkeley's vision of American destiny, Franklin's demographic perspective, and his own personal belief in the progressive unfolding of history in the New World to create the most effective piece of patriotic propaganda of the entire revolutionary crisis. "As I have always considered the independency of this continent, as an event which sooner or later must arrive," wrote Paine, "so from the late progress of the continent to maturity, the event cannot be far off." Paine claimed that it was "repugnant to reason, to the universal order of things, to all examples from former ages, to suppose that this continent can long remain subject to any power." All that Parliament's oppressive policies had done, he observed, was to hasten a foreordained historical process. America was on the threshold of its manhood, so "for God's sake let us come to a final separation," he wrote, "and not leave the next generation to be cutting throats under the violated unmeaning names of parent and child."[31]

Of course, Paine's purpose in *Common Sense* was to generate popular support for the war for independence, not to champion America's cultural coming-of-age. Nevertheless, Paine's enormously influential pamphlet, Berkeley's poetic prophecy, Brackenridge and Freneau's *The Rising Glory of America,* and British apprehensions about the future of the empire all derived their persuasive power from the same source: America's incredible growth rate. More specifically, as more and more colonists became conscious of their spiraling population and economic productivity, a whole range of possibilities which had been inconceivable a few decades earlier began to seem not only plausible but even inevitable.

The gradual development of new, positive attitudes toward America's potential came about because the demographic and economic growth of colonial America was slowly transforming day-by-day life in the towns and rural villages where the vast majority of colonists lived and died. The community studies produced by a rising generation of colonial historians have focused scholarly attention on the several ways in which the stability, harmony, and cohesion of seventeenth-century villages were eroded during the course of the eighteenth century and the bonds that tied communities and families together were gradually unraveled. Doubtless the self-sufficient agrarian communities of seventeenth-century New England were not as placid and free of conflict as some historians would have us believe. And despite population pressures, the declining crop yields of farm land, tensions between propertied fathers and landless sons, increasing social stratification, and the steady commercialization of agri-culture, many villages remained traditional agrarian communities committed to harmony and order through the eighteenth century. Nevertheless, it now seems undeniably clear that colonial com-munities were at various stages of a major social transformation in the middle decades of the eighteenth century, that the ties which bound individuals together were dissolving, and that due subordination of individual interests to communal goals could no longer be taken for granted. Even in rural villages that looked much the same in 1750 as they had in 1650, where ministers and magistrates continued to exalt the old virtues of austerity, def-erence, and self-restraint, new and more liberal attitudes toward authority and personal freedom were crystallizing.[32]

The impact of these social changes made the great mass of ordinary Americans more receptive than they would otherwise have been to the liberal values and the buoyant way of thinking advocated by prominent colonists like Franklin, Stiles, and Paine. The major claim of Paine's pamphlet, and the meaning of its title, was that the awareness of America's demographic and eco-nomic growth had become commonplace, a matter of common sense. Yet the distinguishing feature of the emerging liberal men-tality was a radically new idea—that growth was a product of liberation. By explicitly exalting the benefits of personal freedom and insisting that unprecedented productivity would result if the energies of ordinary Americans were released on the world, Paine and others like him were championing an idea that would have lacked both legitimacy and credibility if the traditional structure of colonial towns and villages had remained intact. In short, po-litical independence and cultural greatness appear to have derived their plausibility and their appeal from a newfound re-spect, even fascination, for the future of individual freedom in an America society already on the road toward capitalism.

Chapter Two

Paradoxes:

Culture and Capitalism

I shall observe then that to know at what precise point and on what principles you should admit the arts and sciences in your nation, it is first necessary to understand its natural tendency; for we may direct the course of rivers, but not turn them back to their sources.... It is sad to confess that it is to a very great inequality in the distribution of wealth that the fine arts are indebted for their most brilliant period.

Marquis de Chastellux, "The Progress of the Arts
and Sciences in America" (1783)

The belief in the power and preferability of individual freedom has become such an unquestioned article of faith in America that it seems almost sacrilegious to notice that it has a history, meaning that it came into existence at a certain time and under certain conditions, that it is not an eternal verity. But it is absolutely crucial to understand how alluringly new liberal values were in pre-revolutionary America, especially if we are to fathom the utopian expectations harbored by the men who came of age during the last third of the eighteenth century. Moreover, a fresh appreciation of how novel and exciting the release from traditional constraints seemed to the revolutionary generation is essential if we are to resolve a critical and as yet unanswered question: granted that many American colonists derived considerable encouragement from a crude but accurate assessment of their growth in population and economic productivity; granted also that this encouragement helped convince many colonists that separation from the British Empire was not a preposterous idea; granted that the social changes sweeping through prerevolutionary America eroded the communal values that had formerly confined individual behavior and thereby "prepared" colonists for liberal ideals; but why did forecasts of inexorable demographic and economic advances lead to the assurance that the *arts* were also about to flower in America? What was the connection between sheer material growth and the imminent arrival of the muses?

The prophets of America's cultural destiny, from Berkeley onward, assumed that the connection was so obvious that it required no explanation. The *translatio studii* and the *translatio imperii* were always coupled in English and European accounts. Berkeley, for example, simply asserted that empires and the arts rise together. John Trumbull spoke of the simultaneous flowering of "arts and arms." Brackenridge and Freneau presumed that America's "rising glory" would include cultural as well as economic prominence. The familiar references to Athens, Rome, Renaissance Italy and Shakespeare's England served as an implicit historical explanation—the arts would accompany American prosperity and power because that was the way it had always happened in the past. But no one spelled out the reasons why economic and cultural development were expected to go hand in hand.

Eighteenth-century Americans felt no need to explain themselves on this issue, because they presumed that the artistic, political, and economic life of any society, including their own, was a single thing and not several different things. They had yet to create a language that would allow them to refer conveniently to a separate, self-contained sphere of aesthetics and refined taste, because they had no need for such a language. And they had no need for such a language because it was literally inconceivable to them that the arts could flourish, or even exist at all, independent of favorable social and economic developments. If we are to understand the revolutionary generation on its own terms, we need to jettison certain modern ways of thinking and their related vocabularies. Our presumption that it is possible to think and talk about the arts as distinct from society—or, for that matter, the isolated individual independent of society—is a legacy of the nineteenth century. Eighteenth-century Americans had not learned to make these distinctions. They lacked our modern understanding of the word "culture" as a transcendent realm of sensibility divorced from the ordinary events of the mundane world; they retained the traditional assumption that social and aesthetic life was indivisible and interconnected. A flourishing high culture was but one manifestation of social health. Economic property was another manifestation of the same health. Politics, the arts, economic development, and demography were not separate spheres of human activity but interlaced strands comprising the social fabric.

A common refrain, running through the Whig literature on both sides of the Atlantic, linked artistic creativity and economic productivity by making them both natural consequences of liberal political conditions. According to this formulation, a nation's health varied directly with the amount of freedom or liberty the government allowed. In one of his early essays, entitled "Of the Rise and Progress of the Arts and Sciences," David Hume had put it unequivocally: "It is impossible for the arts and sciences to arise, at first, among any people unless that people enjoy the blessings of free government." Hume also insisted that as soon as arbitrary and despotic policies became the norm, "from that moment they [the arts and sciences] naturally, or rather necessarily decline, and seldom or never revive in the nation, where they formerly flourished."[1] In a long series of essays, published in England during the 1720s as *Cato's Letters,* John Trenchard and Thomas Gordon made the preservation of civil liberty the prerequisite for commercial prosperity, legal justice, and everything else worth living for, including the arts. According to "Cato," *"Polite Arts and Learning* [are] *naturally produced in Free States, and marred by such as are not free."*[2] The Earl of Shaftesbury had worked out a similar scheme even earlier. In 1710 Shaftesbury argued that the Glorious Revolution of 1688 had established the proper conditions for the flowering of the arts in England. He claimed that it was "easy . . . to apprehend the advantages of our Britain in this particular, and what effect its established liberty will produce in everything which relates to art. . . ." For Shaftesbury, "the high spirit of tragedy can ill subsist where the spirit of liberty is wanting."[3]

Literate colonists like Franklin, Stiles, and Trumbull were familiar with these English writings. *Cato's Letters* enjoyed an especially wide circulation in the colonies during the middle decades of the eighteenth century and played an important role in shaping American attitudes toward parliamentary power in the prerevolutionary era. But here is another instance when printed words only confirmed attitudes that colonists had begun to acquire from their own experience. When Stiles associated the emergence of an American Athens with "the spirit of freedom," when Trumbull linked the rise of indigenous American poetry and painting with "the absence of constraints," and when Brackenridge and Freneau claimed that greatness in the arts appeared only "where freedom holds her sacred standard high," they were not just echoing the essays of Shaftesbury and Hume. They were embracing the new and intoxicating liberal idea that was barely beginning to enter the consciousness of American colonists by the middle third of the eighteenth century: namely, that if all the artificial restraints and regulations imposed on human activity were removed, the result would not be chaos but harmony; moreover, that the religious and political health as well as the economic and cultural productivity of such a society would increase dramatically.

Although the long-range social changes that were slowly eroding the communal ethos of local life operated at different levels and speeds from the region to region, the benign implications of freedom first became visible throughout the colonies in the aftermath of the Great Awakening. As the religious revivals swept through New England and the middle colonies in the 1740s, they left a trail of ecclesiastical wreckage. The power of the clergy had been eroded; established churches were splintered into several competing sects; the communal cohesion that depended on religious consensus deteriorated even further; the bond between church and state was also weakened, since the proliferation of sects made it difficult for any one religious group to maintain that it alone should enjoy political support. For many ministers, the disorder and disarray were ominous symptoms of

God's wrath, and the collapse of religious uniformity was a source of considerable despondency. But for some observers the new arrangement produced unforeseen and extraordinarily positive consequences. As Stiles saw it, for example, the breakdown of the traditional religious order allowed men and ideas to interact in exciting new ways. Stiles did not worry about chaos or religious anarchy, because, he insisted, the multiplicity of sects "will unavoidably become a mutual balance upon one another." He compared the interaction of religious groups with a chemical reaction: "Their collisions, like the action of acids," he wrote, "will subside in harmony and union, not by the destruction of either but in the friendly cohabitation of all. . . . Indeed mutual oppression will more and more subside from the mutual balance of one another." Most importantly, from Stiles's perspective, both the Congregational and Presbyterian churches of New England appeared to be thriving in the new, wide-open atmosphere, and he presented an impressive array of statistical evidence to support this contention.[4]

Other Americans were also discovering that freedom was a safe and many-splendored thing at this time. During a controversy over the establishment of King's College in 1752, for example, William Livingston opposed Anglican domination of the college. When his Anglican critics charged that he was challenging their supremacy only because he wanted to give Presbyterians control over the school, Livingston repudiated the notion that any single interest group ought to enjoy favored status. He argued that the ultimate authority over King's College should be lodged with the New York legislature, where the clash of various factions would serve as a check against arbitrary rule by any one sect. Livingston claimed that "the Jealousy of all Parties combating each other would inevitably produce a perfect Freedom for each particular Party." Franklin, who was a genius at making the most novel and radical ideas sound like folksy, self-evident truths, expressed the same faith in free and unhampered debates. "Light often arises from a collision of opinions," he wrote in 1760, "as fire from flint and steel; and if we can obtain the benefit of the *light,* without danger from the *heat* sometimes produc'd by controversy, why should we discourage it?" Similarly, during a public debate over the imposition of an excise tax in Massachusetts in

1754, several merchants opposed the tax on the grounds that it would discourage industriousness and thereby lower productivity. Regulations were unnecessary, they argued, because the competition among merchants created a harmonious network of interest groups which not only policed themselves but also generated wealth that would benefit the public.[5]

These scattered celebrations of the inherent tractableness and latent power of freedom—usually described as a release from the constraints imposed by religious, political, or economic regulations—were the first manifestations of a genuinely new and modern way of thinking about growth and development. One can discover the early glimmerings of this mentality in late-seventeenth-century England, where advocates of religious toleration began to question the value of religious uniformity and proponents of a free-trade policy began to criticize the mercantile assumptions of the Board of Trade. During the course of the eighteenth century, Scottish thinkers, most especially Lord Kames, David Hume, John Millar, and Adam Smith, made this new attitude toward freedom into the centerpiece of a school of thought for which Smith's *An Inquiry into the Wealth of Nations* represented the culminating philosophical statement. By the 1780s James Madison, who was thoroughly familiar with the writings of the Scottish *philosophes,* used their arguments in *Federalist 10* to claim that the constant clash of interest groups in the new nation would provide a source of stability for the allegedly fragile republican government. And by the third decade of the nineteenth century the principle of *laissez-faire* had entrenched itself as an established feature of an unofficial American creed that glorified the hurly-burly of the capitalistic marketplace.[6]

From a long-range perspective, then, it is possible to see the sporadic endorsements of freedom which first began to surface in America during the middle years of the eighteenth century as the earliest symptoms of a mentality which, in its fully developed form, became the dominant ideology of liberal, capitalist society. It is probably no accident that the initial formulations of what was to become known as the bourgeois or market mentality appeared in the prerevolutionary era, just when the economy was becoming commercialized and when the majority of colonists, farmers as well as merchants, were discovering that their livelihood depended upon the buying and selling of commodities in the marketplace. For our purposes, however, it is critical to recognize that the emerging commitment to the benign and powerful effect of unregulated conditions was not solely or even primarily a commitment to economic development. The crystallizing ideas and attitudes which we now recognize as essential for the triumph of capitalism were originally believed to be all-purpose agents capable of liberating religion, politics, trade, and the arts from past constrictions.

And so another piece of the puzzle falls into place. As we have seen, excessively optimistic predictions of America's cultural growth became commonplace in the middle years of the eighteenth century, at a time when colonists were first becoming aware of the rapid growth of America's population and economy. Moreover, virtually all the predictions of imminent artistic greatness contained some reference to the important role that freedom would play in generating the cultural apotheosis. This emphasis on freedom, usually defined as the release from traditional sources of authority, accompanied the development of a market mentality, which in turn coincided with the emergence of a market-oriented economy in colonial America. The affinity that so many commentators presumed to exist between economic and cultural growth in America, or between the rise of empire and the arts, now comes into sharper focus. Commercial and cultural ascendancy were described as synonymous because they were regarded as the mutual beneficiaries of the same liberating process. Artistic creativity and economic productivity were expected to flourish together in the free and stimulating conditions of the American marketplace.

•

The outbreak of the American Revolution produced additional enthusiasms that also enhanced the prospects for the arts in the new nation. Many of the aspiring artists, poets, and dramatists who came of age during the Revolution—including all the men described in the chapters that follow—were conscious of the Revolution as an historic event worthy of artistic celebration. A French aristocrat who fought for the patriot cause speculated that the American Revolution had generated "more heroes than she [America] has marble and artists to commemorate them."[7] The Revolution served the cause of American culture in an obvious way: it provided the first generation of native artists with inspirational subject material. Kenneth Silverman has provided a detailed and comprehensive chronicle of the arts in revolutionary America that documents this simultaneous upsurge in cultural and national activity. "By the time the country inaugurated its first president in 1789," observes Silverman, it had also produced "its first novel, first epic poem, first composer, first professionally acted play, first actor and dancer, first museum, its first important painters, musical-instrument makers, magazines, engravers—indeed most of the defining features of traditional high culture."[8] In terms of the sheer volume of creative work generated, the optimistic predictions made before the Revolution seemed to be coming true in the 1770s and '80s.

But when the predictions of an American Athens took the form of paintings, poems, and playhouses, when the visible trappings of high culture actually materialized, they were widely denounced as enemies of republicanism and harbingers of social decline. One person's apotheosis, it turned out, was another's apocalypse. After the Revolution, as the arts became more visible, they became the favorite target of ministers, political officials, and pamphleteers who described themselves as guardians of the virtuous principles for which, they claimed, the Revolution had supposedly been fought. It soon became clear that American attitudes toward art and artists were highly charged, that many Americans associated the arts with degeneration rather than progress. The Marquis de Chastellux, who traveled throughout the country in the early 1780s, claimed that public opinion was evenly divided between those who considered "the fine arts and the enjoyments they produced as a delicious ambrosia that the Gods have thought proper to share with us" and those who regarded the arts "as dangerous poison" fatal to the life of the new republic.[9]

Opponents of high culture were often just as scatological in their criticism as early prophets had been effusive in their praise. And, as we shall see, the arguments varied in character and intensity as critics shifted their sights from painting to fiction to the stage. At this point, however, it is worth noticing that there was such a thing as hostility to high culture in general.* While the roots of this hostility were deeply embedded in Western history, the apprehension expressed by Americans of the revolutionary generation emerged out of the same specific social context as the celebrations. And at the nub of the frenzied denunciations of high culture was a fear of the very freedom which looked so alluring to the others and a distaste for the liberal values of the budding capitalist society. Worry and joy, fear and exaltation were closely related responses to the same social conditions, two sides of the same historical coin. Moreover, Americans who insisted that the arts were a serious threat to the stability of the American republic had the bulk of the past's accumulated wisdom on their side.

First, a venerable body of literature criticized the social and psychological impact of the fine arts on public mores. In the fourth century B.C. Plato had warned that poets and artists undermined the morality of the community because they tended to incite the passions instead of reason; he charged that poets such as Homer and Hesiod destroyed public virtue by depicting the gods as selfish and quarrelsome and thereby encouraging ordinary citizens to repudiate the kind of self-sacrifice on which the community depended. In his *Republic*, Plato argued that artists must be banished if the moral health of citizenry was to endure. Jean Jacques Rousseau had constructed a modern version of Plato's classic argument in the eighteenth century; in *A Discourse on the Arts and Sciences* (1751), Rousseau warned that artists and the arts could flourish only in societies glutted with surplus wealth because their support was possible only when men had excess money to spend on luxuries. He noted that Rome and the Renaissance city-states began to degenerate just when the arts began to flourish. Like Plato, he claimed that the fine arts were incompatible with public-spiritedness and self-discipline. Charles Rollin, author of a thirteen-volume *Ancient History* read in abridged form by many well-educated colonists, followed in the

---

* The specific criticism leveled at painting, fiction, and the stage are reviewed in considerable detail in chapters three, four, and five. My intention here is to explore the social origins of these criticisms and to suggest that hostility to all the fine arts was a product of the social conditions that accompanied the rise of a market mentality.[10]

same tradition; Rollin described a "taste for statues, pictures, and other rare curiosities of art" as "a dangerous temptation" that seduced men and then entire nations into indulgent habits that undermined virtue. Edward W. Montagu's *Reflections on the Rise and Fall of Ancient Republicks* (1760) also traced all social ills to self-indulgence and luxury, which sapped the nation of its vitality while providing a fertile but short-lived environment for the arts. Plato, Rousseau, Rollin, and Montagu all agreed on one critical point: the muses were history's buzzards; when they began to gather, the end was near.[11]

Second, New England ministers had been warning their brethren against the seductive dangers of luxury and prosperity for over a century. Puritanism has become infamous as the primal source of American prejudices against the arts; in point of fact Puritan criticisms were usually aimed not at the arts *per se* but at the social and psychological conditions that accompanied the arts. Puritan ministers insisted that godliness was in league with austerity, not with riches, and they incessantly denounced excessive wealth as a burden weighing down Christians in their worldly journey to the hereafter. The familiar message was paradoxical if not perverse: the devout Christian must exert himself in his calling, then spurn the fruits of his industry. One need not be a New Englander or a Puritan to think this way. William Smith, an Anglican minisiter in Philadelphia, described the syndrome most succinctly: hard work gave rise to plenty, Smith observed, "but Plenty begat Ease, and Ease begat Luxury, and Luxury introduced a fatal corruption of every good and virtuous principle."[12] The Puritan jeremiad, which remained the sermonic staple of the day well into the eighteenth century, did not encourage fanatical philistinism so much as fanatical self-control and repression. As a person accumulated more wealth, or as a nation became more prosperous, the very qualities which had generated the prosperity were likely to be abandoned as men and whole societies went spiraling downward into profligacy and sloth. The emergence of a market economy was especially troublesome because it seemed to generate what Richard Jackson called "a commercial spirit" and an insatiable appetite for material comfort. "Steady virtue, and unbending integrity, are seldom to be found where a spirit of commerce pervades everything," Jackson wrote to Franklin, adding that "Luxury and Corruption . . . seem the inseparable companions of Commerce and the Arts."[13] According to Puritan doctrine, then, prosperity was the apex of a moral trajectory. Like Plato and Rousseau, Puritan ministers regarded the proliferation of artists, dramatists, and lyricists as clear symptoms of creeping decadence and imminent social collapse.[14]

Third, and most important for the revolutionary generation, the republican ideology that shaped the colonists' response to British policies in the 1760s and the domestic political debates for twenty years thereafter also encouraged a suspicious attitude toward both individual freedom and the fine arts. As an entire school of American historians has made clear, the republican principles embraced by the leading spokesmen of the revolutionary generation were much more than axioms for a representative form of government; they were the components of a coherent world view that replicated, in a secularized form, many of the traditional values of Puritanism. The watchword of American republicanism was virtue, which was defined as the willingness of the individual to subordinate his private interests for the good of the community; it was also the public-spirited, self-sacrificing quality that the entire populace must possess if government by the people were to have any chance of succes. Two aspects of this republican ideology merit our special attention: first, the criticism of English society and government as corrupt, unvirtuous, and addicted to luxury was, in effect, a criticism of the values produced by a burgeoning capitalist economy; the rapid growth of the colonial population and economy was making this criticism as applicable to America as it was to England; second, although the countless pamphlets, newspaper articles, and treatises generated during the revolutionary crisis put a premium on freedom or liberty, the emphasis was placed on ordered, disciplined freedom circumscribed by the civic obligations imposed by public virtue. Sparta, not Athens, was the historic model for most republican theorists in America. On the one hand, dramatic plays, novels, and portraits were suspect because they were superflous, mere ornaments that pleased the eye or titillated the imagination at a time when the weighty business of waging war and framing constitutions deserved undivided attention. On the other hand, the fine arts were more than just symbols of defiance to public virtue; they were also insidious agents that broke down self-control by overpowering one's mind and senses, thereby destroying the moral fiber of the republican personality. As the modern-day Marxists viewed religion, republicans of the revolutionary era regarded concern for the fine arts an an opiate, a form of "false consciousness" that blinded men and then entire nations to the harsh realities of the world.[15]

Because the American Revolution eventually established the values of the liberal tradition as articles of faith for subsequent generations, and because belief in the almost limitless potential of personal freedom *did* play a crucial role in mobilizing public opinion for independence, it is tempting to read history backward and presume that the revolutionary generation subscribed wholeheartedly to the liberal creed. But it did not. In fact, the republican ideology which came to dominate public debates during the revolutionary crisis formalized a mode of thinking that ran counter to the drift of history by idealizing traditional rather than liberal values, precapitalist rather than capitalist codes of behavior. The American Revolution looked forward and backward at the same time. Liberalism was the wave of the future. Republicanism, however, was based on a constellation of attitudes appropriate for the small, self-sufficient agrarian villages of the past, where the ideal of communal harmony reigned supreme, the economic incentives for a more dynamic, liberated personality had not yet materialized, and individual freedom was easily subordinated to the demands of social order. Republicanism idealized the values of a world that was already fading. It was a nostalgic, backward-looking ideology resting on assumptions that were fundamentally antithetical to the market conditions and liberal mentality emerging in prerevolutionary America. In the language of social scientists, it was not simply "premodern," it was "antimodern."[16]

Republicanism cannot be dismissed as an intellectual anachronism, a cluster of reactionary convictions that might be expected to retire quietly to the graveyard for irrelevant ideologies once the Revolution had ended. The Revolution breathed new life into traditional values by stigmatizing the institutions and attitudes of English society on the verge of the Industrial Revolution. Material wealth became synonymous with luxury; individualism became synonymous with selfishness; high culture became synonymous with imminent decline and fall. And all of these perceptions were hallowed because of the patriotic function they had performed in the successful war for independence.

Moreover, the decisive transformation of America into a full-blooded capitalist society remained fifty years away. Although it is possible to detect the origins of a market-oriented economy and liberal mentality before the Revolution, most Americans of the revolutionary generation remained, as James Henretta has put it, "enmeshed . . . in a web of social relationships and cultural expectations that inhibited the free play of market forces."[17] Social historians have not yet created a language that does justice to the complex configuration of economic forces and social attitudes that characterized American society during this "transitional era." Such terms as "post-traditional" or "preindustrial" are labels for what American society had been or would become. Nor is it customary for attitudes which have commanded the respect of most members of a society for over a century and a half, which have been exalted in a victorious revolutionary struggle, and which continue to make sense for many ordinary men and women on the local level to expire suddenly because they are threatened by portentous economic and demographic changes. More frequently, the proponents of old and venerable convictions intensify their commitment to the traditional order and treat challengers to their abiding beliefs as upstarts who must be shouted down. And this is what happened in late-eighteenth-century America.

The debate over the role of high culture in the new nation was one important manifestation of this clash between prevailing and emerging attitudes. Enthusiasm for the arts was part of a larger enthusiasm for the benign effects of liberation that accompanied the emergence of market conditions in colonial society. Hostility toward the arts was part of a larger hostility toward the liberal values of the marketplace, most especially the release of undisciplined energies, the creation of surplus wealth or luxuries, and the abandonment of communal responsibilities. At the Yale commencement of 1786, in fact, two graduating seniors engaged in a formal debate over precisely these issues. Jedidiah Morse argued that sumptuary laws were essential because they dis-

couraged unnecessary finery and encouraged virtue; he dismissed
excessive devotion to the fine arts as sinful. David Daggett argued
that sumptuary laws reduced economic productivity; he called for
the elimination of legal restrictions on human behavior, the
development of domestic manufactures, and public support for
the arts and sciences.[18] In 1800, when John Marshall told John
Adams that the recent immigration of Frenchmen at least had
the advantage of introducing talented musicians and artists into
the American population, Adams denounced all Frenchmen, but
most especially "schoolmasters, painters, poets, &C." He warned
Marshall that the fine arts were like germs that infected healthy
constitutions and claimed that he would "rather countenance the
introduction of Ariel and Caliban with a troop of spirits the most
mischievous from fairey land."[19]

The conflict over the meaning of the arts and the rise of
liberal attitudes was not always a public affair; it also raged
within particular personalities. In his own private debate with
himself, for example, even John Adams sometimes wavered. He
encouraged Charles Willson Peale during an early stage of his
artistic career, praised John Singleton Copley as the finest painter
in America, and admitted that the beauty of French architecture
almost took his breath away. But by and large Adams felt obliged
to suppress such swells of affection. They were temporary flirta-
tions from which he quickly recovered, preaching the doctrine
of old-fashioned republicanism as a reminder to himself of what
was at stake. "Will you tell me how to prevent riches from becoming the effects of temperance and industry?" he asked
Thomas Jefferson. "Will you tell me how to prevent luxury from
producing effeminancy, intoxication, extravagance and folly?"
Lest there be any doubt where the arts fit in this paradoxical and
fatalistic cycle, Adams spelled it out: "It is vain to think of re-
straining the fine arts. Luxury will follow riches and the fine arts
will come with luxury in spite of all that wisdom can do."[20]

Most Americans were less sure. And if our analysis of the
social and intellectual currents moving past John Adams and his
generation is essentially correct, then we should expect to encounter a larger number of men holding tenaciously to different
sets of antithetical attitudes all at once: applauding the emergence of native American artists and authors while warning

against the seductive power of paintings and novels, celebrating the right of Americans to think and create as they saw fit but bemoaning the loss of stability and standards, denouncing restrictions on individual freedom while expecting artists to produce work that buttressed public mores, clamoring for both republican simplicity and an American Athens.

We should expect to see these systematic inconsistencies because an American who was born before the Revolution and then lived into the nineteenth century experienced a major transformation in the world he knew. It was not simply that colonial America became a separate and independent nation with a political and constitutional framework all its own. Alongside that major change occurred a whole range of social and economic changes that tied the formerly isolated agrarian villages into commercial networks, further eroded the bonds that connected members of families and communities, enhanced the opportunity for financial profits, and carried the new nation to the very edge of what we now call the Industrial Revolution. History, of course, never stands still; but the changes sweeping through America during these years were especially dramatic; they fundamentally altered the shape of our institutions and values. In this historical context a premium was put on the ability to adapt old habits to new circumstances, on what F. Scott Fitzgerald described as "the ability to hold two opposed ideas in the mind and still retain the ability to function." Men who live in an age that straddles a great divide in history are forced to graft new ideals to inherited assumptions in ways that seem to us, who possess the advantage of hindsight, highly paradoxical. The capacity to integrate traditional and liberal attitudes was the hallmark of the "premodern" personality in America, for it created a distinctive cast of mind that gave the era its own integrity and special character.

Aspiring writers and artists were shaped by the same historical pressures that affected other people. The belief that certain artists are superhuman geniuses whose work emerges from the timeless depths of their creative imaginations is itself a nineteenth-century idea inspired by the mounting disenchantment with the world that came into existence after the Revolution.[21] In fact, American artists reflected and refracted the shifting values of the time more sharply than their contemporaries did, in part because they tended to be more thoughtful about their predicament and in part because they were engaged in work that aroused some of the deepest feelings about America's prospects. In the profiles that follow we should expect to encounter men who combined an incredibly optimistic estimate of America's cultural potential with a deep distrust of their own artistic callings, hatred for the pecuniary values of the marketplace with considerable skill as entrepreneurs, intense private ambition with a genuine craving to channel their creative energies into public service. We might be on the lookout for artists who discovered that a highly developed sense of paradox was the foundation of their best creative works. We might ask ourselves if the specific ways in which these cultural pioneers reconciled tensions and fused together the disparate strands of their personalities blocked or released their creative energies. And we might ask what legacy they bequeathed to the emerging American culture.

Part Two

Profiles

⚜

The most difficult thing to get hold of, in studying any past period, is this felt sense of the quality of life at a particular place and time: a sense of the ways in which the particular activities combined into a way of thinking and living. We can go some way in restoring the outlines of a particular organization of life....Yet even these, as we recover them, are usually abstract. Possibly, however, we can gain the sense of a further common element, which is neither the character nor the pattern, but as it were the actual experience through which these were lived.

Raymond Williams, *The Long Revolution* (1961)

Chapter Three

Charles Willson Peale:

Portrait of

the American Artist as

Virtuous Entrepreneur

❧

The intellect of man is forced to choose
Perfection of life, or of the work,
And if it take the second must refuse
A heavenly mansion, raging in the dark.

W. B. Yeats, "The Choice" (1933)

Four years before he died, Charles Willson Peale advised his son to strive for truth in all his paintings. "Truth is better than a high finish," the old man warned. "The Italians say give me a true outline & you may fill it up with Turd."[1] Peale himself saw to it that posterity would possess the raw material for the "true outline" of his own life; he wrote a lengthy and chatty autobiography and preserved his many diaries, notes, and letter books for future historians. In the twentieth century Charles Coleman Sellers used these materials to "fill up" the outline of Peale's many-sided life in a delightful and comprehensive two-volume biogra-

SELF-PORTRAIT WITH SPECTACLES *by Charles Willson Peale* (1804)
Courtesy of the Pennsylvania Academy of the Fine Arts

phy. Peale emerges as an engaging but wholly unassuming colonial painter who became the most prominent artist in revolutionary America; a fervent radical and patriot during the Revolution; a pioneer in taxonomy and founder of "Peale's Museum" of natural history in Philadelphia; an ardent Jeffersonian; an incessant inventor and tinkerer with plows, gunpowder, eyeglasses, false teeth, portable baths, windmills, and even "Moving Pictures"; and a prolific and devoted father who championed the cause of the family with his brush and his pen, advocated liberal child-rearing practices, and endorsed domestic reforms designed to liberate women from traditional stereotypes.[2] One of the most eclectic men in a young republic filled with broad-gauged personalities, "Old Charlie Peale," as one friend called him, was "one of the best men that God ever made, though he will paint portraits with a chisel, marry a fifth or sixth wife every few years, and outlive all the rest of the world."[3]

Of course he did not outlive the rest of the world; he died in 1827 at the age of eighty-five while in active pursuit of wife number four. Whether or not Peale was one of "the best man that God ever made," he was surely one of the most perplexing. The "true outline" of his character is as elusive as the purported order of his beloved museum. There one could find stuffed birds, monkeys and squirrels, a five-foot-long rattlesnake with fifteen rattles, a five-legged cow, the mastodon bones unearthed in Ulster County, New York, a bald eagle, a waxed figure of Meriwether Lewis, scriptural epigrams, magic mirrors, a sawed-off trigger finger, several of Peale's eleven children running about, and portraits of prominent eighteenth-century Americans looking down from the walls. Peale claimed that the items were arranged according to the Linnaean categories, but Federalists who visited the museum reported that it graphically reproduced the natural anarchy of a Jeffersonian world. Both Peale and the Federalists were right; despite Peale's impressive commitment to the enlightened empirical standards of the day, the museum was part science and part circus. Similarly, Peale's character was a blend of several diverse ingredients. He could be seen as a predecessor of Thomas Edison, Norman Rockwell, even P. T. Barnum, who in fact bought most of the items in the museum after Peale's death. But the "true outline" of Peale's personality took shape during the decades immediately before and after the American Revolution and can be understood only within that context.[4]

For Peale was one of the first Americans to apply to the arts the ideological assumptions on which the Revolution was based. His remarkable range of interests and activities was rooted in the eighteenth-century conviction that politics, the arts, indeed all social, economic, and cultural developments, were part of a whole and were governed by the same principles. He did not think of art or an artistic career as a separate sphere of human endeavor hermetically sealed off from politics, family, or even war against England. The same governing influence, called God or Providence or Nature, controlled all events. More specifically, Peale's bubbling optimism derived from his belief that the Revolution had liberated Americans from the artificial constraints and arbitrary authority imposed by English rule; Americans were now free to vote, worship, trade, and create in accord with the truly natural laws. Although he had moments of doubt and despair, he initially expected the arts, and his own career, to flourish in this bracing, wide-open environment. When he encountered the oppressive conditions imposed by the marketplace and began to regard his paintings as profit-making commodities, and when he discovered that the people-at-large were either indifferent or hostile to the arts, Peale began to leave his world and enter ours.[5]

·

Peale was born in Queen Annes County, Maryland, on April 15, 1741. His father, Charles Peale, gave the appearance of being a dignified school teacher with royalist leanings and a fondness for fox hunting who had migrated from England to the colonies. In fact, Charles Peale had been banished from England in 1737 for embezzling almost 2,000 pounds while serving as a deputy in His Majesty's Post Office in London. He had married Margaret Triggs in 1740, but only after she had conceived his child. In 1743 the new family moved to Chestertown, where Charles Peale became master of the Kent County School, campaigned unsuccessfully for local office, fathered four more children, and apprised all who would listen of his English ancestry. Throughout his childhood young Charles Willson Peale was reminded of his father's noble background and of the distant family lands in Oxfordshire that would one day pass to his father and then to him.

It would take several years for Peale to discover that the much mentioned inheritance was not forthcoming. In the meantime his father died and the family moved to Annapolis, where Charles's mother began work as a seamstress. In 1754 Charles Willson was apprenticed to Nathan Waters, the local saddler, to learn a trade. He was to serve until he was twenty-one; then, presumably, he would inherit his fortune. But instead of serving as a convenient way station between childhood and a life of leisured retirement, the apprenticeship initiated a stormy seventy-three-year quest for solvency and public favor.

His decision to become an artist was a blend of sheer chance and personal misfortune. When his apprenticeship was finished he promptly married his sweetheart, seventeen-year-old Rachel Brewer, and made arrangements to establish his own saddling business in Annapolis. On a trip to Virginia to purchase leather, he met a man "who had some fondness for painting." Peale was surprised that the man could sell his paintings, since they appeared "miserably done" to him. As a youngster Peale had drawn pictures of Adam and Eve based on the descriptions in Milton's *Paradise Lost;* his schoolmates and family had praised these early efforts. Now, in 1762, he had the idea to combine his abilities as a saddler, the little he had learned about watch repair, and what he could learn about "the painting Trade." It was a wholly practical idea, free of any aesthetic or intellectual inspirations, intended to diversify his newly founded business and attract customers from the competition. Once back in Annapolis he practiced painting portraits of himself, Rachel, and his friends; then, in December of 1762, he traveled to Philadelphia to buy paints, brushes, and a copy of Robert Dossie's *Handmaiden to the Arts;* and he obtained rudimentary lessons in portraiture from John Hesselius, the most prominent artist in Maryland, in exchange for one of his best saddles. He was now ready to practice his new trade on as many customers as were willing to pay.

Peale's budding career immediately involved him in a tangle of local economic and political problems that proved to be a preview of his later adventures on the national level. He went into debt in order to purchase the tools and wholesale goods for his shop, then watched as declining tobacco prices in the Chesa-

peake region—the result of overproduction and increased ship-
ping costs—produced a recession. Peale's creditors began to press
for their money at precisely the time when customers could not
afford to have their saddles or watches repaired, much less their
portraits painted. This was also the time when Peale threw his
energies into a hotly contested political campaign in which
Samuel Chase opposed the proprietary candidate for the Maryland assembly. Peale drew up banners and placards for the insurgents, who included prominent colonists like Charles Carroll
as well as disaffected farmers and small businessmen like Peale.
Chase won the election, but the losing party promised reprisals
against the insurgents. Peale was an early casualty. Four writs
were served on him for payment of back debts totaling almost 900
pounds. In June of 1765 Peale said good-bye to his pregnant wife,
packed his paints and brushes, and fled to Virginia, where he
hoped to paint his way out of debt.[6]

For the next eleven years Peale was almost constantly on
the move, traveling the colonial roads and rivers from Charleston
to Boston, learning and practicing his trade, and gradually coming to regard art as a more exalted calling than fixing saddles. In
Boston he met John Singleton Copley, already America's most accomplished and prominent artist. "I make as much as if I were a
Raphael or Correggio," Copley wrote in 1767, "and three hundred
guineas a year, my present income, is equal to nine hundred a
year in London." In the 1760s Copley was so secure that he welcomed Peale's appearance "and the fair prospect it affords of
Americas rivaling the Continant [*sic*] of Europe in those refined
Arts."[7]

Peale also discovered that there were wealthy colonists
willing to support a budding artist's education. Charles Carroll,
the same Maryland lawyer Peale had met during the campaign
for Samuel Chase's election, provided most of the money for a
trip to London. Once there he began to study under Benjamin
West, a Pennsylvanian only three years older than Peale but already an acknowledged genius. West was also pleased to assist
an aspiring artist, especially a fellow American who "when he is
not painting, amuses himself repairing my locks and bells." Peale
even posed as Regulus for West's first commissioned painting
for George III, *The Departure of Regulus for Rome*. He also met
Joshua Reynolds, soon to become first president of the Royal

Academy, author of the *Discourses on Art,* and a personal symbol of the stature the arts and artists had recently achieved in England. Reynolds earned about 6,000 pounds a year from his painting, received 200 pounds for each of his full-length portraits, and, when he died, had dukes, barons, and earls as his pallbearers. Peale took it all in. He studied William Hogarth's *Analysis of Beauty* for its technical and aesthetic insights; later he would read Matthew Pilkington's *Gentleman's and Connoisseur's Dictionary of Painters* for inspiration. By the time he returned to the colonies in 1769, he possessed a wealth of knowledge and experience as well as a vision of himself, not as an artisan, but as an artist.[8]

Even before his departure from London, Peale received a letter from his chief patron that served as a reminder of the discrepancy between colonial and English attitudes toward artists. "I observe your Inclination Leads you much to Painting in miniature," Charles Carroll wrote. "I would have you consider whether it may suit so much the Taste of the People with us as Larger Portrait Painting which I think would be a branch of the Profession that would turn out Greater Profit here." Carroll went on to discourage "the study of History Painting" because it was "the most Difficult Part of the Profession . . . and indeed in this Part of the World few have a Taste for it."[9]

From the perspective of an English connoisseur of the arts, miniature, portraiture, and historical painting represented three discrete levels of artistic proficiency; a young artist usually began with miniature, developed his technique, then moved up to portraits. He attempted a historical painting only after his earlier work demonstrated a high level of competence and a capacity for capturing the essence of a sitter or scene. In short, there was an elaborate set of technical and aesthetic rationales for each kind of painting. Yet Carroll's advice referred only to two practical, market-oriented considerations: "the Taste of the People" and "Greater Profit."[10]

Perhaps the most significant fact about young Peale was that he did not need such reminders. He had begun his career as an indebted itinerant painter, an entrepreneur with a brush. He knew that most colonists thought of him in much the same way as he had once thought of himself—as a peddler of painted likenesses trying to earn a living. His exposure to England, Benjamin

West, and the artistic community in London had transformed his own understanding of the arts, but he never presumed that his fellow Americans had changed their minds while he was away. Largely because he had a realistic sense of what he was up against, Peale recognized that he would have to meet his potential customers on their own terms. In spite of his English experience, which provided him with a vision of the moral and philosophical responsibilities of the artist, he remained an artist-entrepreneur sensitive to the vagaries of the American marketplace. "Be sure that your likeness pleases your sitter," he wrote a young student in 1775, "or it will be like a man who pulls down the scaffold before the walls are compleat."[11]

Between 1769 and 1773 he established himself as one of the leading portrait painters in America. During this time he painted over 150 portraits and developed a reputation among the gentry of the middle colonies. Prominent colonists like Benjamin Rush, the Philadelphia physician, noticed his work; Rush even requested Peale to paint a gallery of portraits depicting persons afflicted with various diseases, which could be identified by means of facial expressions. And on May of 1772 George Washington consented to a portrait: "I am contrary to all expectations under the hands of Mr. Peale," wrote Washington, "but in so grave—so sullen a mood . . . that I fancy the skill of this Gentleman's Pencil will be put to it, in describing to the World what manner of man I am."[12] Most sitters were apparently less restrained and more congratulatory. "My reputation is greatly increased by a number of New Yorkers having been here," Peale wrote from Philadelphia in 1772, adding that they "have given me the character of being the best painter in America—that I paint more certain and handsomer likeness than Copley. What more could I wish?"[13]

But the artistic success Peale enjoyed was neither complete nor easily achieved. Several times he was forced to delay commissioned paintings in order to redo earlier portraits in which the colors had darkened because he had not mixed his paints properly. And by 1771 he had exhausted the market in Maryland. "I have very little to do, not worth mentioning," he admitted to Beale Bordley, who advised him to try his luck in the West Indies.[14] He traveled instead to Philadelphia, Williamsburg, and Norfolk in search of customers; he began to feel that he must choose his terrain carefully. "Mr. Copley [*sic*] I hear is now painting at New York," he wrote to Bordley. "This is the time I ought to go to Philadelphia."[15] By 1773 he had decided he could "find full employment" in Philadelphia. "I have my hands full and I believe would always find a sufficiency between this and New York," he told Bordley, then added ominously that he hoped "to be at least clear of incumberances."[16] During the next year, when he decided that Philadelphia was sufficiently promising to move his family there permanently, he remained in debt and was forced to take out space in the *Maryland Gazette* to demand payment for past work so that he might pay his own creditors.[17]

By 1775 Peale's prospects were a strange·mixture of enthusiasm and despair. Copley had gone to Europe the year before, leaving Peale the uncontested leader of the arts in America. But what did that mean? In the absence of institutions like the Royal Academy or wealthy patrons willing to provide long-term support, Peale's six-year experience demonstrated that the colonial artist, no matter how prominent, had to solicit customers, often solicit payment, and fend for himself in a capricious popular market. Peale had only proven that it was possible to survive, not thrive, in this hurly-burly; and survival required adopting the attitudes of a huckster, not the kind of attitudes that allowed for artistic development or aesthetic appreciation. Clearly, if the arts were to rise above the clatter of the marketplace, if serious artists like Peale were ever to become more than traveling salesmen in America, they would have to find powerful allies. Providentially, in the spring and summer of 1775, history conveniently provided Peale with a whole new range of subjects and a potentially new status as artist of that new and all-powerful patron the American Revolution.

•

Even before the outbreak of hostilities at Lexington and Concord, Peale had recognized the historical and artistic significance of the time in which he lived. He was the first American artist to see that the events of the 1760s and '70s constituted the subject material for a new kind of historical portrait.* Rather than search

* Virtually all the major American artists of the time—West, Copley, Trumbull, and Peale—modified the English theory of historical painting; in

for historical scenes in classical Greece or Rome, as did most English and European artists, Peale turned to the events and personalities of revolutionary America, convinced that they were an important chapter in world history that later generations would compare with the rise of classical civilization. In 1772 Peale lamented that he could never become "well acquainted with the Greesian [*sic*] and Roman Statues. . . . These are more than I shall have time or opportunity to know, but as I have a variety of characters to paint I must as Rembrandt did make these my anticks. . . ."[19]

In one sense Peale's vision of his comtemporaries as potential "Anticks" was a shrewd insight into the future art market perfectly in keeping with the capitalistic ethic, a long-range investment that promised to pay dividends in the form of fame as well as money. In another sense Peale's view of himself as an American Rembrandt recording history in paint helped to lift his efforts above the marketplace and rescue the artist from the mundane concern of pleasing customers. He preferred to focus attention on his more disinterested motives, claiming, for example, that he was "ever fond of perpetuating the Remembrance of the Worthies of my Time, as I conceive it will be a means of exciting an Emulation in our Posterity . . . and mankind will receive an advantage thereby, the Likeness being added to the Historic page giving it more force and the Reader more pleasure."[20] But he made no pretense of being wholly disinterested and was usually quite candid about the rewards he hoped would accrue to his descendants and his memory. "I have between 30 and 40 portraits of Principal Characters," he wrote in 1783. "This collection has cost me much time & labour and I mean to keep adding . . . in full expectation that my Children will reap the fruits of my Labours."[21]

No matter what the mixture of his motives, Peale's response to the American Revolution set him apart from other eighteenth-century American artists. Copley regarded the approach of war as a serious blow to his artistic ambitions. "I am desireous of

each case the American artist made use of contemporary scenes and particular, contemporary episodes in their historical paintings. Peale's awareness of the historic significance of his own time carried this tendency even further.[18]

avoiding every imputation of party spir[it]," he wrote, "Political contests being neither pleasing to an artist [n]or advantageous to the Art itself."[22] Copley departed America just before Parliament passed the Intolerable Acts; he never returned. Like Copley, Gilbert Stuart sailed for England before the outbreak of hostilities in order to avoid involving himself or his art in the controversy; he returned after the ratification of the Constitution specifically to paint George Washington, who by then had achieved the status of an icon that transcended political or ideological squabbles.[23] Although John Trumbull was, like Peale, a devout patriot who sensed the artistic potential of the Revolution early on, he spent most of the war years in Europe and deferred most of his historical portraits of the Revolution until the nineteenth century, when American independence was assured, patriotism was fashionable, and Congress was willing to pay 8,000 dollars apiece for the four murals he painted for the Capitol.[24]

Peale, on the other hand, was temperamentally and ideologically disposed to take an active role in the Revolution. The notion that artists could or should be granted immunity from wartime tribulations struck him as absurd. It was a time, he reminded many of his friends, when all colonists would have to choose sides. "Some ask why they may not be left neuter," he wrote Benjamin West, "but I believe [it] is almost a settled point that those who do not enter the fight with us is against us."[25] Although Peale, like Copley and Trumbull, regarded the artistic profession as an elevated calling that benefited from tranquility and artistic independence, he did not believe that any faction or group, including artists, could remain aloof from the political and ideological issues that faced the colonies in the 1770s. He recognized that the artist who committed himself to one side usually lost the patronage of his political opponents; it is likely that Peale's inability to prosper in the early 1770s was directly linked to his association with the patriot cause. But, as he saw it, the colonial artist who left America at this critical moment in history was not opting for artistic freedom so much as placing profit above principle. "I would recommend to you to come immediately to America," he wrote a London friend in 1775, then added sardonically, "unless you are in great Business; if so, London is the best place in the world to make money."[26] Moreover, when the war was over and the colonies were independent—

Peale insisted that British defeat was inevitable—everyone, including the artist, would be scrutinized for the role he played in the contest. The future of the arts in the new nation depended heavily on the way artists conducted themselves during the Revolution.

It was easy for Peale to see things this way because he was deeply involved in the political struggle. By 1775 he attributed the deterioration of relations between England and America to "a set of Jacobites" who misrepresented the colonial situation to their superiors at Whitehall. "These men have had the views of getting lucrative posts, & places to tyrannise over the people. These Muckers are now obliged to fly."[27] And his analysis of the colonies on the eve of war was a blend of patriotic rhetoric and well-founded confidence: "All the people declare for Liberty or Death. They are much used [to] hunting and are all good marksmen even our children.... Is it to be supposed that such people thickly settled at least 1400 miles length can be conquered by all the Troops England can send here [?] No it is not probable."[28] In addition to a long and heavily populated coastline, the colonists had George Washington, "a Man of very few words, but when he speaks it is to the purpose";[29] already Peale had spotted Washington's potential as an American hero. Without any qualms, he helped spread stories of Washington's superhuman strength and wisdom, because he believed them himself. On August 9, 1776, Peale enlisted as a common soldier in the militia and soon found himself elected first lieutenant in the High Street ward company. "I go round the ward to know who will go and who not and their reasons, against the enemy," he wrote in his diary.[30] A year earlier he had written Edmund Jenings of the day "when my brush should fail, that I must take the Musket."[31]

The juxtaposition of the brush and the musket is fascinating for several reasons. First, Peale never really exchanged the one for the other; in fact, he painted more portraits in 1776 than in any other year of his life. Most of the approximately sixty-five paintings he completed that year were miniatures; handy and portable, they came into vogue among his fellow soldiers and helped supplement his income. The paintings done that year also constitued a giant first step toward Peale's goal of capturing the faces and scenes of the Revolution for posterity. And in May he received the first commission offered by the Continental Congress to paint a patriotic portrait of Washington.[32] Second, Peale's service in the militia meant that he experienced the war at first hand and was able to store up vivid impressions for future reference. For example, he visited his family in the winter of 1776–77 after they had fled Philadelphia, then occupied by the British, and described "a girl [who] stood in a corner of an old fashioned fireplace, baking Buck-wheat cakes from morning to night to feed the now increased family." He then added, "Not a bad subject for a picture."[33] Although he never painted it, this was the kind of scene—the impact of the war on a typical American family rather than a military engagement—that he liked best. His personal experiences with troops in battle convinced him that heroic depictions of noble acts of valor in combat were falsifications that would teach future generations the wrong lessons. War, as he saw it, was mud and ice and unburied dead and, most of all, utter confusion: the pickets of the Continental Army being shot by their fellow Americans because they did not know the countersign or password used by militia units; the logistical chaos accompaying a major engagement; the insane tactics of the British, "whose practice it generally was to blaze with their numerous artilery on every wood that might cover our scouting parties."[34] The one combat operation he urged West to paint was "the taking of the Hessians at Trent Town, perhaps the point of time when the Genl [Washington] was returning across the River—it was a stormy morning."[35] But unlike later portraits of Washington crossing the Delaware by Thomas Sully and Emanuel Leutze, Peale emphasized the confusion of the moment. It was, as he recalled to Thomas Jefferson in 1819, "the most hellish scene I have ever beheld."[36] Like Goya, Peale regarded the idealization of war as an immoral distortion of reality. When Benjamin West requested precise information about the appearance of the uniforms worn by colonial troops so that he might do a historical portrait, Peale advised him to dispense with "the Ruffles on the shirt."[37]

And even before the war began to provide him with material, Peale had brandished his brush as a weapon and used it with considerably greater skill than he ever used his musket. In his autobiography he called himself a "zealous advocate for the Liberties of his Country" since the time when "Great Britain first attempted to lay a tax on America."[38] This was bragging, but it was also true; indeed, only part of the truth. For Peale was not only an inveterate patriot with spotless patriotic credentials; he was also an experienced propagandist who made banners, signs, and emblems for the Sons of Liberty in Maryland and Massachusetts. Toward the end of his apprenticeship under West, he had completed a large painting and mezzotint of William Pitt, clad in a Roman toga and speaking in behalf of the colonies while clutching a copy of the Magna Carta in his left hand. The picture was cluttered with political symbols—an Indian representing America waited in the background with a bow at the ready—and demonstrated how easy it was for Peale to let his political convictions overwhelm his aesthetic judgment.[39]

His penchant for propaganda, like his embrace of radical ideas, was not the result of meditation or lengthy study. He seemed to assimilate the popularized version of the natural-rights philosophy by osmosis, then, quite instinctively, to express his views with paint as well as words. The portraits he painted during the late 1760s and early 1770s were usually intended to please the buyer rather than exhibit his own political sentiments, but when a patriotic friend like Beale Bordley requested a portrait, Peale felt free to turn it into an allegory denouncing arbitrary power. By 1774 he was receiving commissions from radical groups in Williamsburg and Baltimore for explicit pieces of propaganda:

the design is liberty trampling on Tiranny and puting off Slavery and taking hold of Death, behind them the figure of Slavery coming with hasty strides, behind her a Sea. By Liberty is a collum to de note Stability & an extent of country. The motto *representation or no Taxation.*[40]

This was explicit propaganda. Like the Pitt and Bordley portraits, it was intended less to please than to persuade, was aimed less at the future than at the present, and was designed less as a visual recording than as a contemporary event. True, within the larger context of Western history there was nothing new about didactic art. Both Plato and Aristotle had insisted that the main value of art lay in its usefulness as an educational force in the community. And Aristotle had called attention to the relatively greater power that colors and shapes had over words in affecting public behavior. In the tenth century the monk Theophilus had argued that visual images made a more lasting impression on the human mind than did either the spoken or written word. Diderot had picked up on this theme in the 1750s, arguing that art vitalized the emotions or passions in ways that made it an indispensable tool for shaping public policy. Joshua Reynolds was able to elevate the status of the arts in England by arguing effectively that the artist was more a philosopher than a craftsman, a moral guide whose work rendered certain general truths more comprehensible to the viewer. And William Hogarth, Reynolds's contemporary, was in the process of revolutionizing the English art market by insisting that the moral messages contained in art be made accessible to a broader audience.[41]

But despite the long-recognized claim for art's social utility, despite the realization that art not only gave aesthetic satisfaction but also channeled thoughts and feelings, there were in fact few established precedents for using art as a weapon on behalf of revolution. Virtually all the systematic efforts to harness the arts to a political or ideological cause had been made by established institutions or authorities—the medieval church, the Italian princes and patrons, the court of Louis XIV—primarily because they controlled the wealth essential for the artists' support. Peale's admittedly spontaneous and sporadic attempts at visual propaganda offered the promise not just of enlisting the arts in a crusade for independence destined to go down in history, but also of effecting a reversal in the role artists had historically played in formenting social change.

Peale's personal efforts did not attract the attention of any officials in the state governments or the Continental Congress. Just as there is nothing so powerful as an idea whose time has come, there is nothing so ineffectual as an idea for which no one is prepared. In France fifteen years later the Jacobins created special committees to plan the various ways of exploiting the artistic talent at their disposal. Jacques Louis David emerged as the pioneer in the use of art as a revolutionary weapon; with the assistance of radical leaders he organized festivals, designed military uniforms, encouraged competition among artists, sculptors and architects, and opposed the conservative policies of the Royal Academy. Subsequent revolutionary leaders in Russia and China took special care to attract artistic support and mobilize it for their political purposes. But in eighteenth-century America, potential propagandists like Peale received little official encouragement or support.[42] Some Americans feared or mistrusted artists; most were simply indifferent to and oblivious of the ways art and artists could serve the Revolution. The extended debates over the strengths and weaknesses of monarchic, aristocratic, and democratic government; the newspaper essays, broadsides, and treatises that explored the proper limits of political authority and the legitimate sources of political power—all showed the sophistication American thinkers had achieved as republican theorists. But they had thought scarcely at all about aesthetics or the revolutionary role of the arts. During the Revolution no one knew what to do with a politically active artist like Peale, except make him a politician.[43]

Between 1777 and 1780 Peale served as chairman or member of thirty-two committees entrusted with the regulation of the government and economy of Philadelphia. "Having unfortunately become popular," he explained in his autobiography, he was "obliged to be a busy active character."[44] A leader in the Whig Society (renamed the Constitutional Society in 1779), which dominated Pennsylvania politics throughout the war, he supported the radical provisions of the new state constitution in the face of opposition from moderates like James Wilson and John Bayard, who feared that the new state government incited popular opinion at the expense of property rights. But Peale also opposed the extreme radicals in his own camp who called for the execution of all Tories and the use of violent tactics against the moderates, whom the radicals regarded as Tories in disguise. And while walking that tightrope, Peale served on the committee charged with the identification and arrest of Tories and the disposal of their confiscated estates. This proved his most difficult job, since loyalty to the Revolution was a relative matter, contingent on the degree of commitment required and the proximity of the British army. "To be asking always who are Whigs and who Tories is troublesome," he told a friend, "and I am Sorry to say uncertain. I wish that some marker were put on the Houses of our well known enemies as the Turks do with Lyars, that is by painting them Black."[45] He helped conduct an investigation of Robert Morris's wartime profiteering and, in 1779, was elected to the Pennsylvania assembly. There he supported the gradual abolition of slavery and currency reform.[46]

This pace left little time for painting. He did miniatures during the winter of 1777–78 while serving another tour of militia duty with Washington's army at Valley Forge. And the Pennsylvania assembly commissioned a full-length portrait of Washington in 1779. In 1780 he had a chance to try his hand at propaganda again when he made an effigy of Benedict Arnold holding a mask in one hand and a letter from Beelzebub in the other. But the bulk of his energies went into politics rather than political art.

Inevitably, he made enemies. After the spring of 1778, when the British army evacuted Philadelphia and the war moved south, political divisions between moderate and radical patriots in Pennsylvania took on the appearance of class warfare. Peale, along with Tom Paine and Timothy Matlock, became visible symbols of the radical notion that postrevolutionary American society should be restructured in order to destroy all social distinctions. Moderates who regarded the Revolution as a war for colonial independence in which the structure of postwar society would remain intact were aghast that Peale should take the words of the Declaration of Independence so literally. And these were the wealthy leaders likely to commission portraits. In short, by 1780 Peale had alienated precisely that group of potential patrons on which his future as an artist depended. As Peale put it, "The difference of opinion here made him enemies of those whom before he had considered his best friends."[47] His successful efforts to prevent undue harassment of Tories and to avert open warfare between radicals and moderates also outraged the more fanatical members of the Whig Society, so that he was forced to carry a large cane made of seasoned ash, which he named "Hercules," for protection while walking the streets during the last two years of the war.[48]

Finally, after his unsuccessful attempt to win reelection to the legislature in 1780 and "finding the party disputes of this State intolerably disagreeable," Peale decided to resume his painting career.[49] "When the merit of each was put in the balance," he later explained, "the peaceful muse outweighed political warfare."[50] Not the kind of man to wallow in cynicism, Peale nonetheless left the political arena disappointed and embittered at the way the war had affected his reputation. "Since the beginning of this dispute with Great Britain," he wrote Edmund Jenings, "I have . . . rather more attended to make my Country than myself Independent."[51] Despite his years of public service, he had acquired a reputation as an irresponsible radical, his talent as a propagandist had gone unnoticed, and, once again, he was heavily in debt.

•

In 1780 he applied himself "with a tolerable share of Industry" and resumed painting "a collection of the portraits of characters distinguished from the American revolution. . . ."[52] Peale conceived of this gallery of American heroes as his artistic legacy to posterity; he felt assured that as the years passed, subsequent generations would crave faithful depictions of America's revolutionary leaders. No less an authority than Joshua Reynolds had advised artists that "Present time and future may be considered as rivals and he who solicits the one must expect to be discountenanced by the other."[53] Peale was more convinced than ever—the American victory had confirmed it—that he was present at the creation of a new era in Western history from which future Americans would draw inspiration. This was Peale's elemental and most enduring insight, and it is worth pausing to explore its sources and what it reveals about Peale's artistic values.

First, Peale's scheme for a gallery of American heroes was not a narrowly nationalistic enterprise; it was not calculated to encourage reverence for the secular saints of a patriotic cult. Although Peale was a committed patriot, he regarded the American Revolution as an important event in world history which reaffirmed eternal values that transcended national borders. His patriotism was cosmopolitan, because he accepted unquestioningly the Enlightenment conviction that the proper standard for law, government, morality, and beauty were universal ideals. The newly founded nation was simply the geographic vehicle for classical virtues that had once flourished in Greece and Rome, before the corrupting influence of medieval princes and priests had clouded men's minds. For Peale the Revolution swept away the obfuscations that had formerly blinded Americans to the natural order of things, thereby allowing a recovery of ancient wisdom; this was what the phrase "an American Athens" meant to him. When he began to paint the most prominent leaders of the revolutionary era, he was wholly uninterested in representing them as unique American characters. He wanted to depict them as classical models of timeless, supranational qualities.

Second, the artistic style that Peale had developed by the 1780s depended upon conventions which reinforced the dramatic, heroic character of his subjects. From West, Reynolds, and the London art world he had learned that the artist had moral responsibilities; a painting should elevate and educate the minds of viewers. But Peale's technique also retained strong reminders of his colonial origins, most especially the influence of Godfrey Kneller and Anthony Van Dyke on prerevolutionary American portraiture. Like Kneller, an eighteenth-century English court painter, and even more like his several colonial imitators, Peale emphasized the easygoing authority and benign dignity of his subjects. In a Peale portrait the sitter's hand is often thrust into his vest or his arm rests jauntily on his side; he almost always wears an expression of self-conscious nonchalance along with a half-smile; and the background, which Peale customarily "filled in" after completing the face and torso, seems distinct and alien, thereby causing the figure to stand out even more prominently. Even the awkwardness and archaic stiffness of Peale's figures help to convey an impression of quaint nobility. For all of his technical limitations as a portraitist—the almond-eyed face and bloated torso are Peale trademarks, there is no concern with a sitter's character or psychological makeup, and even his best portraits have a formulaic quality—Peale's depictions of the revolutionary generation still possess a distinctive charm. Part doll and part demigod, the typical Peale figure suggests a benign otherworldliness that wins our affection because of, rather than in spite of, its naivety.[54]

Third, Peale's way of seeing his subjects was saturated with classical assumptions that caused him to disguise the more radical and controversial implications of the American Revolution behind a facade of ordered serenity. In Peale's paintings the social dislocations, wartime atrocities, and personal agonies that accompanied the Revolution have been screened out. Regardless of what Peale's eyes saw during the Revolution—and we know from his diaries and letters that Peale abhorred the boredom of army life and the arbitrary cruelty of the battlefield as well as the social and political disarray in wartime Philadelphia—the classical idioms which he inherited as a disciple of Kneller, West, and Reynolds served as a lens that refracted these incoming images into idealized patterns. Of course Peale himself did not believe that he was imposing his order on chaos, but rather discovering the order that already existed. Creativity, originality, and virtuosity were not appropriate goals for him, because he saw himself as a recorder of the prevailing unity and order reigning in the universe. He assumed that the benevolent rationality reflected in his portraits was embedded in nature rather than in the mind of the artist. "We realize today more and more," writes Ernest Gombrich, "how long is the road from 'perception' to 'expression.' The original genius who paints 'what he sees' and creates new forms out of nothing is a Romantic myth. . . . [The artist] can no more represent what is in front of his eyes without a pre-existing stock of acquired images than he can paint without the pre-existing colours which he must have on his palette."[55] In Peale's case the aesthetic conventions of the classical tradition blended perfectly with his Enlightenment optimism to produce dignified distortions that made the Revolution appear more tame and reasonable than he knew it to be. Ideological disagreements, political squabbling, and military disasters faded away. The role of mass movements and outraged mobs did not fit the classical prescriptions. The Revolution became a gallery of respectable, middle-class personalities.

It is futile to chide Peale for failing to overturn classical conventions that served as the very foundation of his vision as an artist. No other American or English artist was up to the task either. But it is possible to gauge the artistic opportunities that went begging during the American Revolution by contrasting Peale's work with the paintings and sketches of Francisco Goya (1746–1828). Goya's life span matched Peale's almost perfectly. Like Peale, his origins were humble; he matured as an artist in the midst of a revolution and witnessed the horrors of war firsthand; and he too attempted to record for posterity visual images of what he had seen. Moreover, both Peale and Goya were struck by the confusion and bestiality of revolutionary war. But there the similarity ends. For Goya took the insight of war's mindless inhumanity and made it the basis of his art. In his *Caprichos* (1799) and most graphically in the series entitled *The Disasters of War* (1804–14), Goya revolutionized art by stripping historical events of all heroic artifices. Men became monsters driven by unspeakable instincts and trapped within irrational circumstances. With Goya, the artist was no longer interpreting the natural order; he was a creator, a godlike visionary responsible only to his own perceptions of truth. Goya's achievement helps to define even more clearly the limits of Peale's painterly sensibilities and to dramatize the reassuring character of Peale's American heroes.[56]

Fourth and finally, the plan to paint "a collection of our most illustrious personages" allowed Peale to retain the dual role of artist and public servant. Peale was neither a sophisticated political theorist nor an articulate proponent of complicated ideas, but he was a living advertisement for the values of republicanism, most especially the conviction that individuals should subordinate their personal well-being to the greater good of the community. During the war years Peale liked to remind friends of the sacrifices he was making in his artistic career in order to serve the cause of independence. In the 1780s he began to claim that there was a veritable fortune to be made in private commissions, but that he had opted instead for public service by painting portraits of the revolutionary leaders for little or no remuneration. When he established the museum in the 1790s, he insisted that it was a public institution for which he was prepared to sacrifice his time, health, and personal income.[57] Although Peale had an annoying need to draw attention to his virtuous behavior, and although he exaggerated the financial opportunities being lost, his obsession with public service was no idle boast; it was the dominant theme of his entire career. Peale was psychologically incapable of dedicating himself completely to his personal development as an artist or to the pursuit of lucrative commissions unless both could be linked, at least in his own mind, to projects that benefited the public welfare. He was not just an opportunistic hustler who seized upon the idea of a portrait gallery of revolutionary heroes in order to assure his own fame and fortune. He had a sincere and lifelong need to demonstrate his usefulness to the American republic.

Many of the most perceptive and enlightened thinkers in America—the very men Peale wanted to capture on canvas—believed that the most useful thing artists could do would be to leave the country. Although Peale believed that the Revolution had ushered in a golden age for the arts, men like John Adams and Benjamin Rush drew upon republican ideology to argue that the fine arts were a nefarious influence in the new nation and ought to be vigorously opposed. While Peale regarded each setback to his artistic plans as a temporary aberration that would soon be washed away by a wave of high culture that, naturally and inevitably, must sweep across America, the fine arts were being described as an infectious disease fatal to republican values.[58]

At the most mundane level the hostility toward artists focused on their impracticality. Artists were social parasites who contributed nothing to the essential job of nation building. At a time when continents were waiting to be conquered, fields cleared, roads constructed, and canals dug, art seemed superfluous, its support an unnecessary drain on the national energies. Peale was sufficiently saturated with the republican insistence on utility to share this apprehension himself. His various efforts to demonstrate art's usefulness were intended to silence critics on this point and to remove the personal doubts he harbored about the social utility of his own calling.

But a more serious indictment derived from attitudes inherited from prerevolutionary American society and incorporated into republican ideology. According to this traditional view, artists were not just useless; they were exceedingly dangerous creatures who symbolized the victory of luxury over virtue, the corruption of simple, agrarian values by commercial arrangements, and the waning of self-discipline owing to excessive wealth. Artists, so the argument went, tended to flourish in mature societies like imperial Rome or Renaissance Italy, which had reached that point in their development when wealth became available for luxuries. The most articulate spokesman for this view was Rousseau, who argued that the fine arts blossomed only when a society was on the verge of decline. Rousseau did not claim that artists *caused* moral and social decay, only that they were a clear symptom of degeneration always associated with the erosion of public virtue. But American colonists had not needed to read Rousseau to share this suspicion of the arts. As eighteenth-century America became more populous, as the economy shifted from subsistence farming to commercial agriculture, as the available wealth increased and was distributed more unequally, as large towns and cities replaced rural villages as the social and economic centers of American life, the stability and simplicity cherished by most colonists seemed to deteriorate. The emergence of the arts and artists was yet another distressing manifestation of the social changes sweeping through eighteenth-century America and transforming the established patterns of day-by-day existence. Those Americans who believed that the Revolution was fought to preserve the simple agrarian virtues of the past from English corruption regarded the appearance of artists as a threat to the traditional values they held most dear.[59]

Americans of the revolutionary generation were particularly receptive to this formulation for several reasons: it gave intellectual integrity to their prejudices against European cultural superiority by making cathedrals, palaces, and paintings symbols of social decline rather than of national greatness; it confirmed their reading of history by affirming the symbiotic relationship between the arts and despotic figures like kings, priests, and nobles; it depended upon the same mode of historical analysis that informed the thinking of American republican theorists, who also contrasted public virtue with luxury, republican simplicity with despotic extravagance; it turned American cultural deficencies from a source of shame into a cause for rejoicing by making them hallmarks of social health rather than badges of barbarism. As John Adams warned John Trumbull, "Remember that the Burin and the Pencil, the Chisel and the Trowell, have in all ages and Countries of which we have any information, been enlisted on the side of Despotism and Superstition.... Architecture, Sculpture, Painting and Poetry have conspir'd against the Rights of Mankind."[60]

Peale's entire artistic and political career defied Adams's version of history. Whether he was simply the exception that proved the rule or positive evidence that the Revolution had initiated a new set of arrangements between art and society no one at the time bothered to say. In the end it made no practical difference.

While Peale waited expectantly for art to flourish in a new American Athens, its association in the public mind with wealth, selfishness, decadence, and the irrelevant kept art on the defensive. And in an age of purported rationality, Peale found himself caught in an irrational but highly effective whipsaw: he suffered from the suspicion of artists as agents of tyranny at the same time that he stood accused of taking the rhetoric about "the Rights of Mankind" too literally; his eagerness to harness the arts to American republicanism was squelched by republican fears that artists were despotic mercenaries.

•

This American apprehension toward the arts affected the art market. Peale found it necessary to become an artist-capitalist after the war, searching out customers willing to pay for paintings and badgering them for fees. "I have been very busily employed," he told Beale Bordley, "but not with politics or any kind of public affairs, but with the pensil, labouring hard to give full satisfaction to those who favor me with employment."[61] He was also kept busy writing to request payment for portraits and miniatures done during the war. "If you will please pay me now," he told one delinquent customer, "you may be doing me a greater favor than if you had paid me much sooner."[62] His letters to prominent former sitters like George Washington, John Hancock, and Samuel Mifflin were usually deferential and plaintive in tone, although when Henry Laurens balked at the bill for three portraits, Peale gave him a lecture on the time required to paint, frame, and pack the items and the impact of the currency inflation on creditors.[63] If a customer proved recalcitrant, Peale minced no words: "You had your portrait in miniature from me in Oct. 1781 at which time you promised to pay for the same in three or four Days. I want no more promises, but the money or the picture I expect immediately."[64] With former friends like Benjamin Rush, who had broken off relations during the war because of Peale's association with "the mobocracy," he retained his pride by requesting funds in the form of a joke. "When a person is in Cash," he wrote Rush in 1782, "the people of Maryland use the phraise, [*sic*] such a one is in Blast. . . . I am out of Blast. . . ."[65]

Although he usually tried to put the best face on his situation when corresponding with Benjamin West, in the 1780s even Peale's letters to West reflected his despondency. "I now find it necessary to travel to get business sufficient in the portrait line to maintain my family," he admitted in 1788. "I mention these things to show you that the state of the Arts in America is not very favorable at present, altho' I am so fortunate as to please all that employ me, yet I find it difficult to get wherewith to maintain me."[66] In the winter of 1786 he was forced to request an advance of fifteen bushels of coal from the local dealer, pleading poverty and the support of his wife, mother, seven children, and two kitchen servants. A month earlier he had begged for a similar advance from the grocer: "Want of money for tomorrow's marketing obliges me to ask your acceptance at this time. The Arts are languishing in our City, at least within the circle of my knowledge. And whether I can live here or not, in a short time will be determined . . . I hope you will befriend and excuse this call. . . ."[67] He petitioned for back pay that he claimed was due for committee work done during the war and even recommended himself to Washington as a candidate for the job of postmaster general, all as a way of supplementing the income from his painting and reducing the hardships imposed by an art market that seemed even more capricious than before the war.[68] He continued to work on his gallery of "prominent personages," which remained the chief assurance of his historical reputation. At the same time he began to grope for a strategy that would make him less dependent on the taste and support of wealthy customers.

One answer Peale called "public art." It represented his attempt to put an end to his reliance on individual patrons by casting him in the role of "artist of all the people." The major feature of the scheme was government subsidy of Peale's work in return for art that was intended to exalt the virtues of the new nation and be displayed in public. Copies of Peale's Washington portrait of 1781, which various state legislatures commissioned, represented one form of this new arrangement among artists and government, but Peale clearly envisioned a more permanent and binding alliance than the periodic sale of official portraits.

What Peale had in mind was designed to rescue art from the market by transforming artists into public servants supported by government subsidies. In 1781 he had placed three "illumina-

tions" or transparent pictures in the windows of his house to celebrate the American victory at Yorktown:

In the lower story was a representation of the ship Ville de Paris under
full sail; in the second story were busts (good likenesses) of the excel-
lancies general Washington and count Rochambeau in an elliptical circle
of stars and flowers de luce—the motto LIVE VALIANT CHIEFS;
and in the third story, a label extending across the front of the house—
FOR OUR ALLIES, HUZZA, HUZZA, HUZZA.[69]

He had displayed these "illuminations" at his own initiative and
received no support from the government. In 1783, however,
he attempted to repeat the experiment, this time with financial
assistance from the state. And late in the year, after much lobbying
by Peale, the Pennsylvania assembly agreed to pay him 600
pounds, the equivalent of a year's income for Peale, for the creation
of a huge "triumphal arc" that would serve as the centerpiece for
a public celebration in honor of the signing of the Paris peace
treaty. Peale stopped work on all his other projects and devoted
six weeks to the construction of a frame, fifty-six feet wide and
forty feet high, that spanned Market Street. The structure contained Ionic columns, representations of Washington as the American Cincinnatus, of "Confederated America," of Louis XVI of
France, panels in honor of the war dead, various Latin inscriptions, allegorical scenes, all topped by a goddess symbolizing
peace. The panels were transparent and were to be lighted by
over one thousand lamps.[70]
   If Peale had high hopes that this project marked the start of
increased government support for the arts, those hopes went up
in smoke along with the entire "triumphal arc." On the night of
the celebration, as Peale was putting the finishing touches to his
creation,

A rocket being put too near the paintings unfortunately took fire and in
10 minutes the work of much pains & study was consumed to ashes.
But this was not the worst. One or two persons was killed by a great
number of rockets taking fire . . . I was on the top of the frame and
seeing no prospect of extinguishing the first I endeavored to save myself by descending by a back post.[71]

In the aftermath of the disaster Peale requested the government to finance a reconstruction of the grand design, but the officials balked. "Let the misfortunes and losses of this undertaking be a warning to his children, not to engage in a like enterprise," he advised in his autobiography. "It is much better to trust in the generosity of an Individual than to the public." But he wrote this many years later, after a series of frustrated efforts to obtain state support for his museum and government support for the arts and sciences in general. For most of his life he championed the cause of public art and government subsidies, despite his inability to convince the legislators that American culture required or deserved such support. "I say I am sorry," he wrote in 1797, "but it is not for myself . . . but for America, because this will bring a disgrace on her which I cannot avow."[72]

Soon after the "triumphal arc" episode, Peale concocted yet another scheme designed to bring his art before a mass audience. This time he dispensed with the effort to obtain government backing and decided to sell tickets for admission to an exhibition he described as "a new kind of painting." If the government would not support the arts, perhaps "the people" would come to the rescue on their own. He first called the exhibition "Perspective Views with Changeable Effects; or Nature Delineated and in Motion," which he soon shortened to "Moving Pictures." The idea was to produce transparent pictures that could be manipulated and lighted in such a way as to create the illusion of a realistic scene from nature or history. He worked on the pictures, machinery, and lighting for over a year and added a new room to his house to serve as the theater. By May of 1785 he was ready to show his pictures and discover "how they will take with the public." He purchased space in the newspapers to advertise the exhibition, which could be seen for three shillings ninepence per customer, a price most artisans and mechanics could afford.[73]

It is difficult to categorize the painted scenes Peale presented to the people of Philadelphia, who initially flocked to the show in great numbers. They were an artistic novelty, distant forerunners of the modern cinema, similar to the propagandistic "illuminations" he had done during the war. One of the scenes, entitled *A Grand Piece of Architecture,* showed a thunderstorm appearing over Roman-styled buildings; after the storm subsided a rainbow appeared, a reassuring symbol in the year of Shays's Rebellion. The depiction of the *Bonhomme Richard*'s victory over the British frigate *Serapis* was explicit propaganda designed to arouse patriotic applause from the spectators, which it apparently did. But the chief purpose of the "Moving Pictures" was less to express political sentiments than to bring a broad public into contact with the arts. The high point of the program was entitled *Pandaemonium,* a popularized historical portrait of the confusion and horror of Lucifer's kingdom as described in *Paradise Lost.*[74] This was the kind of subject prominent English artists painted for exhibitions in the Royal Academy, here being presented to an audience of middle-class Americans in a gimmick-ridden format intended to catch and hold their attention. Interestingly, Peale insisted that "there was nothing in the subjects to make the populace laugh," even though an exhibition with more humor and what he called "bustle" might "have been more generally resorted to" and caused "People [to] run mad to see it."[75] Peale was clearly interested in using the "Moving Pictures" as a way of introducing the populace to American art and initiating their visual education. He was willing to make concessions to popular opinion until that opinion became more sophisticated; but he did not want to turn the exhibition into a sideshow that prostituted his artistic talent. "I neglect many little contrivances which might serve to catch the eye of the gaping multitude," he wrote later, "although this direction of my labour may not be immediately so productive of funds, yet it will ultimately be more important . . . and honorable to me."[76]

Neither the initial success of the exhibition nor Peale's enthusiasm for public or popular art could overcome the disheartening fact that ticket sales dropped off as the novelty of "Moving Pictures" waned. A broad, popular constituency proved just as fickle as aristocratic patrons. Peale noted the decline in public interest after two months: "If the profits is not sufficient to enable me to ride in a Coach," he observed, "I can nevertheless be tolerably happy in going on foot."[77] But there was obviously something about the exhibition other than its money-making possibilities that Peale found endearing, since he kept it going for over two years. In February of 1787 he concluded that "the profits of my Exhibition is insufficient for the Expence of labour" and prepared a public announcement that "the Exhibition will end forever."[78] But in March he decided to delay the closing in order to allow the children of Philadelphia to view the show. Then in April and May the delegates to the Constitutional Convention arrived in town; Peale extended invitations to prominent representatives from other states, received a request for a special showing from the Society of the Cincinnati, and kept the "Moving Pictures" alive until the end of the summer. A few years later the pictures and equipment were sold to a traveling showman.[79]

The end of the "Moving Pictures" also marked the beginning of a new career as a naturalist and curator of "Peale's Museum." His interest in public art never disappeared; in 1788 he painted a transparent picture entitled *The Horrors of Anarchy and Confusion, and the Blessings of Order* in honor of Maryland's ratification of the Constitution. And despite the fiasco of 1784, the Pennsylvania Assembly commissioned him to prepare another elaborate arc in 1789; this one was equipped with a device that lowered a laurel wreath to the head of George Washington, who sat astride a white charger provided by the city while on his way to New York for his inauguration as president.[80] But the names he gave his male children accurately reflected Peale's change of interest; after Raphaelle, Rembrandt, Titian, Rubens, and Vandyke, the next two boys were christened Charles Linnaeus and Benjamin Franklin. Although he continued to add to his historical collection and painted some of his most impressive portraits early in the nineteenth century, his main concern became the preservation of natural objects and animals rather than human likenesses. With the announcement of the opening of "Mr. Peale's Museum . . . Admittance *One Shilling*" in July of 1788, his active career as a struggling artist came to an end.

•

Although the museum was a new career and a new obsession, filled with all the surprises, mishaps, and adventures friends came to expect of "Old Charlie Peale," the major themes in his life—one might say its "true outline"—were all well established by 1788. The museum years, which were punctuated by periodic artistic flurries and a try at retirement, repeated the old melodies in a slightly different key: constant indebtedness, frequent appeals for public support in order to avoid dependence on wealthy patrons, government unwillingness to subsidize his various enterprises, the persistent conviction that his artistic reputation and American cultural life would flower at some unspecified time in the future, a conscious sense that he was helping to create a national mythology, an enthusiastic eclecticism that bordered on impulsiveness.

It is tempting to take the last theme as the whole and attribute the diversity of Peale's life to his personality; Peale suggested as much himself. "I am not unconscious that I have mispent much of my time," he wrote to Jefferson in 1815. "It seems impossible to forbear putting my hands to execute what the fancy dictates...."[81] And in 1800 he confessed that "like a child of Nature, unrestrained, I have strayed a thousand ways, as the impulse I have lead [*sic*] me on with little regard to the result."[82] The stops and starts and ingenious schemes that characterized Peale's artistic life were, in this view, a function of his eccentric and idiosyncratic personality. As one nineteenth-century commentator explained it, even when Peale stood among the displayed rarities of his museum, he was "by far the most memorable curiosity."[83]

But the museum should not be seen as a random collection of curios; nor should Peale be remembered as a childlike creature skittering from one unrelated distraction to another. In fact, the museum was a metaphor for the order, stability, and coherence that Peale valued most highly, an institutionalization of Peale's republican ideal, comprised entirely of American artifacts. Like his gallery of revolutionary portraits, the museum represented Peale's effort to capture, then freeze for all time, the benign serenity and harmony of the postrevolutionary American world he longed for. He described the museum as "an institute of laws eternal" and a "Temple of Wisdom" which provided "striking examples of the beneficence of Providence with charming models for every social duty." He loved to tell the story of the chance meeting in the museum between two hostile Indian chiefs who were so overcome with the natural harmony surrounding them that they agreed to sign a peace treaty on the premises. In the museum, if nowhere else, virtue still reigned supreme. A believer in civic responsibility throughout his life, Peale hoped that the ordered replications of the museum would "influence public opinions [so] that republicanism will be highly promoted."[84]

If the museum embodied Peale's dedication to the ideals of republicanism, the fate of the museum serves as a convenient symbol of Peale's lifelong encounter with the capitalistic and democratic forces accelerated by the American Revolution. Over the years Peale was forced to compromise his scientific principles, in part because he collected so many different animals and artifacts that they overwhelmed his Linnean scheme, in part because the continued existence of the museum required concessions to popular opinion. Peale's backyard became a hilarious menagerie of buffaloes, Indian scalps, jaw bones, owls, baboons, rattlesnakes, rare rocks, and plants—all vying for a special place in the "natural order of things." Under Rubens's prodding, Peale agreed to stage shows in the museum in order to attract customers. And so an Italian musician who styled himself "The Pandean Band" played the viola, drums, symbols, pipes, and Chinese bells among the skeletons and petrifications. In 1823 Peale introduced the "Magic Lanthorn" show, designed to illustrate the principles of astronomy and the sciences; it featured mock thunderstorms, collapsing miniature houses, Raphaelle doing sound effects and ventriloquy, and the firing of a brass cannon. Peale cringed at the corruption of science by show business, but, as Rubens pointed out, the people stayed away unless the museum offered special attractions.[85]

In short, Peale's eclecticism was an economic necessity. Throughout his career, he was not so much willing to experiment with different kinds of art and different constituencies as he was forced to do so in order to survive. The Revolution had discredited art's traditional allies. In the process of searching for new ones Peale inevitably developed the habit of adapting his art to his audience, evaluating his paintings against the market rather than against an internalized ideal, lobbying for prominent sitters and government commissions, living by his wits as much as by his brush. Unless he followed the example set by West and Copley and left America, he had no other choice. His decision to remain in America had assets and liabilities: it guaranteed that future generations would overpraise his work because of his patriotism;[86] it also required him to develop commercial in-

stincts that constrained his growth as an artist. It is even possible
to understand Peale's inability to remain solvent as a self-inflicted
punishment for acquiring many of the characteristics of an entrepreneur.*

His efforts to establish a popular foundation for his art followed naturally from his political convictions; and these convictions were not whimsical accoutrements but deeply felt principles shaped in the ideological controversies of the decades
surrounding the Revolution. Although he was not a sophisticated
political theorist, he had a remarkably clear understanding of
the cultural implications of his elemental political values. Ironically, the revolutionary ideology that Peale so ardently espoused
undercut the traditional sources of support for artists and helped
instill a widespread apprehension of the arts in America. Peale
the artist suffered the consequences of policies and values that
Peale the revolutionary championed. But if that irony was lost on
Peale, he *was* acutely aware of the need to adapt the arts to the
republican values of postrevolutionary America. His effort to
forge alliances between the arts and the revolutionary tradition,
the arts and the American public, the arts and the government,
was a pioneering if premature attempt to place American culture,
like American government, on a broad public foundation. In the
end, everything that Peale painted was propaganda, in the sense
that it was intended to show present and future generations that
the visual arts were at worst harmless and at best valuable allies
of the principles rooted in the revolutionary tradition. Virtually
all the social predicaments and economic pressures which were to
afflict American artists over the next century manifested themselves in Peale's career. And Peale's response to these pressures
foreshadowed almost all the maneuvers available to American
artists caught in the freedoms of a democratic and capitalistic
society.

* Peale thought a great deal about his inability to stay out of debt,
especially toward the end of his life, when he worried about debts that
would pass on to his children. "I had nothing when I began the world, and
somehow or other, I have always been poor . . . , he wrote to Henry Moore.
He contrasted his concern for beauty and for the public good with the
broker's concern for money and personal gain: "I consider them [brokers]
the leeches of human society." In his autobiography he asked rhetorically,
"Can it be honest to gain by others' losses?"[87]

Chapter Four

Hugh Henry Brackenridge: The Novelist as Reluctant Democrat

❧

Our American Chivalry is the worst in the World. It has no Laws, no bounds, no definitions; it seems to be all a Caprice.

John Adams to Thomas Jefferson, April 17, 1826

One of Charles Willson Peale's most endearing attributes was his unabounded optimism for the future of the American republic and for his own artistic reputation. Hugh Henry Brackenridge was a prominent postrevolutionary writer who displayed less confidence about the future of the nation and his own impact on posterity. Brackenridge confessed that he had once considered himself an important author "embued with faculties above the capacities of mere mortals" and destined for a place in American literary history. "I would not have made the exertions that I have made," he observed, "unless I believed my work would endure." But by 1806 Brackenridge had concluded that only a twentieth-century reader who was "rummaging amongst old and scarce books" would find any of his works, and that then they would prove valuable only "to see in what manner the human mind had employed itself in times past."[1]

Hugh Henry Brackenridge *by Gilbert Stuart* (*1810*)
Courtesy of the University of Pittsburgh

Although his literary reputation has enjoyed several minor revivals, history has tended to confirm Brackenridge's prediction. His major work, the novel *Modern Chivalry,* went through several editions in the nineteenth century. In 1847 John Quincy Adams even proclaimed that Brackenridge's fictional characters were the American equivalent to Virgil's mythical heroes and that *Modern Chivalry* would "last beyond the period fixed by the ancient statutes for the canonization of poets, a full century."[2] But Brackenridge is scarcely remembered today, much less canonized. Vernon Parrington devoted a few pages of *Main Currents in American Thought* to Brackenridge in 1927. Five years later Claude Newlin published a life-and-times biography, soon followed by a new edition of *Modern Chivalry,* which Newlin called "the most vigorous book of its time and the most penetrating comment on American democracy in the making." Nevertheless, anthologies of American literature mention Brackenridge only in passing, if they mention him at all, and historians of early America seldom recognize his name. Lewis Leary was being overly generous when he said that *Modern Chivalry* fits Mark Twain's definition of a classic, "a book which many people have talked about, but few people have read."[3]

During his own lifetime many people talked about Brackenridge, although few claimed to understand him. A portrait painted by Gilbert Stuart in 1810, when Brackenridge was a judge on the Pennsylvania Supreme Court, conveys the impression of a dignified man of self-conscious propriety. But a young law student claimed that Brackenridge heard cases "with his breast entirely open; his small clothes without suspenders, and neither exactly on nor off; his beard unshaven, and his hair undressed, with large ungainly boots; cravat twisted like a rope, and his whole demeanor anything but attentive to the business of the court."[4] When he was a practicing lawyer in Pittsburgh a prospective client reported that Brackenridge told him, "Go away, sir; no man of sense goes to law—did you ever hear of my going to law?" Brackenridge then responded to the charge of eccentricity by asserting that "he was the only one of his acquaintances like everybody else."[5] The Federalists, who considered him a dangerous radical because of his association with the Whiskey Rebellion in western Pennsylvania, called Brackenridge "President of the

Jacobin Society ... Poet Laureate to the Herald of Sedition, Biographer to the Insurgents, Auctioneer of Divinity, and Haberdasher of Pronouns."[6] Meanwhile, many residents of the frontier considered him an ally of eastern politicians and criticized him so severely that Brackenridge compared his life on the frontier to "the situation of a traveller in the Island of Borneo ... with a thousand monkeys leaping and chattering amongst the trees and incommoding the Caravan by the fall of excrement."[7] Yet, despite his satirical attacks on the crudity of western mores, Brackenridge married an illiterate country girl who first impressed him by leaping a rail fence while running barefoot across a cow pasture.[8]

Much of Brackenridge's eccentricity and apparent inconsistency was an elaborate charade, a self-conscious effort to ridicule westerners who considered themselves pristine embodiments of a romanticized wilderness ideal and easterners who behaved as if they were divinely appointed agents of civilization. Federalists and Jeffersonian Democrats received the same treatment, which usually involved juxtaposing the pretensions of one group and the follies of the other in such a way as to generate laughter. And while the objects of his ridicule were laughing, Brackenridge assured them that he should not be taken seriously. "My business is to speak nonsense," he announced in *Modern Chivalry*, "this being the only way to keep out of criticism." But even the assurances were barbed jokes: "The truth is, I will not give myself the trouble to write sense long," he told his readers, "for I would as soon please fools as wise men; because the fools are more numerous, and every prudent man will go with the majority."[9]

He began his adult life as an enthusiastic young radical, co-author with Philip Freneau of *The Rising Glory of America*, a chaplain with the Continental Army at Valley Forge, and a magazine editor committed to reaching ordinary Americans with the good news that they were all potential Platos and Shakespeares. To the very end of his life he remained a staunch defender of republican principles who joked that the execution of a monarch "affects me no more than the execution of another malefactor" and who insisted that he wrote his books for "Tom, Dick, and Harry in the woods. . . ." But even before the Revolution was over Brackenridge had begun to have doubts about what he would later call "mere democracy" or "the despotism of many instead of one." He was most apprehensive about the erosion of cultural and intellectual standards, the elevation of ignorant and uneducated men to public office, and the burgeoning belief that truth was best served by a poll of the people. He became skeptical of the values coming into existence in the marketplace and the legislatures. Like Captain Farrago, the main character in *Modern Chivalry*, Brackenridge retained affection for the classical ideals of antiquity, for deferential rather than egalitarian principles, for chivalry more than modernity. In this sense he had much in common with Federalist critics who wrote scathing critiques of democratic policies and values for magazines like the *Port Folio* and the *Monthly Anthology*. But—and with Brackenridge there is always a "but"—Brackenridge loathed the Federalists and made them the recipients of some of his most biting satire. He had the capacity to stand outside the various ideological and political groupings of his day, to lob explosive jokes into the different camps, and to laugh at his own follies while doing so. "The comic," wrote Henri Bergson, "comes into being just when society and the individual, freed from the worry of self-preservation, begin to regard themselves as works of art." Brackenridge developed his capacity for humor and his affinity for paradox just when American society began to become the liberal, democratic world that Brackenridge had once found so alluring.[10]

•

Only a few shreds of evidence about Brackenridge's childhood survive, and they are invariably the kind of nostalgic recollections and secondhand reminiscences that comprise the stuff of democratic mythology. He was born in Scotland in 1748, the son of an impoverished farmer named William Brackenridge and the grandson of a tenant farmer who was killed in the battle of Culloden. The family migrated to America in 1753. Brackenridge grew up in Peach Tree Township, one of the Scotch-Irish frontier settlements just west of the Susquehanna River in colonial Pennsylvania. There, according to family lore, he demonstrated an early preference for books rather than the plough, learned Latin and Greek in the Slate Ridge School, cried when a cow chewed up his only copy of Horace, and walked thirty miles each Saturday to borrow books from the Reverend John Blair. His teachers and several neighbors encouraged his love for books, and eventually his mother "began to look forward with fond hope to seeing her favorite son one day a minister of the Gospel," then regarded as the appropriate career for a scholar. In 1763 the fifteen-year-old prodigy left the family farm to become school-master in Gunpowder Falls, Maryland, where he put down student rebellions with an authority that belied his age, and continued to read the classics. After five years of teaching, at the somewhat advanced age of twenty, he was admitted as a student at the College of New Jersey at Princeton.[11]

Princeton had only recently come under the control of John Witherspoon, a Scottish clergyman who exposed Brackenridge, and eventually an entire generation of future American statesmen, to the major ideas of the Scottish Enlightenment. Witherspoon's course in moral philosophy introduced Brackenridge to the works of David Hume, Francis Hutcheson, Lord Kames, and Adam Smith, and to two heady notions: that both human nature and society were governed by immutable laws; and that only the scholar-statesman capable of discovering these laws was properly equipped to govern. Brackenridge and the other Princeton students could not help interpreting this message as a call to public service. For the rest of his life Brackenridge retained the conviction that a rigorous education was a prerequisite for political office. In the prerevolutionary years, however, Loyalists argued that Witherspoon's classes bred a seditious brand of skepticism. When Jonathan Boucher charged that Princeton was a hotbed of a "Mischievous kind of knowledge," Witherspoon replied that his students were not defective in their "loyalty to our most excellent sovereign." This proved a rather lame rejoinder, especially after Witherspoon became a member of the Continental Congress and a signer of the Declaration of Independence.[12]

Brackenridge had probably opposed British policies toward the colonies before his arrival at Princeton, but his college experiences intensified and channeled his patriotic zeal and helped prepare him for an early career as revolutionary propagandist. Witherspoon's lectures on moral philosophy and the reading he did for courses developed Brackenridge's familiarity with both modern and classical justifications for republicanism.[13] But extra-curricular life, what James Madison called "recreation and release from business and books," fired up Brackenridge's ambitions and launched his literary career. In 1769 he joined with Madison, Philip Freneau, and William Bradford to form the Whig Society, a student organization that matched wits and words with the rival Tory group. Brackenridge, the precocious western farm boy, enjoyed the friendship of a future American president, the foremost poet and radical propagandist in the new nation, and a future attorney general of the United States. In this select company and in the heated political climate of prerevolutionary Princeton, Brackenridge first tried to make a mark on history with his pen.[14]

Like Peale's early paintings, Brackenridge's student writings were crude and naive productions in which aesthetic concerns were drowned in a flood of revolutionary rhetoric. In his contributions to a series of student poems entitled "Satires against the Tories" he ridiculed Tory writers who tried to support their cause with verse:

> *Ye Gods! What pitiful pretence!*
> *What vile unheard of impudence!*
> *What Daemon from the realms of night*
> *Has bid your glowing poets write?*

He implied that the correctness of a writer's political principles, rather than the quality of his language, was the essential prerequisite for an aspiring man of literature. He even made fun of the opposition by writing foolishly trite verses from the Tory perspective, suggesting that those who supported the Stamp Act and the Townshend duties were capable only of "dirty things in prose" and "tawdry rimes." A literary critic on the lookout for early evidence of Brackenridge's mature style would discover a few noteworthy items: he was most clever and witty when ridiculing the pretensions of his ideological enemies; and in a short piece of prose fiction entitled "Father Bombo's Pilgrimage" he wrote dialogue based on the patterns of speech used by Irish and Scotch settlers on the Pennsylvania frontier. Both of these tendencies would be more fully developed in *Modern Chivalry*. But during the Princeton years Brackenridge's written verses and stories were juvenile imitations of classical authors, especially Lucian, and represented Brackenridge's effort to defend his Whig political convictions with a classical style that masked his back-country origins.[15]

In 1771 Brackenridge graduated—he was salutatorian of his class—and at the commencement ceremonies read from a poem that he and Freneau had written for the occasion. The last third of the poem, which was entitled *The Rising Glory of America,* sketched Brackenridge's vision of an America "not less in fame than Greece and Rome." He predicted that colonial America would eventually become a "seat of empire" where the sciences, literature, and the arts would flourish and "fair freedom shall forever reign." Here was the standard Whig belief that the expansion of personal freedom and political liberty paved the way for literary and artistic greatness, Bishop Berkeley's uplifting vision of an American Athens, and the inevitable westward drift of civilization. And like Peale, Brackenridge regarded the looming conflict with England as the prelude to epochal events that would provide American artists and writers with a set of patriotic heroes fit for enshrinement:

> *I see a train, a glorious train appear,*
> *Of patriots plac'd in equal fame with those*
> *Who nobly fell for Athens or for Rome.*
>
> .   .   .
>
> *I see a Homer and a Milton rise*
> *In all the pomp and majesty of song,*
> *Which gives immortal vigour to the deeds*
> *Achiev'd by Heroes in the fields of fame.*

While Brackenridge's Princeton classmates, who reportedly greeted *The Rising Glory of America* with "great applause," wondered if they might become the new American heroes, Brackenridge himself had begun to entertain the hope that he was an American Homer.[16]

This preposterous and presumptuous idea had its roots in something more substantial than Brackenridge's schoolboy enthusiasm. The chauvinistic vision of *Rising Glory,* Brackenridge's belief that history was on his side, grew naturally out of the Enlightenment doctrines that Witherspoon propagated at prerevolutionary Princeton and reflected the optimistic mentality that accompanied the demographic and economic growth of prerevolutionary America. Brackenridge attributed the "great inferiority of the moderns to the ancients in fine writing ... to this veil cast over mankind, by the artificial refinements of modern monarchy." Once America earned its independence and the imperial shackles that restricted colonial commerce and culture were broken, a flood of talent would be released and "America will produce poets, orators, critics, and historians, equal to the most celebrated of the ancient commonwealths of Greece and Italy."[17] In effect, Brackenridge was not claiming that he possessed an extraordinary supply of literary ability so much as he was claiming to be part of a critical mass of American cultural energy about ready to explode onto the world.

Unfortunately for Brackenridge, American literary culture proved to be less like an explosion that went off with the Revolution than a tender plant that required over fifty years of cultivation before it blossomed. But no matter how illusory Brackenridge's expectations proved to be—and his career is a window into the frustration of the generation of American writers who came of age with the Revolution—they were plausible. Indeed, there were more reasons for an aspiring author to expect glory than Brackenridge could possibly know.

Put simply, a larger proportion of America's population were potential readers of books than was the case in any other country in the world. Two developments had combined to create this situation in prerevolutionary America. The first was a remarkably high literacy rate. By the time Brackenridge graduated from Princeton, England, which Samuel Johnson called "a nation of readers," had a male literacy rate of about 60 percent; France had a male literacy rate of about 50 percent. Although American literacy rates varied from region to region—New England led the way, followed closely by the middle colonies and then the South —approximately 70 to 75 percent of the white male population knew how to read. In the emerging urban centers, the percentage was considerably higher. In Boston, for example, over 70 percent of the women were literate. Even in the back-country counties of Pennsylvania, where Brackenridge was raised, the male literacy rate had reached 65 percent by mid-century. If it was not a nation of readers, America was, even more than England, a nation populated by men and women with the technical ability to read.[18]

In addition to being literate, a large proportion of Americans had sufficient incomes to afford books. In many prerevolutionary communities wealth was becoming less evenly distributed as the eighteenth century wore on. By 1774, for example, the richest 10 percent of the population in the middle colonies owned 40.6 percent of the wealth and the poorest 10 percent were in debt. But despite the appearance of growing numbers of rich and poor, the overall standard of living was rising steadily, and the middle 70 percent of the population had sufficient income to afford at least a few luxuries, including the two to six shillings required to purchase an inexpensive edition of a book.[19]

English writers had already shown that a change in the size and character of the reading public could have a dramatic impact on literature. A gradual increase in the literacy rate, along with an equally gradual increase in the number of middle-class artisans, shopkeepers, and tradesmen, had combined to alter the center of gravity of the reading public and put England's middle class in a dominant position for the first time. The appearance of a new literary form, appropriately named "the novel," the popular success of such novelists as Daniel Defoe, Henry Fielding, Samuel Richardson, and Laurence Sterne, the emergence of Grub Street booksellers and professional writers turning out essays for new periodicals and monthly magazines—all these developments were largely attributable to the expansion of the popular market for the written word. In short, at some point during the middle third of the eighteenth century, English social conditions had become sufficiently favorable that publishers and writers had begun to benefit from the growing public appetite for books and had begun to feed that appetite with new and inexpensive literary forms, which in turn produced an increased demand for more books and authors. Here was an auspicious precedent for the emergence of American letters.[20]

From our perspective in the twentieth century, of course, the literary prospects of revolutionary America appear less promising. Despite the high literacy rate and income level, the American reading public totaled less than two million people. Philadelphia was about the size of modern-day Poughkeepsie, New York; Boston had fewer inhabitants than Emporia, Kansas, has today.

Although the American population was doubling in size every twenty-five years, it remained pitifully small by modern standards; it was also spread out over a countryside lacking the kind of roads and canals that would allow people and opinions to move about easily. And the ability to put books into the hands of a mass American market awaited the establishment of publishing companies that would make Philadelphia and New York the centers of a flourishing book trade by the 1830s.[21] Most important, we know that Nathaniel Hawthorne and Herman Melville did not produce their classic works of American fiction until the middle of the nineteenth century, that James Fenimore Cooper's *The Last of the Mohicans* was not published until fifty years after the Declaration of Independence, and that Ichabod Crane and Rip Van Winkle did not appear in our fiction until Washington Irving published *The Sketchbook* in 1819-20.

Here, however, is a case in which our awareness of what did, in fact, happen impairs rather than improves our appreciation of the mentality shared by Brackenridge and his generation. Brackenridge's enthusiastic estimate of America's literary prospects certainly proved premature. The belief that cultural independence was synonymous with political independence, that American literature would develop naturally and immediately once the colonies broke free of English imperial rule, was based on the erroneous assumption that the elimination of restrictions was all that was required to generate a national literature. But nefarious comparisons with present-day readerships or with the "American Renaissance" of the nineteenth century err on the other side by imposing fundamentally ahistorical standards on eighteenth-century America. To do so is to read history backward, to wrench the revolutionary generation of writers out of its historical place and thereby ignore the intentions, illusions, and expectations of men like Brackenridge.[22]

•

In the 1770s his most immediate and pressing problem was to find a job that provided an adequate income but also allowed him time to write. He taught school at Somerset Academy in Maryland, read theology in preparation for a career in the ministry, served as a chaplain with the Continental Army from 1776

to 1778, founded a magazine in Philadelphia devoted to literature and politics in 1779, studied law with Samuel Chase—Peale's
old patron—and finally moved to Pittsburgh in the spring of 1781
to set up his own legal practice. When he reviewed this ten-year
quest for a calling, Brackenridge insisted that his true love was
literature; he described himself as a broken-hearted suitor searching for a marriage of convenience. "I have loved *Miss Theology,*"
he wrote in 1780, "yet we both saw the necessity of ceasing to
indulge any fond thought of a union." Although he retained a firm
belief in the existence of God, he could not abide the doctrinal
disputes over theological distinctions he regarded as inconse-
quential. He never submitted to ordination, in part because of his
religious skepticism and in part because he felt that *"Miss
Theology"* deserved a completely committed, full-time mate. He
admitted that "the present object of my soft attentious..., *Miss
Law,*" although a "comely young lady" who promised him financial security, was also a half-hearted choice "a little pitted with the
small pox." He confessed that he most wanted to be a professional
author, even though his hopes for a permanent relationship with
the muse of literature "has long since vanished." Then he added:
"The circumstances of this small affair must remain a secret to
the world. Perhaps when I die some hint of it may be found
amongst my papers; and some friend may inscribe it on my
tomb."[23]

Before the end of the Revolution, Brackenridge had discovered what Freneau, Joel Barlow, Robert Treat Paine, John
Trumbull, and a generation of aspiring authors would discover in
the 1780s and '90s, namely, that it was impossible to be a professional author in eighteenth-century America. Authors were expected to be aristocrats whose wealth allowed them the leisure
time to write. They published their books in limited editions,
which were usually purchased by a small number of patrons who
had subscribed for their copies beforehand. Authorship, in short,
was an avocation rather than a profession, and serious literature
was reserved for an elite rather than for a mass readership.[24]

Brackenridge had presupposed that the American Revolution
would fundamentally change this situation. He envisioned a
vastly expanded American readership comprised of farmers and
artisans eager "to obtain some knowledge of the history and

principles of government." The establishment of a republican government in place of monarchy, he reasoned, meant that "the mechanic of the city, or the husbandman who plows his farm by the river's bank, has it in his power to become, one day, the first magistrate of his respective commonwealth, or to fill a seat in the Continental Congress." In this new order of things, authors had the responsibility "to conciliate the minds of the audience, and, in the words of Cicero, to render them *teachable, attentive, benevolent....*" The stability of the American republic required that the great mass of Americans "become more deep and solid scholars by reading systematic writers, and *diving deeply* into the fountain head of classical information." He saw himself as "a republican author," a modern interpreter of the ancients who would enlighten the broad mainstream of the American populace, a writer whose publications would guarantee that "the greater part [of the public] be moderately instructed" and enabled "to speak with great propriety and fluency on any subject." He explained that his "language may appear romantic, but I have seen the case exemplified." In sum, Brackenridge thought that the Revolution would usher in social and cultural changes that would make authors, as much as officeholders, representatives of the public interest and recipients of public support.[25]

These were not isolated or idiosyncratic expectations in revolutionary America. As Gordon Wood has shown in great detail, "throughout the war, nearly every piece of writing concerned with the future ... was filled with extraordinarily idealistic hopes for the social and political transformation of America. The Americans had come to believe that the Revolution would mean nothing less than the reordering of eighteenth-century society and politics as they had known and despised them...."[26] Brackenridge happened to be one of the many Americans who regarded the Revolution as something more than a colonial war for independence from England; it was a genuinely revolutionary struggle for a new set of social arrangements. And just as Charles Willson Peale developed his view of art and artists within this highly charged ideological atmosphere, Brackenridge shaped his view of literature and authorship according to the dictates of his republican principles. In the 1770s this meant that he willingly and consciously subordinated personal and aesthetic concerns to his public responsibilities as an author.

The result was not literature but propaganda. In fact, Brack-enridge became one of the most prolific and zealous propagandists of the war. His *Poem on Divine Revelation* (1774) harked back to the same patriotic themes that John Adams had first articulated in his *Dissertation on the Canon and Feudal Law* (1765). Brack-enridge located the source of the American love for liberty in the English Reformation and, like Adams, credited the Puritan set-tlers with carrying that same spirit to America,

> *Where birds of calm delight to play, where not*
> *Rome's pontiff high, nor arbitrary king,*
> *Leagu'd in with sacerdotal sway are known.*

William Bradford, Brackenridge's former classmate, predicted that the public would cheer the political message of the poem but would not appreciate it as literature. "I am afraid he has pub-lished it at an improper time," Bradford wrote to Madison, for "the political storm is too high for the still soft voice of the muse to be listened to."[27]

Between 1775 and 1779 Brackenridge published two revo-lutionary plays and seven short prose pieces. In each of them the "soft voice of the muse" was sacrificed for propagandistic pur-poses. As the British troops advance on the colonists in *The Battle of Bunkers Hill* (1776), for example, Brackenridge had the American officer deliver a patriotic speech:

> *Fear not, brave soldiers, tho' their infantry*
> *In deep array, so far outnumber us.*
> *The justness of our cause will brace each arm,*
> *And steel the soul, with fortitude; while they,*
> *Whose guilt hangs trembling, on their consciences,*
> *Must fail in battle and receive that death,*
> *Which, in high vengeance, we prepare for them.*[28]

In *The Death of General Montgomery* (1777) the American commander stands before the ramparts of Quebec and delivers a soliloquy that begins, "What says my friend, to the heroic thought, of storming this fair capital to day?"[29]

It seems clear that Brackenridge had become so caught up in the war effort, so committed to the rightness of the revolution-ary cause, that he had little capacity to distinguish between his obligations as a serious-minded author and his goals as a patriotic propagandist. And as the war dragged on, he became less temperate, more savage in his political judgments, and wholly incapable of recognizing the human drama and tragedy of the conflict. George III became the "fierce, cruel, unrelenting, and bloody king" more wicked than "the Hun, the Vandal, or the Goth, and all the cruel, persecuting, bloody princes. . . ."[30] (Many years after the war, when George III died, Brackenridge retained his bitterness. He imagined the British monarch "coming down to the borders of the Styx, and claiming an immunity from ferriage on the score of being a customer of so long standing, and to so great an amount, in sending down shades.")[31] He insisted that all colonists who did not support the Revolution were Tories and ought to be shot. "These men have out-savaged the Indian and out-tygered the fiercest beast that roams upon the mountains," he wrote. "They have forgot the fathers of which they are descended." British soldiers were "*dogs of hell*" who fought "in the manner of the Canibals of South America," ravished virgins, and tortured prisoners. American soldiers, on the other hand, were animated by "the pure love of virtue and of freedom, burning bright within their minds, that alone could engage them to embark in the bold and perilous undertaking."[32]

The same partisan spirit affected the writing he did for the *United States Magazine,* a monthly journal he founded in 1779. The frontispiece of the magazine referred to an emerging American empire that would stretch "From the cold *Canadian* skies . . . to the noble *Mexican* bay." He imagined the North American continent liberated from British occupation and filled with "millions of the virtuous peasants, who now groan beneath tyranny and oppression in three quarters of the globe." He wrote an open letter to the "Poets, Philosophers, Orators, Statesmen and Heroes of Antiquity," assuring them that the American revolutionaries were keeping their spirit alive. And he published regular accounts of the military campaigns being waged in the South, in which acts of American bravery received extended attention.[33]

On occasion Brackenridge found it possible to put aside his patriotic fervor and poke fun at wartime eccentricities. After several American officers suffered minor wounds in duels, usually fought over women or accusations of cowardice, Brackenridge suggested that future duelists agree to put their noses in the barrels of the opponents' pistols in order to assure at least one fatality per duel. He also wrote several satires on "the paperwaster, ragborn, kite-faced fellow, *Continental Currency.*" His most revealing effort at detachment was a series of fictional essays entitled "The Cave of Vanhest." Here Brackenridge interviewed an imaginary hermit named Vanhest who had fled from the chaos of the war in order to practice the classical virtues while living in a mountain retreat in the West. But if part of Brackenridge longed for a similar serenity, readers of the *United States Magazine* would never have guessed it. He was an engaged editor, committed to the republican principles of the Revolution, the sworn enemy of all Tories, critical of redcoats, neutrals, and American leaders like Robert Morris and Silas Deane, whom he suspected of wartime profiteering. Although his sense of humor peeked through the pages now and then, the vast bulk of his writing for the *United States Magazine* continued in the patriotic tradition of his plays and sermons.[34]

Unlike Peale's patriotic portraits, which achieved a measure of historic significance as time passed, Brackenridge's wartime writing was out-of-date the moment the Revolution ended. Nor was Brackenridge's fate unusual; the Revolution did not produce a single piece of imaginative literature that has endured. The generation of writers who came of age during the Revolution breathed in a supercharged ideological atmosphere; they pressed themselves and their art into the service of their country, only to discover that a republic could be as demanding a patron as a wealthy prince. Several of Brackenridge's contemporaries spent the remainder of their literary careers composing patriotic epics, such as Timothy Dwight's *The Conquest of Canaan* or Joel Barlow's *The Vision of Columbus,* which today read as if they had been written by the same person. "The unanimity of men at war," Edmund Wilson has written, "is like that of a school of fish . . . or like a sky-darkening flight of grasshoppers . . . all compelled by one impulse. . . ."[35] Throughout the 1770s Brackenridge's voice was part of the American chorus that chanted patriotic litanies. If he had anything distinctive to say or a distinctive way of expressing himself, he did not share it with his readers.[36]

What did distinguish Brackenridge from other young American authors was not the literary quality of his wartime writing but the lessons he learned from the experience. After celebrating the patriotic cause for several years, Brackenridge did a sudden and startling turnabout. In his final editorial for the *United States Magazine,* he announced that the writing he had done in the 1770s had been misguided. Although he continued to support the American cause against England, he no longer believed that the mass of Americans, once freed from British rule, were prepared to take full advantage of their independence. From being an unrestrained champion of the American Revolution and its chief beneficiaries, the people-at-large, Brackenridge had become a cynical critic of popular taste and the people's capacity for freedom. He had reluctantly come to the conclusion, he announced, that the bulk of the people "inhabit the region of stupidity, and cannot bear to have the tranquility of their repose disturbed. . . ." After lamenting the lack of public support for his magazine and for authors, like himself, who had committed all their energies to republican principles, Brackenridge promised that he would allow his readers to *"sleep on and take your rest."*[37] He claimed that he would never write again.

Brackenridge's denunciation of "the people-at-large" was as unpredictable and impervious to logical analysis as a conversion experience, except that Brackenridge experienced a conversion-in-reverse. He did not bother to offer extended explanations of his newfound skepticism about the capacities of the American public. Nor did he leave behind any letters or personal documents that would allow the historian to reconstruct his intellectual and psychological development during those crucial months in 1779. It does seem reasonable to surmise that the two years he spent in war-torn Philadelphia exposed him to the ideological and political quarrels that divided the radical and moderate factions in the city, both of which claimed to represent patriotism and the people; Peale had been similarly disillusioned by the same experience. In later years Brackenridge remarked that the economic instability produced by the currency inflation was his chief worry and the major cause of his magazine's failure. And as an editor he undoubtedly was subjected to abuse from zealots of various persuasions who believed that his magazine was prejudiced against their favorite causes. Revolutionary Philadelphia was a factious city, riddled with class conflicts and political intrigues that drove an artist like Peale out of public life. It is not impossible to imagine the impact of these same circumstances on a young and optimistic champion of "the rising glory of amer- ica" as he listened to a cacophony of vices, each claiming to be the voice of "the people."

Whatever the cause or combination of causes, Brackenridge lost his innocent faith in the future of America in 1779 and never regained it. In its place he began to fashion a brooding temperament, an appreciation for paradox, and a budding curi- osity about the unforseen implications of popular sovereignty. These characteristics, it turned out, proved to be more efficacious influences on his development as a writer than patriotic zeal. But in the spring of 1781 literary considerations seemed irrele- vant; the disillusioned author who headed west to the frontier town of Pittsburgh to set up a law office claimed he would never write again.

•

Pittsburgh was the St. Louis of the eighteenth century, the gate- way to the West for postrevolutionary pioneers and a haven for hucksters eager to sell essential supplies at inflated prices. In 1790 a traveler described Pittsburgh as a town of 150 log houses, 50 frame or brick houses, and 1,000 inhabitants "who act as if possessed of a Charter of Exclusive Privilege to filch from, annoy and harrass her [*sic*] Fellow Creatures...."[38] Brackenridge pre- dicted that the settlement "would one day be a town of note, and in the meantime might be pushed forward by the usual means that raise such places." By 1786 he had a wife and son and a growing reputation as the best lawyer in western Pennsylvania, and had helped found the *Pittsburgh Gazette,* paved the way for the Pittsburgh Academy (later the University of Pittsburgh), and announced his candidacy for the Pennsylvania legislature. And despite his vow to "swear off writing," he had begun to send es- says to various newspapers for publication.[39]

As Brackenridge's prominence grew, his position on the issues of the day and the writing he did about them began to as- sume a new and distinctive shape. On the one hand he became an enthusiastic advocate of western interests, arguing for increased representation in the state legislature, a more aggressive policy toward the Indians, American navigation rights on the Mississippi, and government support for westward expansion. In his essays on Indians, for example, Brackenridge lent an air of respectability to the greed and racism of western whites by ridiculing the arguments of Indian supporters in the East. He apprised the legislators of Philadelphia that they were "like young women who have read romances, and have as improper an idea of the Indian character . . . as the female mind has of real life. . . ." Eastern politicians who considered the Indians *"Children of the Forest,"* he wrote, were "tortured with Jean Jacques Rousseau and other rhapsodies." Any assertion of *"the original right* of these aborigines to the soil," Brackenridge argued, "is like the claim of children; it is mine, for I saw it first—or what that of the buffaloe might be—it is mine, for I have first run over it."[40]

But Brackenridge also confounded his western friends by defending Indians accused of crimes and insisting that Indian rights be protected under the law. When one settler challenged him to a duel because of his defense of two Indians accused of murder, Brackenridge responded that he did not duel and he did not love Indians, although he respected their legal rights. He then broke a chair over the settler's head and tossed him into the fireplace.[41]

He began to develop a reputation, which soon grew into a local legend, for inexplicable and unpredictable behavior that frequently wavered between eccentricity and lunacy. During his term in the Pennsylvania legislature, despite the judgment of other representatives that he was the most effective spokesman for western interests in the assembly, Brackenridge shocked his constituents by opposing a bill that would have allowed settlers to pay for lands in state certificates of indebtedness. He argued that eastern speculators had bought up most of the certificates at depressed prices, so that creditors rather than farmers would benefit from the proposed bill. But the *Pittsburgh Gazette* was soon filled with letters denouncing Brackenridge as a traitor. Brackenridge then had the audacity to respond in kind, informing his constituents that they were poorly informed and asserting that "a representative is not supposed to be a mere machine, like a clock wound up to run for many hours in the same way; he is sent to hear from others, and were it a new case, I would do it again."[42]

If this statement made it likely that Brackenridge would be turned out of office, his actions during the final session of the assembly made it certain. The federal Constitution had just been drafted and sent to each of the states for approval. Brackenridge was the only representative from western Pennsylvania to support it. Again he argued that his constituents were not the best judges of their own self-interest, that some of them believed that "reason is an erring guide, while instinct, which is the guiding principle of the untaught, is certain." He published comic accounts of western representatives in the state legislature who tried to block a vote on the Constitution by absenting themselves from the debate so that there would not be a quorum. And while the Pennsylvania ratifying convention was deliberating approval, Brackenridge published a parody of the Antifederalists' arguments, insisting that voters reject the Constitution because the sex of the president was not prescribed, the Scotch-Irish were not given preferential treatment, and no provision guaranteed that men would be required to wear pants in the senate.[43]

Several of Brackenridge's contemporaries regarded his contempt for popular opinion and his proclivity for ridicule as symptoms of some mysterious mental illness. His abrupt manner and sudden outbursts—he would often chase clients out of his law office while they were trying to explain their problems—supported this view of "madman Brackenridge." Exaggerated stories about his family life also fueled the local gossip, stories that Brackenridge could not remember his infant son's name, or that he had purchased his new wife, a beautiful country girl named Sabina Wolfe, for ten dollars from her father. Others claimed that Brackenridge was simply a two-faced politician who had sold out his western supporters to the eastern establishment in Philadelphia. Still others believed that Brackenridge was an intensely independent man whose defense of Indians or the Constitution reflected a stubborn commitment to personal principles that would not be influenced by public opinion.

None of these opinions was the whole truth, although all of them, especially the last one, contained elements of the truth. But Brackenridge was more than an abrupt lawyer, or a negligent father, or a westerner who admired the sophistication of eastern colleagues in the legislature, or a fiercely independent thinker. He had developed a personal perspective and style that defied conventional explanations or stereotypes; in fact, his dissatisfaction with the political or ideological labels available in postrevolutionary America was central to Brackenridge's perspective. In place of the youthful enthusiasm and advocacy of the 1770s, he had fashioned a new way of seeing the emerging American society that anticipated many of the insights Alexis de Tocqueville would achieve in the 1830s. And like Tocqueville's hopeful but critical analysis, the quality of Brackenridge's vision derived from his position as an outsider; he was neither an easterner nor westerner, a Federalist nor a Jeffersonian, an aristocrat nor a democrat.

In fact, Brackenridge is a significant figure in our literary history precisely because he was the first postrevolutionary author whose fiction explored the anomalies and contradictions of American culture without trying either to reconcile them or to champion one side against the other. No longer an advocate, as he had been in the 1770s, Brackenridge could develop the aesthetic and literary advantages made possible by his discovery of what Nathaniel Hawthorne would call "a neutral territory." Of course, later American novelists discovered different kinds of neutral territory: for James Fenimore Cooper it was the border between the wilderness and civilization; for Herman Melville it was the *Pequod* at sea; for Mark Twain it was Huck Finn's raft on the Mississippi; for William Faulkner it was Yoknapatawpha County. Brackenridge's strategic position was simultaneously a geographic place, the semicivilized west, and a temporal place located somewhere between the classical eighteenth-century America of the founding fathers and the modern nineteenth-century America of the Jacksonian Democrats. In 1788 he began to write about this time and place.*

* Lionel Trilling's essay "Reality in America" was the first attempt to focus attention on the contradictions and tensions that so many American writers made the main concerns of their work. See his *The Liberal Imagination: Essays on Literature and Society* (New York, 1950). Then, several other studies, most notably Richard Chase's *The American Novel and Its Tradition* (New York, 1957) and Leo Marx's *The Machine in the Garden: Technology and the Pastoral Ideal in America* (New York, 1964) developed

In the same year that Brackenridge began writing what became *Modern Chivalry,* Philip Freneau published an essay entitled "Advice to Authors." Freneau observed that American authors "are at present considered the dregs of the community; their situation and prospects are truly humiliating." He distinguished between political independence, which "was accomplished in about seven years," and cultural independence, which "will not be completely effected in as many centuries." He then advised prospective American writers "to graft their talent upon some other calling" and specifically recommended that they try something "more profitable," like bricklaying.[44] Freneau's lament did not go unchallenged. In the late 1780s and early 1790s the editors of several magazines remained optimistic about the prospects for American literature and continued to celebrate the imminent arrival of "an American genius" who would do for American prose what the revolutionary heroes had done for American politics. In 1794 one editor bragged that some American authors were already "as highly esteemed, even by foreigners, as . . . a Butler, a Milton, a Pope, or even an Addison."[45] Nevertheless, Freneau's despondency was symptomatic of a decided shift in opinion that began in the late 1780s and that infused the public debate over the state of American literature well into the nineteenth century.

In place of the unrestrained enthusiasm for a national literature that was expected to follow quite naturally on the heels of political independence, commentators became obsessed with what they called "the literary delinquency of America."[46] Within the pages of the approximately two hundred periodicals founded between 1790 and 1820, the boundless optimism for American

Trilling's suggestion more fully. More recently, Michael Kammen has pursued this same theme back into the seventeenth and eighteenth centuries in his *People of Paradox: An Inquiry into the Origins of American Civilization* (New York, 1972). My intention here is twofold: first, to link Brackenridge to a literary tradition that scholars have come to regard as central to the American experience; second, to suggest that Brackenridge's novel, *Modern Chivalry,* emerged out of a specific historical context in which the radical implications of republican ideology were first becoming visible. *Modern Chivalry* is, then, both part of a long-standing American literary tradition and a book that crystallizes the social and political tensions of a particular era.

letters gave way to excessive despair. Federalist magazines like the *Monthly Anthology* described American literature as "all desert, a wide African sand garden, showing brambles, and rushes, and reeds" and apprised American writers that "no greater punishment [was] due them while in this world than to be continually surrounded by their own works." Although the emergence of national political parties in the 1790s influenced the public debate over cultural development—Federalists tended to attribute American literary deficiencies to the crudity of popular opinion while Jeffersonians, including Freneau, blamed the failure on Federalist efforts "to recolonize this country to England" —both sides agreed that American literature was an embarrassment. "Nothing can more obstruct American improvement," wrote one typical observer, "than the absurd persuasion in defiance of all truth and philosophy, that she has acquired an extent of knowledge which renders her as independent in her literature as she is her government." "Gracious heaven," exclaimed another critic, "is this the fate of American genius? poverty, contempt and obscurity!... and yet—who would be an American author?"[47]

In short, Brackenridge returned to writing just when the public attitudes toward American authors, at least as reflected in the magazines and periodicals of the day, began to shift from chauvinism to defensiveness and despair. Moreover, he had decided to write a novel, precisely the kind of book that most enlightened Americans considered the most worthless and even dangerous form of literature. Brackenridge's former mentor, John Witherspoon, was only expressing a widespread opinion when he claimed that "novels not only pollute the imaginations...but likewise give...false ideas of life...." Even Thomas Jefferson, who prided himself on his broadmindedness, argued that a novel "infects the mind, it destroys its tone" and produces "disgust towards all the real business of life." Men like Jefferson and Timothy Dwight, who occupied different ends of the political and ideological spectrum in late-eighteenth-century America, agreed that novels were insidious influences.

Few, if any, American commentators had an elaborate or formal definition of "the novel" in mind. A novel, quite simply, was a lengthy piece of fictional prose that usually took the form of a story. What seemed to be most worrisome was that the story was untrue, the product of the author's imagination, a tale that seduced the reader into a fictitious world where factual sign-posts were obliterated and titillating concoctions masqueraded as reality. In his *Retrospect of the Eighteenth Century,* for example, Samuel Miller bemoaned the appearance of novels, claiming that they "have a tendency to dissipate the mind, . . . to excite a greater fondness for the productions of imagination than for sober reasoning and practical investigations of wisdom." In 1806 Samuel Jarvis told Yale's graduating class that novels were prosaic daydreams and that "the evil consequences attendant upon novel reading are much greater than has been generally imagined." An anonymous contributor to the *Weekly Magazine* in 1798 explained that novel-reading was addictive because people "read of characters which never existed" and cannot "avoid falling in love with the phantom." Several American novelists, concerned that potential readers might be scared away by these warnings, insisted that their novels were based on true or real events. Some writers even had fictional characters in their own novels deliver soliloquies against novel-reading.[48]

The hostility toward novels was similar in several respects to the hostility toward the fine arts. Like paintings, works of fiction were frequently denounced as impractical and wasteful endeavors, not the kind of interests appropriate for Americans who should be up and doing. And America's "literary delinquency" reassured those cultural commentators who regarded artistic or literary accomplishment as a symptom of imminent social decay. But because the novel, unlike painting, was a relatively new form of literature whose appearance and development in eighteenth-century England was made possible by an expanded popular readership, the apprehension about novels also had roots in the recent past. Whereas artists were associated with such old and familiar enemies of virtue as the papacy, royal princes, and aristocratic patrons, novelists seemed worrisome because of their association with new and unfamiliar threats to republican virtues, namely, the base instincts and inferior taste of an unrefined popular audience.

Critics sometimes described novel-readers as poor and uneducated. More frequently, they linked novel-reading with the

intellectually undeveloped minds of youth or women. Noah
Webster, for example, characterized novels as "the toys of youth;
the rattle boxes of sixteen." Anonymous contributors to magazines
worried about "an effect of the general style of Novels on un-
tutored minds" or a novel's "tendency to enervate the youthful
mind. . . ." But the most frequently mentioned victims of novels
were young women. Throughout the criticism of fiction ran the
refrain that novels "have contributed more than any other cause
to debauch the morals of the fair sex" or were "the powerful
engines with which the seducer attacks the female heart."
Timothy Dwight observed that while boys "read history, biography and the pamphlets of the day, girls sink down to songs,
novels and plays," presumably because the female mind was
more prone to "receive ideas without exertion." A male speaker
at the Young Ladies Academy of Philadelphia indicated that
warning women about the evils of novel-reading had become an
obligatory ritual. "There is a species of composition, young ladies,
which were I not to mention on such an occasion as the present,"
he said, "the omission might be considered a studied one, and
censured as improper. You already anticipate the mention of
novels."[49]

We do not yet know enough about the reading habits of
postrevolutionary Americans to say with any certainty whether
women read a disproportionate share of novels. The establishment of many new schools designed explicitly for female education undoubtedly increased the literacy rate among American
women in the late eighteenth and early nineteenth centuries.
And it is possible to conclude, on the basis of fragmentary and
impressionistic evidence, that women constituted a larger percentage of the reading public than ever before. But a majority of
the reading public were certainly *not* women, and the presumption that novel-reading was primarily a female activity seems
unwarranted.[50]

The persistent association of novels with youthful and feminine stereotypes, then, is less a measure of the actual readership
than a clue to the deeper sources of apprehension about a new
and popular form of literature. Novels were troublesome because
they were aimed at and appealed to Americans who had traditionally been excluded from cultural life and whose judgment,

taste, and experience were undeveloped. Like women and children, or rather stereotypes of them, this emerging mass readership could not be counted on to handle responsibly the complex social and moral issues raised in books.

Brackenridge wrote *Modern Chivalry* with many of these concerns in mind. He disarmed potential critics by proclaiming that his novel was intended only for "weak and visionary people" who wanted "something to read without the trouble of thinking," adding that "it is better to make the patient laugh than think." Since his alleged purpose was only "to talk nonsense eloquently," he insisted that his book "cannot be the subject of criticism." Instead of bemoaning the prospects of American authors, Brackenridge predicted that his novel would make him rich and famous. Instead of worrying about the depressed condition of American literature, he described *Modern Chivalry* as a classic, "an opus magnum.... Were all the books in the world lost, this alone would preserve a germ of every art." The Bible was probably the greatest book of all time, he admitted, and Homer, Shakespeare, and Plutarch came next, "but I flatter myself that my performance may occupy the next grade." *Modern Chivalry*, he joked, was intentionally comprised of writing that was "pretty good" and "a good deal of trash," because it was "calculated for all capacities" and all seasons.

But beneath all the jokes and jibes and masks, Brackenridge maintained the same deadly serious purpose that had possessed him in the 1770s. He now wrote fiction rather than wartime propaganda, but he was using a popular literary form, the novel, to instruct a mass audience in the principles of republicanism. What worried so many other Americans, namely, that novels appealed to a broad public constituency traditionally excluded from cultural affairs, actually motivated Brackenridge. "It is talk out of doors that I respect," he declared. "And this is the fountain which is to be corrected. It is therefore into this pool *that I cast my salt. It is to correct these waters that I write this book.*"[51]

•

Modern Chivalry does not fit neatly into any of the categories that literary critics customarily employ. Whether it is a satiric, didactic, realistic, or picaresque novel, indeed whether it is a novel at all, are questions that can inspire spirited disagreement among knowledgable scholars. Part One of *Modern Chivalry* is a series of loosely connected tales that issued forth from the presses in Pittsburgh and Carlisle in four separate installments between 1792 and 1797. Part Two is an even more episodic and inchoate collection published between 1804 and 1815. The reader encounters two main characters, Captain John Farrago and Teague O'Regan. Neither character changes or develops as the story proceeds. Farrago remains a learned, middle-aged American whose ideas "were drawn from what may be called the old school: the Greek and Roman notion of things." Teague remains his Irish servant, a "bogtrotter" of boundless ambition and no principles whose primary business is to get into trouble. As Swift did in *A Tale of a Tub* and Fielding did in *Tom Jones*, Brackenridge inserts chapters "containing observations and reflections" throughout the text. He interrupts the narrative to publish a favorable mock review of the preceding installments, threatens to satirize Federalist leaders unless the government agrees to purchase five hundred copies from his publisher immediately, and expresses disappointment that no government official has attacked his book as "insipid, libelous, treasonable, immoral, or irreligious." "What? Ho," he asks, "are ye all asleep in the hold down there at Philadelphia?"[52]

There is no story line, only a series of adventures and encounters that befall Farrago and Teague as they journey through postrevolutionary America. Teague survives on savvy, good luck, and the Captain's bumbling generosity. By the end of the book a tarred-and-feathered Teague has been shipped to France by the American Philosophic Society on the mistaken impression that he is a natural curiosity; he arrives in Nantes during the French Revolution, is taken for a *sans culotte,* and is welcomed as a hero. In earlier episodes Teague aspires to be a lawyer, a minister, a member of the Society of Cincinnati, a writer, and an actor. Farrago accompanies him through a college, a whorehouse, a presidential levee, and a session of the federal Congress, and rescues him from several enraged mobs, women, and duelists. Everything and everyone they encounter become the butt of ridicule. When one Major Jacks challenges the good captain to a duel, for example, Brackenridge has him respond with a formal letter. "Sir," he writes,

I have two objections to this duel matter. The one is, lest I should hurt you; and the other is, lest you should hurt me.... That being the case, I think it most advisable to stay at a distance. If you want to try your pistols, take some object, a tree or a barn door about my dimensions. If you hit that, send me word, and I shall acknowledge that if I had been in the same place, you might also have hit me.[53]

And so it goes throughout each chapter and in every niche of America the two travelers visit.

What the characters in *Modern Chivalry* say is often funny; moreover, the way they speak reproduces the speech patterns of ordinary Americans on the frontier. When Teague hears a Scotsman address Farrago, he complains about the impurity of the Scotsman's language in words that are equally undignified:

plase your honor, where did you pick up dat teef-luking son o'd a whore, dat has no more manners, dan a sheep-stealer in Ireland. . . . By saint Patrick, if your honor had given me leave in de road, I would have knocked his teet down his troat. . . . I will go out and take him by de troat, and make him talk to himself like a frog in de wet swamps; de son of a whore, to spake to your honor wid a brogue upon his tongue, in such words as dese.[54]

When a black slave by the name of Cuff is invited to address the American Philosophical Society about the origin of differences in skin color, the content of his speech is no more and no less ridiculous than the observations of educated white members of the society, but his dialect is his own:

Now, shentima, I say, dat de first man was de black a man, and de first women de black a woman; an get two tree children; de rain vasha dese, and de snow pleach, an de coula come brown, yella, coppa coula, and, at de last, quite fite; and de hair long; an da fal out vid van anoda; and van cash by de nose, an pull; so de nose come long, sharp nose.[55]

When Brackenridge was asked how he invented the dialogue of these ethnic characters, he claimed that he was merely recording the voices he heard around him and "dipping my pen in the inkstand of human nature." He then added that he had wanted to give his readers a typically American character who was neither a recently arrived Irishman, nor an African, but that such a creature had not yet come into existence. "The American has in fact, yet, no character," he observed, "so that I would not take one from our own country; which I would much rather have done, as the scene lay here."[56]

In the end, the most significant feature of *Modern Chivalry* is the perspective that Brackenridge, as narrator, brings to "the scene [that] lay here." For although Farrago and Teague do not learn much about themselves during their odyssey, the reader learns a great deal about American society. "The whole book from beginning to end, has a moral," said Brackenridge, "which, if anyone has not found out, let him begin again." Federalist readers like John Quincy Adams, who praised *Modern Chivalry* to his friends, undoubtedly regarded the book as an amusing put-down of democratic excesses and popular ignorance. But that was not the point of the story. The butt of many jokes, Teague cannot be laughed off the stage. It is Teague, not Farrago, who is elected to office. Even Farrago realizes that Teague is symptomatic of America's democratic future, that "when the present John Adamses, and Lees, and Jeffersons, and Jays, and Henrys, and other great men . . . have gone to sleep," their places will be filled by the likes of Teague.

This did not make Brackenridge happy. He himself had been one of the patriots who believed that the Revolution would usher in an age when "genius and virtue are independent of rank and fortune; and it is neither the opulent, nor the indigent, but the man of ability that ought to be called forth to serve his country." But such beliefs have been overtaken by events and exposed as shibboleths. Farrago is the decent, gentlemanly, republican past; Teague is the ill-mannered, popular, democratic future. "Now it may be said that this is fiction," writes Brackenridge in an aside, "but fiction or no fiction, the nature of the thing will make it a reality." *Modern Chivalry* is a book about the ironic, unforeseen, but inevitable consequences of the leveling forces unleashed by the American Revolution.[57]

A thesaurus of Americana, a panorama of the social landscape, and a harbinger of democratic values, *Modern Chivalry* is also the first American novel to describe American culture as a bundle of polarities, a set of irreconcilable contradictions and tensions. "I perceive, Captain," says one of the characters, "that you are no slouch at supporting a paradox." Neither was Brackenridge. Throughout the novel Brackenridge inserts epigrams and maxims that express his personal preference for "a middle course" between the extremes represented by eastern and western customs, aristocratic and democratic values, the hierarchical social order of the past and the egalitarian ethic of the near future: "There is a medium in all things"; "the best men are the most moderate"; the wise leader is one who recognizes when "active and uninformed spirits are useful or perhaps absolutely necessary" and when "deliberate reason, and prudent temperament are necessary."

But in the world through which Farrago and Teague ramble, moderation does not work. "It is a strange thing," says the captain, "that in the country, in my route, they would elect no one but a weaver or a whiskey distiller; and here [in Philadelphia] none but fat swabs, that guzzle wine and smoke cigars. . . . Something must be wrong, where only the inflate, and pompous are the objects of choice." Farrago becomes a ridiculous figure whenever he forgets this lesson and tries to reason with a mob or behave benevolently toward merchants. The result is inevitably comic disaster. Farrago achieves his objectives only when he uses guile and trickery to dupe Teague, the voters, or the politicians. Unlike Don Quixote, whose pathetic illusions reside within his own imagination, Farrago is an eminently rational and sensible character who has the misfortune to be living in an unstable world seized with "Teagueomania." And like James Madison in *Federalist 10*, Farrago hopes that the competition between various factions, fools, and popular favorites will produce equilibrium. "When we see, therefore, a Teague O'Regan lifted up," he muses, "the philosopher will reflect that it is to balance some purse-proud fellow, equally as ignorant, that comes down from the sphere of the aristocratic interest." And that, Brackenridge seems to argue, is the only form of chivalry the modern world will allow.[58]

If, as Richard Chase has suggested, American novelists have

often been stirred by "the aesthetic possibilities . . . of alienation, contradiction, and disorder," if "much of the best and most characteristic American fiction has been shaped by the contradictions and not by the unities and harmonies of our culture," then *Modern Chivalry* qualifies as the first distinctively American novel. Brackenridge was an author who repudiated both the national chauvinism of Barlow and Freneau and the defensiveness and Anglomania of the Federalist *literati*. He was most interested in exposing the ironies and anomalies that were embedded in late-eighteenth-century American culture. He claimed to have many more insights into the inconsistencies and follies of his time, but "the more forward of them I have actually knocked on the head, having reason to believe that they might do more harm than good. . . ; dearies, said I, you must go. It is better you should die than your father. So they went, poor things." Although he might have longed for some land east of the frontier and west of civilization, inhabited by virtuous people and governed by natural aristocrats, he never confused his own longings with social and political realities. With the outbreak of the Whiskey Rebellion in 1794, he found himself caught between the very forces he was trying to describe in his fiction, in desperate need of all the narrative skills and the same capacity for ironic detachment that he exhibited in *Modern Chivalry*. Brackenridge's role in the Whiskey Rebellion became an extended nonfictional illustration of his capacity to orchestrate the social forces unleashed by the Revolution. For once, art and life coincided.[59]

•

The Whiskey Rebellion was triggered by an excise tax on grain alcohol passed by the federal Congress in 1791. Approximately 25 percent of the stills in the United States were located in southwestern Pennsylvania; there farmers traditionally processed their rye crop into whiskey in order to facilitate its transportation across the Alleghenies for sale in the East, where "Monongahela rye," as it was called, sold for fifty cents a gallon. Westerners claimed that "it was good for fevers, it was good for ague, it was good for snake bites. . . ." It was the beer and wine of the West, as well as an accepted form of currency. The excise tax was not a heavy economic burden—officials estimated that it would cost each family a dollar-fifty annually—but it affected every settler, rekindled several smoldering resentments against the financial policies of Alexander Hamilton, and almost led to a civil war.[60]

Westerners regarded the tax as unjust. They compared it to the Stamp Act and Hamilton to George Grenville. "A breath in favor of the law," wrote Brackenridge, "was sufficient to ruin any man. It was considered as a badge of toryism." In 1794 radical clubs, calling themselves Democratic-Republican Societies, appeared in western Pennsylvania and became the centers of opposition to the excise. Members claimed to be ideological descendants of the Sons of Liberty; they set up liberty poles, terrorized tax collectors and expressed kinship with the Jacobins in the French Revolution. After fighting broke out between some of the more militant rebels and the excise collectors, the Washington administration threatened to dispatch federal troops to restore order. The rebels organized a five-thousand-man army of their own, occupied Pittsburgh, and even threatened to march on Philadelphia. Washington's cabinet split over the crisis, a split that led directly to the creation of two political parties. But eventually Hamilton assumed command of a thirteen-thousand-man federal army, which crossed the Alleghenies in October of 1794 only to discover that the rebel army had disbanded and support for the rebellion had dissipated.[61]

Brackenridge was working on the fourth installment of *Modern Chivalry* when the Whiskey Rebellion erupted. Although he opposed the excise tax and had defended a group of rioters against a suit by an aggrieved tax collector, he regarded the rebels as irresponsible radicals, "the Sans Cullottes of the country. . . , a large and enraged body of men, under the command of one as mad as themselves, or under no command at all."[62] At first he tried to find some neutral territory from which he could view the developments as if they were a fictional tale and he was the narrator. But in real life, as Brackenridge quickly discovered, neutral territory is often a no-man's-land between opposing armies. And that, figuratively and literally, was where Brackenridge found himself in the summer of 1794.

On three separate occasions Brackenridge faced precisely the kind of dilemma that Captain Farrago encountered in *Modern Chivalry*. The first occurred on July 23, 1794, when the rebels asked him to attend a meeting of the Democratic-Republican Society at Mingo Creek in order to provide legal counsel. A week earlier the rebels had attacked and burned the home of an excise officer and were now circulating petitions for the creation of a dissident army. "My situation was delicate," Brackenridge recalled, for "I was but a moment between treason on the one hand, and popular odium on the other." He decided to attend so that he might exercise a moderating influence on the insurgents. But once present at the meeting Brackenridge realized that the advice he intended to offer the rebels—namely, to recognize that they had committed treason, to appeal to President Washington for amnesty, and to oppose the excise tax through legal channels —was not what they wanted to hear. Spirits were running high at the meeting, and most of the participants carried rifles. So,

in order to put them in good humour, and at the same time lead to the point I had in view, the practicability of obtaining an amnesty, I indulged a good deal of pleasantry at the expense of the executive [Washington], on the subject of Indian treaties. I introduced General Knox on the one side, and Cornplanter [the Seneca chief] on the other; and made them make speeches. Now, said I, if Indians can have treaties, why cannot we have one two [*sic*]?

He then made more jokes about the cowardly behavior of excise officers. The rebels were roaring with laughter when he told them that, under the law, they were all guilty of high treason and that the president could call out the militia to arrest them. "I saw this struck them greatly," he reported. He left the meeting after his speech, observing that he "was not about to be the subject of eulogium."[63]

A week later, on July 30, he faced off with the rebels again. An army of between five and seven thousand Pennsylvania farmers was gathering in Braddock's Field outside of Pittsburgh. "The idea of the people at the time," recalled Brackenridge, "was that the law was dissolved, and that the people themselves, in their collective capacity, were the only tribunal." As the rebel leaders debated whether or not to attack Pittsburgh, on the grounds that the residents there had evidenced only lukewarm support for the insurrection, Brackenridge led a party of townsmen out to Braddock's Field to confer with the rebels. He reported the following exchange with one of the more rabid insurgents:

> *Insurgent:* "Are we to take the garrison [Pittsburgh]?"
> *Brackenridge:* "We are."
> *Insurgent:* "Can we take it?"
> *Brackenridge:* "No doubt of it."
> *Insurgent:* "At a great loss?"
> *Brackenridge:* "Not at all; not above a thousand killed and five hundred mortally wounded."

A member of Brackenridge's party leaned over and whispered, "You have a great deal of subtility [*sic*], but you will have occasion for it all." Brackenridge then met with David Bradford, the rebel leader, whom Brackenridge called "the Robespierre of the occasion," and persuade him that the rebel army ought to march through Pittsburgh in an orderly and peaceful fashion so as "to impress the government that we are no mob." He assured the rebels that the inhabitants of Pittsburgh sympathized with their cause, then told off-color stories about the women and whiskey awaiting them in town. The "Battle of Pittsburgh" became a parade that ended with a wild celebration. "It cost me four barrels of whiskey, that day," Brackenridge claimed, "and I would rather spare that than a single quart of blood."[64]

Brackenridge's ability to moderate and manage public opinion was put to a third test on August 14, when two hundred and twenty-six delegates, plus hundreds of armed spectators, gathered at Parkinson's Ferry to decide on the direction of the rebellion. By then the federal government had begun to mobilize an army to crush the insurrection and had sent commissioners to Pittsburgh to administer oaths of loyalty to the government of the United States. On August 8, Brackenridge had sent a private letter to Trench Coxe, commissioner of the revenue, pleading for federal restraint. He noted that the excise was part of "a funding system detested and abhorred. . . . There is a growling, lurking discontent with this system that is ready to burst and discover itself elsewhere." Then he warned Coxe:

Should an attempt be made to suppress these people, I am afraid the question will not be whether you will march to Pittsburgh, but whether they will march to Philadelphia, accumulating in their course, and swelling over the banks of the Susquehanna like a torrent, irresistible, and devouring in its progress.

At the Parkinson's Ferry meeting, however, his strategy was to prevent the rebels from voting for military action against the federal government. "I wished to evade it," he wrote, "and endeavored to divert attention by keeping them laughing." Albert Gallatin, another advocate of moderation who had been shouted down by the rebels, did not understand Brackenridge's purpose and observed, "He laughs all by himself." But, as usual, Brackenridge knew what he was doing. Although the majority of delegates undoubtedly wanted to fight, he succeeded in referring all decisions about policy to a committee of safety, on which he served. After two weeks of deliberation the committee recommended that the rebels submit to arbitration with the federal commissioners. In effect, the insurrection was over.[65]

The ironic and at times comic climax to this frontier drama occurred when the federal troops arrived at Pittsburgh in October. Brackenridge, who had done more than anyone else to avert violence, was accused of being a leader of the insurrection. His letter to Trench Coxe implicated him; witnesses also testified that he had slandered President Washington at the Mingo Creek meeting; and several of the rebel leaders, who now realized that Brackenridge had manipulated them, sought revenge by claiming that he had recommended an attack on Pittsburgh during the parlay at Braddock's Field. But Brackenridge was not without allies. One of the principal federal commissioners charged with investigating the uprising was William Bradford, his old college friend. The officer in charge of the federal army was Henry Lee, whom Brackenridge had tutored at Princeton. Both men testified that Brackenridge was a man of character, but found the situation awkward and left the interrogation of their old friend to Alexander Hamilton.

Brackenridge claimed that Hamilton received him "with that countenance which a man will have, when he sees a person, with regard to whom his humanity and his sense of justice struggles—he would have him saved, but is afraid he must be hanged." After one day of testimony Hamilton changed his mind. Brackenridge had the foresight to bring to the Mingo Creek meeting friends who testified that his slander of Washington was a ploy to restrain the insurgents. And when Hamilton asked about his role at Braddock's Field, Brackenridge answered, "Was it any more than Richard the second did, when a mob of 100,000 men assembled on Blackheath?"[66]

Although Hamilton dismissed all charges against Brackenridge, the court of public opinion was more severe. Local settlers concluded that he had to be guilty of something: either he had supported the rebellion and deserved punishment from the government or he had opposed it and should have suffered at the hands of the rebels. An incensed excise officer, who had lost his property during the insurrection, called Brackenridge "the most artful fellow that ever was on God Almighty's earth" and convinced an army officer to challenge him to a duel. Brackenridge simply ignored the challenge. Clients for his law practice dropped off noticeably, even though he outraged the commissioners by agreeing to represent local settlers in damage suits against federal soldiers soon after he himself was released from custody. In May of 1795, he traveled to Philadelphia to testify as a government witness at the trials of insurgent leaders accused of treason, only to discover that easterners thought him a rebel turncoat. Old friends in Philadelphia avoided him on the streets and he described himself as a man "forced to contemplate the buildings a good deal, casting his eyes to the upper stories of the houses. . . . A stranger would have thought me a disciple of Palladio, examining the architecture."[67]

•

When Brackenridge's son, Henry Marie, sat down to write an affectionate memoir of his father in 1842, he described the Whiskey Rebellion as the critical event in his father's life. In the lives of most people," he noted, "there is a crisis, which, like the turning incident of the drama, fixes the denoument or catastrophe."[68] But, in fact, the Whiskey Rebellion was less a turning point in Brackenridge's life than it was an occasion to put into practice ideological convictions and political principles that had taken shape years earlier, during and immediately after the Revolution.

Nor was the Whiskey Rebellion a catastrophe for Brackenridge's career. Although his law practice suffered from a lack of clients, he remained active in Pennsylvania politics, became the leader of the Jeffersonian party in Pittsburgh and, in 1799, received an appointment as justice of the Pennsylvania Supreme Court after a Jeffersonian governor came into office. During his remaining years he cultivated his image as an irascible sage, terrorized the young lawyers who appeared in his court, wrote poetry, opened a correspondence with Jefferson, and even published a book on Blackstone's *Commentaries,* in which he argued that American law must be freed from the vestiges of feudalism that survived in English common law. Fresh installments of *Modern Chivalry* appeared in 1804, 1805, and again in 1815. "The people of Pennsylvania are so sensible of the use that it has been in the state," mused Brackenridge, "that there's scarcely a parlour window without a MODERN CHIVALRY." He claimed that "five booksellers have made a fortune by it," even though he himself had "never asked a cent from any of them for the privilege of printing an edition. . . ." At the time of his death, in 1816, he was preparing another installment in which Teague O'Regan would become the American ambassador to the Court of St. James's. He bequeathed to his son the entirety of his estate, which consisted of "his small library and a purse of a hundred dollars or so."[69]

His legacy to American culture was more substantial. But an understanding of that legacy must begin with an understanding of the historical context within which he lived and worked. His career exposes the insurmountable problems facing the first generation of American authors. The liberal values celebrated during the Revolution generated two problems which, ironically, Brackenridge and most aspiring authors initially regarded as opportunities. First, it discouraged an aristocratic conception of authorship and encouraged writers to aim their prose and poetry at a large public audience. However inspiring and liberating this may have seemed at the time, it made the private and lonely pursuit of imaginative insights seem selfish and unpatriotic, and it inadvertently required American writers to adopt political instead of aesthetic standards for their work. Moreover, although the potential readership in America was sizable, the dispersed population and the absence of publishing houses that could market books meant that postrevolutionary writers were ideologically committed to a popular constituency they could not possibly reach in their lifetimes.

Second, the Revolution politicized literature by sweeping Brackenridge and his generation toward a doctrinaire defense of republican principles in which the imaginative concerns of the artist were subordinated to the pressing issues of the day. Writers were expected, and in most cases expected themselves, to justify the Revolution, celebrate the new nation, help create a national mythology. This, indeed, was "virtuous behavior," the subordination of personal interests to the larger needs of the community, the kind of behavior that a host of American political theorists regarded as the critical element in a republic. No matter how politically and socially efficacious the elevation of virtue proved to be in revolutionary America, it was disastrous for literature, for it channeled creative energies toward propaganda just as surely as the emphasis on utility and the mass readership equated literature with journalism.

These were not the kind of problems that Brackenridge, or anyone for that matter, could be expected to solve. Social conditions and habits of mind with roots deeply embedded in the past do not allow for solutions; they define the parameters within which artists work or against which they rebel. Brackenridge did both. He remained an ardent advocate of republican principles throughout his life, believing that all serious writers had public responsibilities and insisting that American literature must be directed toward a popular rather than an elite readership. But he also recognized that an affection for the rights of the people-at-large must be coupled with a devotion to intellectual and aesthetic standards that existed independent of any market or constituency. By the 1780s Brackenridge had concluded that his primary responsibility as an author was to defend those standards against debasement at the hands of popular majorities as well as aristocratic minorities. Brackenridge was the first American author to adopt an equivocal and ambivalent attitude toward national ideals, simultaneously to celebrate and criticize the emerging commitment to popular sovereignty, social equality, and unbridled economic opportunity. His personal and literary perspective on postrevolutionary America made psychological but not logical sense. And his sense of humor depended upon the paradoxical insights he had into the historical crosscurrents of his time.

Despite his disdain for mass vulgarity and his worries about the doctrine of popular sovereignty, Brackenridge knew that the social and cultural changes initiated by the Revolution were irreversible. He foresaw that public opinion was destined to exercise an unprecedented influence on arts and letters in America. Moreover, he never completely discarded the idealism of the 1770s, the belief that popular opinion was susceptible to instruction and gradual but steady improvement. *Modern Chivalry* represented his extended effort not only to record the democratization of America in all its ironies, but also to show that it was possible to write a book which a mass readership could appreciate, enjoy and—even as they were laughing—learn from. After Brackenridge, Mark Twain and Will Rogers come as no surprise.

Chapter Five

William Dunlap:
The Dramatist as
Benevolent Patriarch

❧❧

*The tastes and propensities natural to democractic
nations ... will therefore first be discernible in the drama,
and it may be foreseen that they will break out there
with vehemence. In written productions the literary canons
of aristocracy will be gently, gradually, and, so to speak,
legally modified; at the theater they will be riotously
overthrown.*

Alexis de Tocqueville, *Democracy in America*, II (1840)

William Dunlap and Noah Webster—the subjects of the next two
chapters—became friends in 1788 when both were struggling
authors in New York City and charter members of the Philological Society. Dunlap even wrote a play in which Webster
served as the inspiration for a character named "Noah Cobweb,"
who was described as "a curst boring fellow" whose "very looks
give gentlemen the hip" and whose sole aspiration in life was "to
teach the dunces grammar." Characteristically, Dunlap claimed
to be one of the dunces. He invariably coupled criticism of others
with disparaging estimates of himself. This lifelong habit, plus
his bubbling geniality, enabled him to chide Webster without

WILLIAM DUNLAP *by Charles C. Ingham* (*1838*)
Courtesy of National Academy of Design

suffering the usual fate of Webster's critics: burial beneath an avalanche of verbiage. Webster went on to become the leading spokesman for a distinctive brand of American nationalism, the author of some of the most popular and enduring books of the era, a man of unquestioned influence and historical significance. Dunlap's legacy is less visible and less secure. But if we were able to ask their contemporaries which man they liked best, Dunlap would have won easily. He was one of the best-known and best-loved men in postrevolutionary America.[1]

Throughout his long and checkered career as an artist, dramatist, theater manager, novelist, biographer, and historian, Dunlap displayed a knack for making and keeping friends. In 1830, when he was impoverished and ill, an anonymous contributor sent him a one-hundred-dollar bill along with a note, allegedly from his deceased friends in heaven. "As we have everything up here without money and without price," the note read, "several of your old friends thought it best to send it down to you . . . from ABOVE." Three years later the owners of the Park Theater in New York arranged a benefit to celebrate William Dunlap, "artist, author, and the honest man." Despite a severe snowstorm, over two thousand friends attended. Along with Charles Willson Peale, whom of course, he knew, Dunlap was one of the most lovable gadflies in postrevolutionary America.[2]

His sociability and the capacity to listen to hostile opinions with visible earnestness allowed him to make friends without sacrificing his integrity. In 1797, for example, a Methodist minister asked him what church he attended. Dunlap, a deist, replied that he did not attend public worship at all, but would be pleased to accompany the minister to the local Methodist services and receive religious instruction. During the sermon, Dunlap noted in his diary, "the different degrees of sinfulness were enumerated, the last & greatest (all vices & crimes being mentioned before) being Deism—crime of horror! mentioned in a thundering voice accompanied by blows of vengeance. . . ." Dunlap thanked the minister, then went home and spent the rest of the day reading David Hume.[3]

The following year a similar incident occurred when Timothy Dwight, brother-in-law of Dunlap's wife and president of Yale, paid a visit. Dwight read to Dunlap from a polemical poem he had written "against all frenchmen, innovators and infidels." Dunlap listened attentively and, Dwight thought, approvingly. In the privacy of his diary, however, Dunlap confided that Dwight's thoughts were "an inveterate farrago of falshood and abuse." He even made Dwight the model for his "bigoted religionist" in an unpublished novel entitled *Anti-Jacobin*, which satirized all the values that Dwight and Yale embodied.[4] Dunlap's affable and inoffensive temperament, in short, was not a symptom of unprincipled adaptability; it was often an effective mask for strongly held personal convictions.

In addition to being likable, he was also a ubiquitous character who was likely to turn up in the most far-flung and unexpected places. In the 1780s, he could be found conversing with George Washington, studying art at Benjamin West's London studio, or marching alongside Noah Webster in a parade celebrating the ratification of the Constitution. In the 1790s he was helping Charles Brockden Brown revise the manuscript for his next novel, drafting abolitionist platforms with Benjamin Rush, talking law with James Kent, and managing, berating, and comforting the actors and actresses of the American Company. In the early nineteenth century he was championing the prose of Washington Irving, swapping anecdotes about artists with Gilbert Stuart, encouraging James Fenimore Cooper to write, and arguing with John Trumbull about the proper relationship between American artists and businessmen. Dunlap's presence was often fleeting, and his influence is difficult to gauge, but he usually moved somewhere between the center and the edge of postrevolutionary American culture.

Quite understandably, historians have not been sure how to handle him. Because he wrote a three-volume *History of the Rise and Progress of the Arts of Design in the United States* (1834), art historians have labeled him "the American Vasari," while simultaneously concluding that his own paintings are undistinguished. Most histories of the American stage or drama devote an early chapter to Dunlap, who is often described as "The Father of the American Theater." But none of the approximately seventy-five plays that he wrote—thirty original dramas and the rest adaptations or translations—are deemed worthy of revival. His *History of the American Theatre* (1832), in which Dunlap incessantly denigrated his abilities as a dramatist, is regarded as his most valuable contribution to our theatrical history. Surveys of early national culture customarily refer to him in passing as a kind of charming troubadour for the arts in America—Harold Dickson has even identified the cultural history of the young republic as "The Age of William Dunlap." But Dunlap emerges from the standard surveys devoid of flesh and blood and his own convictions; he becomes the symbol for an attractive but superficial versatility, a gregarious but shallow American *philosophe*.[5]

Dunlap himself published two autobiographical essays. These accounts, plus the full-length narrative published by Oral Coad in 1917 and the shorter, more recent biographical studies by Robert Canary and Lewis Leary, provide all the essential information of his life without explaining the reasons for its shape, direction, and the sources of its energy.[6] One comes away from all these histories and biographies murmuring. What did Dunlap think he was doing? Why did he skitter across the surface of American culture with such enthusiasm? How was he able to declare himself a failure so cheerily? What was he measuring himself against? Why, in heaven's name, was this ally of everyone so enamored with America's cultural prospects?

Dunlap was a complex personality whose career was founded on a simple faith; it was a faith akin to Peale's and young Brackenridge's, a faith that the unprecedented freedom unleashed by the Revolution assured America of cultural greatness. "If, as we believe," he wrote, "the world is to be in future a democratic world, and the people thereof hereafter to be governed by those who form and compose the nation . . . it is expedient that every source of knowledge should be *opened* to the governors, *the people*, every obstacle to their improvement removed. . . ."[7] He saw himself as a man called to open all the sluices and kick over all the obstacles between the arts and the public. Despite his loathing of "religionists" like Dwight, Dunlap himself was a crusader on a lifelong moral mission, as he put it, "to set proper exhibitions before a free and well-ordered people."[8] It is an accurate measure of Dunlap's abiding republican faith that he fully expected a free people to be well-ordered, the exhibitions to be proper, and the entire crusade to be managed by leaders he called "the wise and the good."

As a man who came of age during the decade after the Revolution, Dunlap's expectations were not exceptional: on the one hand, he believed that the unprecedented individual freedom possible in postrevolutionary America would generate a flurry of artistic activity; on the other hand, he presumed that artists would behave responsibly and audiences would crave only the best. What proved exceptional was his ability to cling tenaciously to these expectations in the face of popular disapproval, bankruptcy, and massive evidence that America's new natural aristocrats—the men whom Dunlap described as "the wise and the good"—cherished money more than moral or aesthetic truth. One of his biographers has charged that Dunlap, much like Peale, "had a gift for tumbling down financial stairways." In truth, Dunlap was a shrewd and clever fellow, but he had his eyes riveted on loftier objects, despised what he called "pecuniary values," and kept insisting that someone, preferably the federal government, ought to fill in those financial pitfalls; he became the most persistent advocate of federal support for the arts in the new nation. Although there is no evidence that he ever met Hugh Henry Brackenridge or read *Modern Chivalry,* Dunlap's adventures mirrored the fictional exploits of Captain Farrago, bumbling his way across the American landscape full of naive optimism and noble republican ideals.[9]

.

Virtually all that we know about Dunlap's childhood comes from his own autobiographical essays, which are notable for at least two reasons: first, they are unusually detailed and revealing; second, they have been cast into the mold of a melodrama. Dunlap's desire to make himself useful was all-consuming; it extended to his personal history and included a willingness to manipulate the facts of his early life to fit a fabricated, lesson-laden pattern. The central lesson of Dunlap's story was that excessive freedom, especially at an early age, led inevitably to habits of indolence and a selfish, aimless character. His various autobiographies are all morality plays designed to dramatize the danger of self-indulgence and the importance of self-control and discipline. His compulsion to fit his own life into this theme is itself revealing, for it exposes his ultimate disenchantment with the emerging liberal values of nineteenth-century America and his preference for the traditional values associated with republicanism. But in order to extract unadulterated information about his childhood from these accounts, one must lift the evidence free of its moralistic mold, shake it briskly so as to remove melodramatic dust, then examine the features that emerge.[10]

There is no doubt about certain essential facts. Dunlap was born on February 19, 1766, in Perth Amboy, New Jersey. His father was a retired British army officer named Samuel Dunlap who had left Londonderry, Ireland, to fight in the French and Indian War, had been wounded during the battle of Quebec, then settled in Perth Amboy as a shopkeeper and merchant. His mother was a third-generation colonist and native of New Jersey named Margaret Sargeant, an unpretentious woman who disappears from Dunlap's historical record soon after she is introduced.

The rest of the story is saturated with Dunlap's backward-looking biases. He described himself as "the only and indulged child" of doting parents, a boy who was "petted, indulged, spoiled" by the several black slaves in the household because he was "the only child of the master of the family." Although he was sent to the local dame school to learn reading and writing, then on to a grammar school run by a graduate of Oxford to learn Latin and Greek, Dunlap insisted nevertheless that his young mind was uncultivated. "Education I had none," he recalled, "and most of what is to the child most essential education, was essentially bad."[11]

Two men play crucial roles in Dunlap's version of his childhood. The first is his father, who is always described as the embodiment of benign authority, while Dunlap himself is described as the wholly dependent and adoring son. "[M]y earliest recollections," he wrote in 1832, "are those connected with sickness, and the relief derived from being carried in my father's arms." The second person was "a small, thin old man, with straight gray hair hanging on each side of his pale face." His name was Thomas Bartow, and he lived in the center of Perth Amboy. Dunlap described Bartow as "truly venerable," a man "who was yet untainted by the world which he seemed to shun." Bartow read to him from Pope's *Iliad*, Dryden's *Virgil*, and Milton's *Paradise*

Lost, explaining difficult passages and commenting on the plates that illustrated the famous scenes. Dunlap credited Bartow with igniting his lifelong love for books and ideas. Although he only knew him for three or four years and never saw him again after 1775, when Bartow moved inland to avoid the approaching war, Dunlap was haunted by his memory. "For years," he claimed, "I saw him vividly in my dreams, and awoke, like Caliban, with the disposition to weep for a renewal of my dreams." On another occasion Dunlap used even more striking language to express his feelings for Bartow: "Through a long life," he confessed, "his image has visited my hours of sleep—always changed—generally sick—or insane—or confined to his chamber and forbidding my approach to him."[12]

Dunlap, of course, did not have access to the works of Sigmund Freud or to the voluminous literature generated by twentieth-century psychiatrists and psychologists on the significance of dreams, subconscious drives, and the child's early encounters with parental authority. We do, and we also know that in his dramatic career Dunlap was preoccupied with domestic conflicts, most especially conflicts between fathers and sons. In *The Father; or American Shandyism,* later revised and renamed *The Father of An Only Child,* then again in *The Italian Father,* Dunlap publicized his interest in the titles. But in all of his best plays, regardless of title, he explored the tension inherent in the father-son relationship and usually focused attention on the conflict between strong fathers and sons who oscillated between obedience and rebelliousness. In *André,* his most impressive play, he was able to bring these personal preoccupations together most effectively and relate them to larger ideological questions about national authority, popular rebellion, and deference. The thematic concern of his dramatic works, the language he used to characterize the memories of his real father and of Thomas Bartow, his surrogate father, and the constant reiteration of his various autobiographies that he was a "bad" child all suggest that Dunlap's early relationship with paternal authority was traumatic.

For our purposes, which is to say for an understanding of Dunlap's adult behavior and his impact on early American culture, a clinical diagnosis of his emotional problem is unnecessary.

What is essential, however, is the recognition that Dunlap's life-long ambivalence toward authority had its roots in his childhood; his unresolved response of love and fear toward his father was both the emotional wellspring for his most creative dramas and the prototype for his mature attitude toward freedom and authority in national politics.* More specifically, his childhood experience influenced his later career in at least two crucial ways. First, it made him doubt his own importance and crave the approval of friends. Dunlap's renowned knack for making friends was also a need. He even called it "my monomania." With persons of my own age and station, he observed, "I was always full of life and gaiety; and moved by a strong desire to please." With older and more authoritative persons, however, he was reticent and shy. "I had an awe of distinguished men . . . a bashfulness that required encouraging," he wrote, adding that he usually remained silent "in presence of those, whom I considered my superiors."[14] When he himself became older and distinguished, he went out of his way to put acquaintances at ease. He was always most comfortable in relationships based on mutual respect and muted forms of authority, and he worked hard to create those conditions whenever young actors or writers tried to put him on a pedestal. He became a benevolent father figure, a Thomas Bartow if you will, to an entire generation of American authors and artists.

Second, Dunlap's emotional sensitivity to the danger or desirability of paternal authority made him unusually receptive to the shifting values in postrevolutionary America. He was able to straddle the divide that separated the eighteenth from the nineteenth century, republicanism from democracy, classicism from romanticism, virtuous self-restraint from liberating self-expression, because his own feelings about freedom and authority were

---

* Psychohistory suffers from one crucial deficiency—we are not able to resurrect the subject and ask him or her the questions that must be answered in order to fill the inevitable gaps in the evidence. Historians share the problem with psychohistorians, but since the latter frequently claim to be offering scientific conclusions, the absence of evidence is more damaging to their cause. In Dunlap's case, only a clinical hypothesis based on the striking but scanty evidence that survives is possible, namely, that Dunlap feared rejection by his father and developed what Freudians would describe as a repressed oedipal complex.[13]

fundamentally at odds with each other. Eventually Dunlap discovered that his deepest commitment was to the older, less liberal attitudes, and that the new freedoms of the emerging society were harmful agents, like blissfully ignorant but potentially destructive children who must be constrained by enlightened patriarchs. But he was ever tolerant of those who disagreed, always hopeful that democracy would outgrow its youthful excesses and discipline itself, because part of him genuinely believed it was possible.[15]

•

History, of course, did not come to a halt while young Dunlap stumbled his way through childhood. In 1775 the British regiment stationed in Perth Amboy received orders to depart for Boston. The following year Dunlap learned that the regiment had been decimated at the Battle of Bunker Hill. The family moved to Piscataway when war between England and the colonies was officially declared, but Dunlap was too young to understand what was happening, except to rejoice that he no longer was required to attend school. He spent his time, he recalled, "swimming and fishing in the creeks of the Raritan, rambling the fields and woods. . . . The Declaration of Independence caused a sensation which I distinctly remember, but my sports and rambles had more interest for *me*." In the summer of 1776 he "read the whole of Shakespeare" while most Americans prepared for war.[16]

Dunlap's latter-day recollections of the American Revolution tended to take the form of two historical portraits, or perhaps two scenes from a melodrama. In the first scene that Dunlap remembered, British soldiers were plundering the town of Piscataway. The wives and prostitutes who accompanied the army were standing guard over huge piles of frying pans, kitchen utensils, and furniture, while "the women of the village [were] trembling and weeping, or flying with their children." Off to the side, several British deserters were being flogged. "This scene," wrote Dunlap, "was a lesson." And so was the other scene, the return of the British forty-second regiment from a skirmish near Perth Amboy in 1777. Dunlap recalled that the soldiers had marched out of town with all the "pride, pomp, and circumstance of glorious war." One tall and distinguished grenadier had particularly captured his attention. But the troops straggled back in the evening, "their wagons loaded with wounded," and the night air filled with "the groans of those who were borne to the hospitals." The tall grenadier limped by, "his musket on his left shoulder, his right hand bound up . . . but no longer looked like the hero I had admired. . . . I had now seen something of war."[17]

In 1777 his family moved to New York City, a refuge for Tories because it served as the garrison for the British army in North America. There Samuel Dunlap, a moderate Tory whose major concerns were the safety of his family and the continuation of his business, waited for the war to end. Dunlap remembered that most of the city was "a mass of black unsightly rubbish" created by the huge fire following the rebel evacuation in 1776, and that a prominent statue of George III had been removed from its pedestal, melted down, and used for bullets by the patriots. He also remembered that British officers staged plays during the winter months; the first play he ever saw was Farquhar's *Beaux' Stratagem.* Most of all, he remembered one afternoon in June of 1778, when he was hit in the right eye by a piece of wood while playing with friends. He was a one-eyed man for the rest of his life. Soon after the accident, as if to spite his new handicap, Dunlap began to draw pictures and make portraits with crayons and pastels and to talk of becoming an artist. He whiled away his time drawing, playing the flute, and reading until 1783, when the war officially ended.[18]

Dunlap experienced the American Revolution at an awkward age: he was old enough to witness the war and to store up memories which he would draw upon later as a playwright and chronicler, but he was too young—only fifteen when the fighting ended—to participate directly in the military or ideological conflict. He had seen enough to know that war was gruesome and terrible; that was the extent of his understanding. He did not, as one biographer has claimed, emerge from the Revolution "an ardent American." Dunlap remained a political and ideological innocent who had liked the British soldiers when they ruled the city, and who was now eager to like, and be liked by, the victorious American patriots. In his subsequent career he became an avid republican and a spokesman for American cultural achievements. But he discovered these commitments later and in his own unusual way. In the early 1780s he was a rather rare creature—an apolitical young American. When the time came to write plays about the American Revolution, Dunlap, unlike Peale and Brackenridge, had no deep and powerful ideological commitments to draw upon and no political grievances to renounce or control; his emotional and aesthetic convictions could mold his political message, not the other way around.

In 1783 he was ripe for any cause capable of making a strong impression. Late in the summer of 1783 he was traveling on his own through New Jersey, the first time in six years he had journeyed outside the confines of New York City. On the road between Princeton and Trenton, he encountered Washington, "the man whom all men spoke—whom all wished to see." Later in life he remembered the encounter as a tableau:

It was a picture. No painter could have grouped a company of military horsemen better, or selected a background better suited for effect.... [A]sending [*sic*] a hill suddenly appeared a brilliant group of cavaliers, mounting and gaining the summit in my front. The clear autumnal sky behind them equally relieved the dark blue uniforms, the buff facings, and glittering military appendages. All were gallantly mounted—all were tall and graceful, but one towered above the rest, and I doubted not an instant that I saw the beloved hero.... They passed on, and I gazed as at a passing vision. I had seen him.[19]

Washington's headquarters were only a mile from the house where Dunlap was lodging. An introduction was arranged and the general apparently became fascinated with the boyishly bashful young man who had only one eye and who said he wanted to become an artist. Dunlap began to take his meals with the general and his wife. He played his flute for them and did crayon sketches of each. Once he even saw Washington laugh out loud. When he returned to New York he painted an oil portrait of Washington, standing "heroically alone" at the battle of Princeton while another American officer expired "in precisely the same attitude that West had devised to picture the dying of General Wolfe."[20]

As much as Washington, Benjamin West had become one of Dunlap's heroes and much admired father figures, a worthy heir to the fantasies first generated by Thomas Bartow. Throughout the winter and spring of 1784 Dunlap divided his time between assiduous preparation for studying art with West in London and equally assiduous preparation for a life of total irresponsibility at the card tables and billiard rooms. The man-child sailed for England in May of 1784.

He remained in London for slightly more than three years, frolicking with friends, spending his father's money lavishly, and avoiding the art studio and criticism of the great West. Dunlap craved approval. West was prepared to provide encouragement, but he mixed his gentle praise of Dunlap's work with a heavy dose of criticism that rendered the young artist speechless. Soon after his arrival, as West commented on the strengths and weaknesses of one of his drawings, Dunlap concluded that his artistic ambitions were futile. "I stood in the presence of the artist and wondered at his skill," he recalled, "but I stood silent, abashed, hesitating—and withdrew unenlightened;—discouraged by the consciousness of ignorance and my monomaniacal want of courage." He then gathered together his portfolio, chalks, and paints and "delivered them to the porter . . . and walked off: I never entered the school or saw my portfolio again."[21]

For the next three years a typical day began with Dunlap rising late in the morning. He would then spend the middle of the day lounging and chatting at the New York Coffee House, a gathering spot for Americans and young British officers who had served in America. From there he and West's son, Raphael, would amble over to the Cock Eating House for a long dinner, followed by port and conversation and an evening at the theater. Dunlap became an enthusiastic and knowledgeable playgoer who saw all the prominent actors and actresses of the London stage. Drama replaced art as his chief obsession, although he was content to admire the productions without contemplating a serious commitment to dramatic writing. During his London years, in fact, Dunlap was not prepared for a serious commitment to anything except youthful comradery and the affection of other dilettantes. After attending the theater, he and whoever could be persuaded to come along would ramble from club to club. "I strove to shine," he jotted in his diary over a decade later, "[and] I remember . . . that having learned a new song & sung it with the applauses of my companions, I, after singing it at a club in the Strand . . . went, tho' pretty late, to the Bucks-lodge in the hopes of being asked to sing." He pursued approval from all quarters. "And many a time," he remembered with embarrassment, "I sate & listen'd to stupidity & ribaldry in the shape of song or story in the impatient hope that my turn would soon come. . . ."[22]

This could not last. In November of 1786 Dunlap and Samuel Latham Mitchell, a friend from New York who had just received his medical degree from Edinburgh, took a walking tour to Oxford. They encountered an old British soldier along the route who had once been stationed at Perth Amboy and who remembered Dunlap's father. At Oxford they laughed at the ceremonial etiquette in the dining hall, where the students and fellows bowed to one another, *"shaking their heads like Mandarin figures on a chimney piece;* a more ridulous scene Oxford does not afford," Dunlap observed, "and that's saying a great deal." But soon after he returned from the trip, his one and only journey outside London, the inevitable letter demanding his return arrived from his father. After some stalling and last-minute scurrying, Dunlap sailed for New York. He arrived home in October of 1787 without the faintest glimmer of what he might do with himself.[23]

When Dunlap looked back at this critical moment in his life, he saw it as an occasion to deliver a moral lecture on the evils of youthful idleness and self-indulgence. "Between three and four years I had been principally a resident in the metropolis of Great Britain at the most critical time of a man's life—between the ages of eighteen and twenty-two," he wrote, and had returned to America with "no education or habits fitting one for any definite pursuit."[24] The pattern that Dunlap imposed on his early life contained all the essential elements of the standard sentimental melodrama: the indolent young hero arrives home, is lectured by his father, but disregards paternal wisdom and embarks on a life of carousing in New York; enter a virtuous young woman named Elizabeth Woolsey; the hero falls hopelessly in love with her and promises to mend his ways and be a responsible husband; they are married in February of 1789; immediately, the happy rigors of domestic bliss produce a sudden transformation. "I was now rescued from inevitable destruction," Dunlap announced. "My character was fast changing, and the monomania I have complained of was vanishing, until by degrees I learned to appreciate myself and others with some degree of justice."[25]

Love conquers all in melodrama, but seldom in real life. Dunlap was never a willfully intransigent, self-centered young man; he was a reticent, shy child who skittered from club to coffeehouse in search of encouragement and who was emotionally incapable of breaking free of his father's control to discover a direction of his own. Although his marriage to Nabby Woolsey, who brought a respectable family background and considerable love to the relationship, was Dunlap's declaration of personal independence, by itself it would have changed little. For Dunlap remained under his father's control, working in the family import business on Queen Street.

What changed Dunlap's life and released his creative energies was the death of his father. As long as his father remained alive, Dunlap was incapable of using his freedom and talent productively. Soon after the marriage to Nabby Woolsey, Dunlap's father became ill and began to decline steadily until he died in 1791. As his father's vitality waned, Dunlap's own spirits soared. He began to rise early in the morning and set goals for each day. He drew up a structured reading program designed to improve his knowledge of history, political philosophy, and science. Most important, he put away his paints—dreams of an artistic career were vestiges of his past fantasy world—and searched for a new calling. When he looked inside himself for burning interests, he discovered that the most "inflammable material brought from abroad" was his love for the theater. In a sudden burst of activity Dunlap wrote his first play, a comedy entitled *The Modest Soldier, or Love in New-York.*[26] The liberated son of Samuel Dunlap had decided to become a playwright.

•

Many of Dunlap's contemporaries, and later on a good many historians of the American theater, considered it an auspicious time to begin a dramatic career. The same optimistic attitude that had buoyed up the spirits of artists, poets, and novelists during and after the Revolution also raised the hopes of aspiring playwrights and thespians. In his own *History of the American Theatre* Dunlap observed that civilization was on the march and was bringing the public taste for theater along in its baggage. In the first decade of the seventeenth century, he recalled, English America was only a cluster of primitive settlements; by 1751 Benjamin Franklin had estimated the colonial population at one million. "Such was the increase in one hundred and forty years, and the arts, following in the train of civilization, already prepared to rear the standard of taste."[27] Here was the familiar vision of the westward drift of the muses, the widespread conviction that cultural greatness was inextricably linked to social and economic development. Robert Treat Paine, a young American playwright, saw the muses as a flock of birds which had departed the cold and tyrannical European continent and "cast a fondly wistful eye on the pure climate of the western sky." They were supposedly landing all over America in the last quarter of the eighteenth century. "Behold, Appollo seeks this liberal plain," Paine insisted, "And brings the thespian goddess in his train."[28]

Dunlap's *History of the American Theatre* confirmed this enthusiastic vision. From small and meager beginnings, so the story went, and after a century of legal harassment, the American theater seemed about ready to blossom in the 1780s. The first known play to be acted in colonial America was *The Bare and the Cubb*, an amateur production written and staged by residents of Virginia's eastern shore in 1665. Virginia also claimed the first playhouse, which opened in Williamsburg in 1718. But every colony except Virginia and Maryland eventually enacted legislation prohibiting stage plays. A handful of itinerant actors occasionally challenged these laws, or simply ignored them, and thereby kept the theater alive, although the quality of the native plays and the skill of the players seemed to confirm the wisdom of the legislators. In 1752, however, Lewis Hallam brought a company of English players to America and toured coastal towns and cities from Charleston to Boston. In 1767 Hallam's professional actors, now led by David Douglass and called the American Company, staged Thomas Godfrey's *The Prince of Parthia* in Philadelphia. This was the first play written by an American to be performed by a professional company of actors; it marked the start of a native dramatic tradition in America.[29]

The coming of the American Revolution provided some temporary setbacks: in New York City the Sons of Liberty burned down the theater, which they saw as a symbol of licentiousness; and in 1774 the Continental Congress passed a measure prohibiting "all kinds of gaming, cock-fighting, exhibitions of shews, plays, and other expensive diversions and entertainments." But dramatic presentations continued during the war despite the prohibition. In addition to the plays put on by the British officers in New York and Boston, Hugh Henry Brackenridge and Mercy Otis Warren turned out patriotic dramas that glorified American military heroes and demonstrated the utility of drama as propagator of republican ideology. When the war ended, the American Company, now headed up by Lewis Hallam, Jr., and John Henry, reestablished its tour of American cities and challenged the state laws against the theater. In New York, as the legislature debated the propriety of "theatrical demonstrations," it received a referendum signed by 1400 residents who insisted that plays were 'innocent and rational amusements" and should not be outlawed. Similar appeals found their way to legislators in Massachusetts and Pennsylvania as they debated the same question. Moreover, supporters of the theater began to employ a liberal argument that was just becoming an article of faith in late-eighteenth-century America, namely, that no government should have the power to limit the freedom of individual citizens. "The same authority which proscribes our amusements, may, with equal justice," one Philadelphia commentator warned, "dictate the shape and texture of our dress or the modes and ceremonies of our worship." This was an argument with a bright future; the theater was one of its earliest beneficiaries.[30]

By the time Dunlap had returned home from England, old playhouses were being reopened and new ones were being constructed in most American cities. Dunlap arrived back in New York in time to hear the excited talk about a recently performed comedy entitled *The Contrast* by Royall Tyler. This play featured a character named Jonathan, who became the prototype for the Yankee figure destined to dominate early American literature and drama. Jonathan produced some of his loudest laughs when he asked, "Ain't . . . the play-house the shop where the devil hangs out the vanities of the world upon the tenterhooks of temptation?"[31] The evidence seemed conclusive: the old prohibitory statutes were falling, playhouses were going up, native American characters were appearing onstage to deliver jokes that mocked the criticism of the theater. Both Dunlap and the American drama seemed to be coming of age simultaneously.

Unfortunately for Dunlap and the development of American theater, the attitudes and apprehensions responsible for legal opposition to the stage during the colonial period and the war years lived on even after the laws themselves were revoked. In fact, the elimination of legal constraints caused opponents of the stage to intensify their criticism in the late 1780s and '90s. During the debates in the state legislatures, in broadsides and pamphlets and in the newspapers, all the old arguments that had been used against artists and novelists were trotted out once more and directed against playwrights. Moreover, the stage proved vulnerable to a hallowed and long-standing set of prejudices and worries. Plato had banished the theater from his ideal republic; the church fathers had denounced it during the Middle Ages; in seventeenth-century England the Puritans had outlawed it. The social and psychological sources of this intense and persistent hostility to the stage were deeply embedded in Western history. As a result, the theater was unquestionably the most hated of all the fine arts in eighteenth-century America.

First of all, said the critics, attendance at theaters was "a criminal waste of time" in republican America, where so much essential work waited to be done. But the argument that plays were "mere amusements" and therefore superfluous luxuries that distracted Americans from more important chores was usually accompanied by the more serious charge that theaters were "powerful and destructive emblems of dissipation, profaneness, and corruption." Critics of the theater disputed the close connection between social progress and high culture by insisting that the fine arts lagged at the rear of the grand march of civilization; in the life cycle of a society the fine arts blossomed late, just when social order and self-restraint were about to collapse. During the debate over the theater in the Pennsylvania legislature, for example, several speakers asserted that theaters were symptoms not of national health but of national decay, because "they only flourished when states were on the decline." Like all the other fine arts, the theater suffered the stigma of being a harbinger of national decrepitude and therefore an alien presence in a youthful republic.[32]

Second, the plays themselves were susceptible to all the charges directed at novels. Indeed, after his lengthy strictures against novels, John Witherspoon noted that such books produced "as much hurt as any composition . . . excepting plays themselves." Like novels, plays were described as inherently dangerous because they were fictional fabrications which enticed otherwise decent people into unreal worlds where truth was subordinated to extravagant flights of the imagination. Harvard undergraduates were forbidden to witness "Stage Plays, Interludes, or Theatrical Entertainments" on the grounds that exposure to "flighty nonsense" would erode the logical and reasoning capacities that had been built up in the classroom. Critic after critic warned that plays "DISSIPATE THE MIND" because they "chiefly address the inferior powers of our nature and lay us open to the inroads and government of vice and folly, and vitiate our moral sense." By "inferior powers" most hostile observers meant the passions or the emotions, faculties they associated with weak and undependable men or, more typically, with women. "The head is filled with heroes, and heroines," reported one disenchanted playgoer, and "women, seeing the adorations which, in them are given to their sex, have that sort of life so much impressed on their minds, that the affairs of their family and of common life, become unsupportable to them." Most playgoers were not presumed to be women, but the plays themselves were described as appealing to the weaker and allegedly more feminine side of human nature. Samuel Miller contended that "the universal maxims of the theatre are, that *love* is the grand business of life: that *present gratification* is to be preferred to suffering virtue . . . that *human praise* is the highest reward. . . ." These were the romantic illusions of a woman's world, said the male critics. Rousseau had said much the same thing when he argued that the effect of most plays was "to extend the empire of the fair sex, and to make women and girls the preceptors of the public. . . ."[33]

Third, unlike art or literature, the theater brought a mass audience together physically in one place. When Lewis Hallam and John Henry petitioned the Massachusetts legislature for repeal of its law against theaters in 1792, they boasted that the theater joined "all ranks of the people together." This fact might have pleased some Jeffersonians, but it terrified most Federalists. "And let me ask you," Webster wrote in one of his patriarchal polemics,

what sort of entertainment is that in which a thin partition only separates the nobleman from his lackey and the dutchess from her kitchen-maid, in which the gentleman and the lady associate at the same board with the footman, the oysterman, the woman of the town, and all partake of the same fare! With what sentiments must superior beings look down on this motley school of morality?[34]

Typically, Webster exaggerated to make his point; for American theaters, like English theaters of the era, did not lump all playgoers together in one undifferentiated mass. In fact, the seating arrangements mirrored the social divisions and class assumptions of the day. Servants, slaves, prostitutes, and "the rabble" usually occupied the gallery, a balcony section at the rear of the building which usually cost fifty cents for admission. Artisans, shopkeepers, and "men of the middling sort" filled the pit, which was located directly in front of and below the stage; a ticket for the pit cost seventy-five cents. Gentlemen, merchants, and their ladies sat in the boxes, which were behind the pit and below the gallery and cost one dollar.

But once the lamps were dimmed, the curtain raised, and the play had begun, the fact that all these different social groupings were together in one room, sharing the same experience in the dark, troubled observers who believed that social distinctions must be preserved. Because the occupants of the gallery frequently showered the actors and the rest of the audience with apples, nuts, stale gingerbread, and obscene epithets, critics of the theater could depict the situation inside the theater as a perfect illustration of how easily the "democratical element in society can reduce all to their own vulgar level and destroy . . . refinement with mobbish noise." Washington Irving, writing under the pseudonym "Jonathan Oldstyle," found the raucous mood of the gallery quite humorous and recommended that the inhabitants of the gallery be given "less grog, and better constables." His sympathy went out to the steady artisans and yeomen in the pit; they needed only "clean benches, patience, and umbrellas."[35]

Opponents of the theater did not laugh. Just as the plays themselves were associated with the "weaker" and more emotional side of human nature, the theatrical audience conjured up all the worries about the expanding power of the uneducated lower orders, exemplified by the unrestrained residents of the gallery. Even though the separate sections of the theater symbolized the persistence of a hierarchical society in which social inequality remained the norm, the theatrical audience was seldom described as a model of republican order. Defenders of the theater tended to skip over references to the audience altogether; the interior of the playhouse was a subject dominated by hostile observers who described the audience as a potential mob. From their perspective the theater seemed to be a place where matters usually got out of control, where the doctrine of popular sovereignty assumed its most ghastly shape, where the egalitarian implications of republicanism began to shade into unfettered democracy. The theater, in short, became a convenient screen onto which Americans troubled by the onrush of democracy and the waning of traditional values projected their grim vision of the future. And the single most noted feature in this picture—guaranteed to heighten apprehension—was the section of the gallery reserved for prostitutes. Theaters were called "massive whorehouses," "Hot Beds of Vice," and "disguised Brothels" because they admitted known prostitutes, allowed them to display their wares in a special section of the gallery, and even permitted them to shout solicitations to gentlemen in the boxes during intermissions. Between the enticing seductions of the play and the sexual suggestions from the gallery, a moral man had no chance.[36]

Fourth, and finally, there were the actors. Almost all the professional actors in postrevolutionary America were Englishmen who had learned their trade in the provincial theaters outside London. Even Dunlap was forced to admit that "the life of a strolling player in England" was "an education in the school of folly, thoughtless dissipation, or positive vice. . . ." The wonder of it all, he thought, was that so many actors and actresses turned out to be moral and virtuous folk. A small but highly visible minority of every acting company, however, were derelicts addicted to alcohol, drugs, and sexual promiscuity, and they tended to give all actors a bad name. Samuel Miller warned that playgoers who paid for theater tickets were financing "A SET OF PERFORMERS IN A LIFE OF VANITY, LICENTIOUNESS AND SIN." To those who accused him of prejudice against his fellowman, Miller responded by quoting Rousseau: "You will say that these incontestible facts result only from prejudices; I agree to it; but these prejudices being universal, we must seek for an universal cause; and I do not see where we can find it excepting *in the profession itself."* As itinerants who appeared in town for a few performances, then departed, actors suffered from the same suspicions as other transients, although, as Dunlap observed, circuit judges, preachers, cobblers, and country lawyers did not risk arrest whenever they arrived in a community. Actors did.

For there was something nefarious about acting itself. "What is the talent of the actor?" asked one minister, but the "art of counterfeiting himself, of putting on another character than his own, of appearing different than he is. . . ." And what did an actor do but "perform for money . . . and put his person publicly on sale." There was good reason, argued an anonymous critic, why Athens fell soon after Pericles established a theater in the city and why no Roman could appear onstage and retain his citizenship. While Noah Webster seems to have been the only critic who worried that the Anglicized diction and accent of most performers would corrupt the American manner of speaking, audiences were sometimes aroused when they thought they detected a British bias in a scene intended to exalt American patriotism.[37]

These apprehensions and prejudices kept playwrights and theater managers on the defensive. During the prerevolutionary years it had become customary for actors to recite lengthy prologues which proclaimed the wholly moral purposes of the drama, to insist that playwrights were really moral philosophers and the playhouse but another schoolroom or church in which actors delivered animated lectures or sermons. In order to evade the laws against stage plays that remained on the books after the Revolution, managers heralded their plays as "Moral Lectures"; even as the Massachusetts legislature debated the repeal of the existent statute against the stage, a theatrical company was presenting a play in Boston under the guise of "a Sermon in Dialogue."[38]

Although such evasive contrivances were designed primarily to avoid fines and the jailhouse, the insistence that dramatists had to prove their respectability and that the theater, even after it was legalized, was on trial before the guardians of public virtue, imposed severe constraints on the development of native American drama. In a pamphlet entitled *Effects of the Stage on the Manners of the People,* William Haliburton assured his readers that American playwrights realized that they were "under a moral obligation to oppose vice and demonstrate their usefulness . . .

to the public good." A contributor to the *American Magazine* re-iterated the dominant view that playwrights must use the stage as a pulpit and present plays which show "not just a true picture of life . . . [but also] what life itself ought to be." When a person left the theater, one newspaper writer observed, he should "have no doubt about what was right and what was wrong, who the hero was . . . and should testify . . . that he came away a better man than he went." Every play that an American saw, wrote Judith Sargent Murray, must show "Virtue . . . adorned with all her native loveliness, and vice exhibited, deformed, and mis-shapen. . . ." Here was a prescription for caricature rather than character, for melodrama rather than drama, for truisms rather than truth, and it haunted the American stage throughout Dun-lap's career.[39]

•

That career actually began on September 7, 1789, when the American Company performed *The Father, or American Shandy-ism* at the John Street Theater in New York. (Dunlap's first play, *The Modest Soldier,* had been rejected because it did not con-tain suitable parts for the head of the acting company and his wife.)[40] *The Father* ran for three weeks and was immediately published in the *Massachusetts Magazine* as "an important new work written by a Citizen of New York." In the prologue Dun-lap showed that he was aware of the moralistic arguments against the theater and how to blunt them. He described his play as "homespun fare," "a frugal plain repast" unlike the "high-season'd food" of European dramatists. He suggested that hostility toward plays and theaters was understandable, given the degenerate con-dition of the European stage. But Americans need not worry:

> The comick muse, pleas'd with her new abode,
> Steps forth in sportive tho' in moral mode;
> Proud of her dwelling in our new-made nation,
> She's set about a serious reformation,
> For, faith, she'd almost lost her reputation.[41]

Much of the sport derived from Dunlap's willingness to chide himself and to mock his own efforts. At the end of the play an actor delivered an epilogue in which the residents of the gallery were asked why they had not torn the theater apart to protest the drivel they had just witnessed. And the occupants of the pit were ordered not to applaud:

> *Pray, don't encourage these young writers more;*
> *For if you do you'll have them by the score,—*
> *They're mighty fond, 'tis known, of 'yet encore!'*
> *Each blockhead's brain and printer's press is teeming;*
> *All write, none read, and each dull dunce is dreaming.*[42]

Between the reassuring prologue and the self-deprecating epilogue, the audience was treated to a briskly paced comedy that marked Dunlap as the leading American playwright of his time. Not that *The Father* was distinguished by dramatic originality or creativity. These were not Dunlap's gifts. He was, instead, a skillful borrower with a knack for synthesizing and adapting stock characters and familiar plots, then blending the borrowed ingredients to produce a distinctive American alloy. He lifted several situations from Sterne's *Tristram Shandy;* the minor characters in *The Father,* especially Susannah, the maid, and the various servants and miscellaneous visitors, were modeled on the stock characters of British social comedy; and the central plot was a staple story line of sentimental drama—a father, Colonel Duncan, is finally reunited with his long-lost son, Captain Haller, despite the intrigues of a villainous impostor named Ranter.[43]

But the plot is almost incidental to the action of the play. It merely provides the occasion to introduce characters and dialogue. There is Mrs. Racket, a flirtatous and caustic woman who brags that New Yorkers are "a match for the most polish'd people in Europe; we can shew you lawyers without common sense, soldiers without courage, gentlemen without politeness, and virtuous ladies without modesty." There is Jacob, the German butler, a bumbling dictator of domestic routines who tells the servants to "git into de kitchen and mind your own pisiness." There is Mrs. Grenade, a militaristic widow who arranges the food on her plate into a series of fortifications which she then attacks with knife and fork. There is the Van-brot-wagenhauf family, a Dutch brood of considerable wealth and little grace. Mr. Van-brot-wagenhauf takes off his wig at the table in order to wipe the sweat from his bald head. "Cot pless me, I am all of a muck," he exclaims. "Law, pappa!" cries his daughter, "how can you use such vulger

dispressions?" Finally, there is Doctor Quiescent, the most humorous character in the play, who is introduced as an eminent
physician and "a travelled American, who . . . cannot prevail upon
any two ideas to become acquainted with each other." He rambles throughout the different scenes, mistakenly believing that
women find him irresistible, mumbling incoherently about broken
skulls and magic cures, a harmless nitwit whose doctoral thesis
at Edinburgh concerned a new technique to revive drowned cats.
All these characters tumble over each other in the climactic
scene, when Dunlap has the entire cast groping about in a darkened room unable to find their correct partners. Eventually the
lights come on, Mr. and Mrs. Racket are reconciled, father and
son are reunited, and everyone lives happily ever after.[44]

It was good theater, all in all a better play than Tyler's *The
Contrast*, and just as good as the plays currently being turned out
by English dramatists. *The Father* revealed that Dunlap possessed
several talents that would serve him well as an aspiring American
playwright. First, he was extremely skillful at borrowing situations, characters, and story lines, mostly from English plays, then
fusing these borrowed elements together by means of his own
lively sense of humor and his ability to write clever dialogue.
Second, he had an intuitive grasp of stagecraft, a surprising gift
considering his lack of experience and his later insistence that
he "knew nothing about what went on behind the curtain." The
action in *The Father* was adroitly managed, the different scenes
required no expensive costumes or scenery, and the characters
made excellent use of the range of talent available in the American Company. The role of Doctor Quiescent, for example, appears to have been tailored for Thomas Wignell, the best comic
actor in the company and the same man who had played Jonathan in *The Contrast*. Third, Dunlap had the ability to sense
what the audience wanted, to know what would please the public and make people happy. His personal craving for approval
had made him an acute student of popular opinion and the various ways to win it over to his side. The gallery of characters in
The Father offered something for everyone. And how could any
spectator object to the silliness of a German butler or a Dutch
family when the author reserved his most digging comments for
playwrights, in other words, for himself?

Finally, Dunlap showed his ability to disarm enemies of the

stage without surrendering his own integrity as a dramatist. His play was so obviously harmless, a piece of good-natured fun designed to amuse, that only an inveterate theater hater could have found fault with it. And if such a critic charged that *The Father* was mere entertainment, a useless waste of time, then Dunlap could point to the fact that virtue triumphs in the end: Mr. and Mrs. Racket realize that they love each other; the dastardly Ranter is exposed as a blackguard; the noble Colonel Duncan is rewarded for his nobility. All the moralistic bases are touched. Nevertheless, Dunlap does not allow *The Father* to become a melodrama that oozes with sentimentality. He maintains control over the moralistic messages and makes them subordinate to the comic purpose of the play.

·

Dunlap was ecstatic about the play's success. "Filled with youthful ardour, and pleased with the applause of the public," he wrote, now he "thought only of future triumphs; and tragedies, comedies, operas and farces, occupied his mind, his time, and his pen."[45] In 1792 he placed the shop he inherited from his father in the hands of a member of the Woolsey family under terms that guaranteed him a percentage of the profits.[46] He left no doubt about his attitude toward a life devoted to buying and selling: he loathed it. "I have been myself a shopkeeper but I never was a thorough bred one," he observed in 1797, adding that, despite the pressure to maximize profits, he "never forgot the dignity of man" and always tried to treat customers as human beings rather than potential sources of profit.[47] When he read Bernard Mandeville's *Fable of the Bees,* he concurred with the author's charge that only the "vilest and most hateful qualities" could thrive in commercial societies; he interpreted Mandeville's book as a condemnation of merchants, entrepreneurs, and all occupations "whose very existence depend upon vice."[48] Dunlap's hostility toward commercial or capitalistic values was rooted in his republican belief that a life devoted to making money was simply "incompatible with virtue." If money accrued to a playwright in the course of his work, well, that was another matter.

Dunlap used his newfound freedom well. He freed all his deceased father's slaves—a highly symbolic act—and became active in the abolitionist movement in New York. In keeping with

his moderate temperament, he favored gradual rather than immediate emancipation of all slaves and reimbursement of the
owners. That way, he insisted, all sides would be happy in the
long run. But despite his instinctive preference for racial policies
that minimized offensiveness, he had no patience with paternal-
istic rationales of slavery. While reading an account of the slave
trade, he noted that the "blessed Author, is fully of [the] opinion
that the Europeans by buying up the Africans for their plantations have done humanity an infinite service by preventing them
from eating one another! There are many pages of this kind of
stuff."*

He became a regular participant in the literary discussions of
the Friendly Club, an informal group of young New York intellectuals, many of whom had formerly belonged to the Philological
Society. Dunlap, a practiced friend maker and a natural clubman,
formed his closest ties with three bachelors who often visited his
home: Elihu Hubbard Smith, a physician who also wrote poetry
and plays; William Johnson, a lawyer and classical scholar; and
Charles Brockden Brown, a brilliant but erratic novelist and journalist. In part because of their prodding, he began to write articles on dramatic and literary subjects for the *New York Magazine
or Literary Repository.* And the wide-ranging discussions of the
Friendly Club turned him into a voracious reader of history and
philosophy. During a four-month period, for example, Dunlap
read the histories of Thucydides, Edward Gibbon, and David
Hume, Mary Wollstonecraft's *The Rights of Women,* Tom Paine's
Agrarian Justice, William Godwin's *Political Justice,* then selections from Condorcet and Rousseau. In subsequent months he
moved on to Erasmus Darwin's *Zoomania,* Voltaire's *Philosophical Dictionary,* and Jonathan Edwards's treatise *Freedom of the
Will.*[50]

---

* Dunlap's release of the slaves owned by his father is the kind of act
that offers a splendid opportunity to indulge in psychological speculation
(i.e., the son, at last freed from his father, also liberates the other members
of the household). But the relationship between Dunlap's attitude toward
parental authority and his abolitionism, while suggestive, is by no means
clear. Although it is plausible that he was predisposed to endorse emancipation because of his own emotional background, it is also true that his thinking about slavery was greatly influenced by the reading he did in the 1790s
and the opinions of his intellectual friends.[49]

By the middle of the 1790s, under the influence of books and intellectual friends, Dunlap began to develop his own personal philosophy, or at least to commit himself to several identifiable philosophic traditions. First, he became a staunch advocate of deism. For Dunlap, deism meant that God was in heaven and the best way for those of us on earth eventually to join him there was to behave rationally, which Dunlap equated with morality. He criticized ministers and devout churchgoers, whom he began to call "religionists," because, he claimed, they "believe or pretend to believe the necessary connection between religion and morality: with what impudence inculcate that without Religion a man cannot be virtuous."[51] He saw himself as a secular defender of virtue.

Second, he embraced a diluted and highly idiosyncratic version of utilitarianism, probably derived from his reading of William Godwin. He used the word "religionist" to describe not only ministers but also all zealots, be they impassioned abolitionists or self-righteous Federalists, Jeffersonians, or opponents of the theater. What rankled most about such crusaders was their moral arrogance, which he attributed to their mistaken belief that particular men, political parties, and institutions were inherently or intrinsically evil. Although Dunlap agreed that there were absolute values very much worth defending, he insisted that the creatures and creations of this world were invariably mixtures of good and bad. Rather than argue that the theater was of its very nature moral or immoral, he recommended that observers examine the positive and negative consequences of theatergoing. That way sensible and rational men could balance the good against the bad effects and eventually legislate reforms that eliminated undesirable practices. In short, Dunlap adopted a moderate and pragmatic point of view perfectly compatible with his own personality, while affirming his belief in ultimate, eternal principles that—like his God—existed somewhere "out there" beyond any one person's field of vision.[52]

Third, and finally, he developed a fresh appreciation for the potential of the arts in America. He initiated a correspondence with Thomas Holcroft, a prominent British playwright, in which Holcroft advised him to leave the country. "I consider America as unfavourable to genius," wrote Holcroft, "not from any qualities of air, earth, or water: but because the efforts of mind are neither so great, so numerous, so urgent, as in England or France."[53] Dunlap ignored the advice, because he had reached precisely the opposite conclusion on his own. Although he conceded that American artists and playwrights lacked the kind of nourishment available in Europe, Dunlap maintained that this was a temporary problem. In the long run, Dunlap claimed, America would become the cultural center of the world because all its people, not just a privileged aristocracy, were potential consumers and creators of culture.

Both Peale and Brackenridge had said much the same thing in the 1770s, when the fervor of the Revolution had inspired optimistic estimates. Dunlap's perspective was slightly different, for the obvious reason that he discovered the cultural implications of republicanism late, after the revolutionary fires had burned down and the problems as well as the promise of a popular audience for art, literature, and theater had become more visible. As a result, he emphasized the *potentiality* of the American people, the *latent* appetite for paintings, books, and plays that was still in the process of maturing. Already, he noted, Americans were "less passionate or less under the dominion of passion, than other people." The slow but steady growth of an enlightened populace was the result of the Revolution, which produced "liberty & its immediate consequences, a habit of thinking and its attendant tranquillity. Thinking gives way to reason and before reason the passions fade away." Although this "Desirable State" had not yet been achieved, Dunlap insisted that America was "nearer [it] than any other Nation" and therefore tantalizingly close to unprecedented cultural greatness. His job, at least as he saw it, was to help remove the remaining impediments to popular enlightenment and usher in the new era.[54]

The best way to accomplish that job was to write plays, then hope that people would come to see them. Between 1792 and 1798 that is precisely what Dunlap did. After *The Father* he wrote a comedy entitled *The Miser's Wedding* (1793), followed by a tragedy based on Shakespeare's *Macbeth* entitled *Leicester* (1794). Then came *Fontainville Abbey* (1795), a tragedy in which Dunlap lifted incidents from the gothic novels of Ann Radcliffe, a popular British writer, to create an uneven American mystery play. The following year he wrote an opera based on the myth of William Tell, which he called *The Archers*. In 1796 he completed *The Mysterious Monk,* another gothic mystery, which was later revised and published as *Ribbemont.* Then, in 1798, he finished a play on which he had been working off and on for nine years. Entitled *André,* it proved to be the best drama he ever wrote and the most eloquent statement of Dunlap's deepest intellectual convictions.[55]

The plot of *André* was based on an actual episode of recent American history. Major John André was a British army officer who disguised himself as a civilian in order to bribe General Benedict Arnold of the Continental Army. Although Arnold defected to the British, André was captured, tried, and convicted as a spy, and executed in 1780. Dunlap obtained a copy of André's court-martial proceedings from James Kent so as to guarantee historical accuracy. At the same time he claimed "every Poet's right,/ To choose, embellish, lop, or add, or blend/Fiction with truth, as best may suit his end."[56] In the preface to the play he noted that he had been fascinated with the subject for many years, but had delayed his work "because of the prevailing opinion that recent events are unfit subjects for tragedy."[57] Several previous American playwrights, most notably Hugh Henry Brackenridge and Mercy Otis Warren, had written dramas about the American Revolution. But these earlier plays had all championed the American cause and, in the process, used the stage to exalt patriotism and vilify the British. *André* was the first play about the American Revolution that went beyond patriotic rapture and celebration to investigate the human dilemmas and ideological quandaries raised by the conflict. Although it has its melodramatic moments, *André* was the first play by an American to deal with the Revolution as a morally complex piece of history.

When the play opens, André has already been captured and condemned to death. One of the American sentries shouts "All's well," but a middle-aged officer contradicts him:

> *Alas! All is not well;*
> *Else, why stand I, a man, the friend of man,*
> *At midnight's depth, deck'd in this murderous guise,*
> *The habilment of death, the badge of dire,*
> *Necessitous coercion. All is not well.*[58]

Instead of depicting the war for independence as a glorious and ennobling crusade, Dunlap distinguished between the goals of the Americans in the war, which he saw as noble, and the war itself, which he saw as barbarous and inhuman. "War," cries one character, "hath made men rocks." It has also intensified the pressure under which men must act and think. For Dunlap the American Revolution was an excellent subject for drama, not because it provided material for a nationalistic morality play in which good defeated evil, but because it afforded an opportunity to glimpse human beings under extreme stress, trying, often unsuccessfully, to cope with adversity and behave virtuously.

André is Dunlap's meditation on the meaning of virtue, set against a wartime backdrop that dramatized the issues at stake. The focal point of the drama is André himself, who is described as a generous and fair-minded young officer, in all ways the very paragon of virtue, except that he has made one tragic mistake and now must pay for that single blunder with his life. André's nobility derives from his recognition that the attempt to bribe Benedict Arnold was an act "Against my reason, my declared opinion;/Against my conscience, and a soldier's fame." For one moment, André confesses, he "Forgot my former purity of thought',/And high-ton'd honour's scruples disregarded."[59] He makes no effort to justify or excuse his behavior. Throughout the play, André himself is reconciled to his fate. He goes to his death composed and without rancor, the most admirable British character yet created by an American author.

Captain Bland is a young American cavalry officer who insists that it is unjust and cruel to execute so obviously virtuous a man. Bland had been captured and imprisoned by the British earlier in the war, and André had tended to his needs. Not only does Bland feel that he owes André a favor, but he has also learned that his father is a British prisoner and will be executed in retaliation for André's death. Bland's central contention is that the execution of André would itself be an unvirtuous act:

> *The country that forgets to reverence virtue:*
> *That makes no difference 'twixt the sordid wretch,*
> *Who, for reward, risks treason's penalty,*
> *And him unfortunate, whose duteous service*

Is, by mere accident, so chang'd in form,
As to assume guilt's semblance, I serve not.[60]

The essence of virtue, pleads Bland, is charity. He argues that all men are frail creatures who fall victim to their frailties in weak moments. Dunlap makes it clear that Bland's defense of André is partially motivated by personal gratitude and fear for his own father's life, but he also allows Bland to articulate a persuasive case in André's behalf. In fact, André is precisely the kind of appealing character, and Bland's pleas for André are precisely the kind of heartrending soliloquies, that most British and American dramatists employed to win the sympathies of their audiences. In the standard sentimental melodramas of the day, only the most dastardly villain could have sent an André to the gallows.

In Dunlap's play, as in history, the man who orders André's death is George Washington. "I know the virtues of this man," Washington tells Bland, "and love them./But the destiny of millions, millions/Yet unborn, depends upon the rigour/of this moment. . . ."[61] Washington's decision is obviously not a villainous act. Indeed, Dunlap structured *André* so as to contrast two different versions of virtue, two different national ideals, one on the wane and the other on the rise, neither palpably ridiculous.

Washington insists that André's attractive personal qualities and Bland's emotional ties to André must be subordinated to larger, more impersonal considerations. The essence of virtue for Washington is the ability to replace personal and individual preferences with rational judgments of the communal welfare, in this case not only the welfare of the present generation but also of generations to come. Dunlap uses another character, a senior American officer named M'Donald, to express the strongest case against Bland's scheme of values. M'Donald argues that Bland is the victim of "Misleading reason," which places stumbling blocks in the way of "true virtue." Bland's affection for André, claims M'Donald, is rooted in the passions and in personal sentiment. "These things prove gossamer, and balance air," he warns. Bland's version of virtue is man-created" and generates "Perversions monstrous of man's moral sense." His pleas for André's life are "dictates of the heart and not the head."[62]

Although Dunlap clearly endorsed M'Donald's criticism of

Bland, the ultimate embodiment of virtue is Washington. For M'Donald has been hardened by the war and therefore lacks the compassion for André's predicament that would allow him to comprehend the tragedy of the situation. Washington reminds M'Donald to "ever keep in mind that man is frail;/His tide of passion struggling still with Reason's/Fair and favourable gale." André must die, Washington observes to M'Donald, but "it is not Virtue's voice that triumph's/In his ruin."[63] M'Donald recognizes that Washington possesses the capacity for virtue in its highest form, because he combines a staunch commitment to rational judgment with the ability to feel. Washington is

> *By nature, or by early habit, grac'd*
> *With that blest faculty which gives due force*
> *To every faculty, and keeps the mind*
> *In healthful equipoise, ready for action.*[64]

In the context of American cultural and political history, *André* was a backward-looking play, an appropriate drama to close out the eighteenth century. Dunlap exalted the classical rather than the romantic conception of virtue, traditional over liberal values. He chose sense over sentiment, self-control over self-expression, communal responsibility over individual freedom. During the first half of the nineteenth century the American stage would be dominated by melodramas in which heroes like Bland poured out their emotions and victims like André were rescued from fate in the last scene of the last act. Dunlap's Washington was part of an older dramatic world that reflected the traditional values of republican America, a world in which political leaders were expected to be for but not of the people and deference had not been overwhelmed by the belief in social equality. As such, Dunlap's Washington was also the ultimate patriarch, the supreme founding father whose decisions were always guided by rational principles and a disciplined concern for his children. In terms of Dunlap's own psychological development, this was an important statement: the thirty-two-year-old playwright had reaffirmed his belief in the need for paternal authority. Even when they sent young men to their death, virtuous fathers knew best.[65]

•

By the middle of the 1790s Dunlap's life had fallen into a comfortable rhythm. The family import business was flourishing and earning Dunlap enough money to allow him to maintain two homes. Most of the year he and Nabby remained in New York, where he could work on his current play, see it performed at the John Street Theater, meet regularly with his cronies from the Friendly Club, and take personal responsibility for the education of his two children. In the summers he and the family retired to Perth Amboy. There he usually worked in his garden from sunrise to breakfast, took his boy hunting or fishing, read history or philosophy in the afternoon, then wrote in the evening. Charles Brockden Brown or Elihu Hubbard Smith might drop by at Perth Amboy for a few days and stay a week. Work and play, family and friends—all blended together imperceptibly for Dunlap, who was without doubt the most distinguished and prolific dramatist in America.

In the spring of 1796, however, Dunlap made a decision that drastically altered the pattern and direction of his career and that he eventually regarded as the biggest mistake of his life. The two owners of the American Company, Lewis Hallam and John Hodgkinson, invited him to become a partner. In return for his initial investment, Dunlap would own one fourth of the oldest acting company in America. Even more alluring was "the tempting bait of having the sole control of the pieces to be brought before the company." As the new manager of the company he would have total responsibility for selecting and casting all plays; he would also serve as chief producer and director as well as manage the finances of the company. "If the effects of the stage are as great as its friends and enemies have concurred in representing it," Dunlap noted in his diary, "surely I should have the power to do much good." In his *History of the American Theatre* he admitted that private considerations affected his decision: Hodgkinson had assured him that the company had turned a handsome profit the previous season; the construction of an even larger theater on Park Street promised larger audiences and greater profits; and he was enamoured of the prospect of directing his own plays. But Dunlap insisted that he accepted the offer for public-spirited reasons. "The enthusiastic dramatist seriously persuaded himself," he recalled, "that it was his duty to take the direction of so powerful an engine as the stage. . . . The power to direct it he ought to have doubted."[66]

He probably began to have doubts soon after he signed the agreement with Hallam and Hodgkinson. Hallam had been the principal actor in the company prior to Hodgkinson's arrival and therefore usually played the leading parts. But Hodgkinson, an extremely popular and versatile actor who had learned the trade in the provincial theaters of England, now demanded top billing. Dunlap found himself trapped between two contentious and inflated egos. "His ambition for applause was inordinate," Dunlap wrote of Hodgkinson, "and he was as rapacious for characters as Bonaparte has since been for kingdoms." Although Dunlap was officially responsible for all casting decisions, it had become customary for actors to regard their roles as private property, their "line of business"; once a man played Othello or Iago, the part was his and could not be taken away without his consent. "Hallam gave up most that Hodgkinson wanted," noted Dunlap, "but he wished all." Hallam pouted, Hodgkinson increased his demands, and each man refused to speak to the other except through Dunlap. To make matters worse, Hallam's wife was an aging actress who frequently appeared onstage drunk. Eventually, Hodgkinson demanded her removal from the company and refused to appear onstage with her. One evening Hallam packed the audience with his allies, who booed and shouted at Hodgkinson when he made his entrance, accusing him of uncivil behavior toward a lady. Whereupon Mrs. Hallam emerged from behind the curtain to thank the audience for its support. Hodgkinson threatened to sue Hallam after the incident; Hallam responded to the threat by locking himself in the city jail and refusing to leave even after Hodgkinson dropped all charges against him.[67]

In his *History of the American Theater* Dunlap devoted considerable space to a description of the feuds and foibles he encountered behind the scenes of the American Company. The Hallam-Hodgkinson dispute, he concluded, was a classic example of the evil consequences of "the starring system." "What is called '*starring*' is one cause of the degredation of the drama," he wrote. The belief that an acting company needed a star player or "a succession of *stars* [to] keep up attraction and fill the treasury" inevitably generated conflicts within the company.[68] Dunlap described it as yet another illustration of the evil produced by institutionalized inequality. In the republican theater of the future, he prophesied, "there will be no starring." But at the time it was not just the clash between two jealous stars that troubled Dunlap; it was the apparently endless bickering, irresponsibility, and eccentric behavior of all the people he was supposed to manage.

There was, for example, Sir Richard Crosby, a onetime Irish gentleman who had taken up acting after a series of personal misfortunes that included the loss of his reputation in an ill-fated scheme to cross the North Sea in a balloon. Crosby reminded Dunlap of "a greyhound that has the dropsey" because of his frequent bouts of depression, many of which ended in drunken stupors that forced Dunlap to have an understudy ready at all times.[69] The members of the orchestra were equally undependable. The bassoon player killed the sheriff, who had tried to arrest him for unpaid debts. The horn player murdered his own mistress and then committed suicide. Almost the entire orchestra was composed of Frenchmen who had fled the guillotine in Paris or the slave insurrection in Santo Domingo; they considered themselves the victims of democracy and periodically refused to play songs that glorified popular uprisings.[70] One evening in November of 1796, "Two sea captains, doubtless intoxicated, being in one of the stage boxes, called during an overture for Yankee Doodle." Members of the orchestra got into a shouting match with the audience, who rushed onto the stage. A constable was seriously injured trying to suppress the disturbance, and the sea captains threatened to organize their sailors into a wrecking crew that would demolish the building.[71]

Although Dunlap consistently defended the theater against charges of immorality, his experiences during the first year as manager of the American Company helped him to appreciate the reasons for public apprehension about the stage. Indeed, he shared some of these apprehensions himself. Very few of the actors or actresses in the company lived lives of sober, republican simplicity. Dunlap winced when he had to walk the streets with Hodgkinson, who wore powdered curls, breeches, and stockings instead of pantaloons, and outrageous suits. "Go to Hodgkinson's," he jotted in diary, adding in a parenthesis, "If any stranger was to read this might he not say are you thus constant attendant on Hodgkinson & does he never come to you? the truth is, I wish to keep my house free from visits which partake of the theatre...."[72] Dunlap was incapable of priggishness or haughtiness; nevertheless, he took pains to maintain a discreet distance between his private life and his managerial duties and seldom formed close friendships with actors or actresses. That way he protected his moral standards from potential corruption at the same time as he stood ready to arbitrate the endless quarrels with paternal equanimity.

By 1797 money problems had replaced the human drama behind the curtain as his chief concern. Hodgkinson's assurance that the company had been earning sizable profits prior to Dunlap's arrival was, quite simply, a lie. (Hodgkinson was the kind of man who frequently told barefaced lies when it suited his interests, then convinced himself that the lies were true and treated accusations of unreliability as libelous assaults on his character.) In fact, it is highly possible that Hallam and Hodgkinson invited Dunlap to become a partner, not because of his reputation as a dramatist or because they recognized the need for an arbitrator of company squabbles, but because they wanted his money.

During the first season Dunlap discovered that the size of the audiences was not sufficient to meet expenses. He began to count the house each evening and make pessimistic comments in his diary: "In the house Ds [dollars] 324 by which we lose upwards of Ds 90"; a week later he noted, "We lose upwards of a hundred Dols: tonight." Dunlap found it necessary to borrow money, using his own property as collateral, in order to pay the actors' salaries. "Not well," he admitted, "and my mind much disturbed by the difficulty of borrowing money, more by the necessity." Hodgkinson claimed to have the answer to their financial problems: he would take the company to Hartford and Boston during the summer; the recent completion of the Haymarket Theater in Boston, intended to serve as a rival to the Federal Street Theater—which allegedly favored Federalist patrons and plays— offered the promise of large summer audiences. But Hodgkinson ran up expenses of over 1,100 dollars a week and took in less than half that amount at the box office. "Mr. Hodgkinson's partner [Dunlap] sent on money and advice," Dunlap remembered; "the one was taken, the other rejected." The longer Hodgkinson stayed in Boston, "saving" the company, the more Dunlap went into debt. "All parties appear to have been playing at cross-purposes," Dunlap observed, "and every step was leading to ultimate bankruptcy."[73]

Dunlap placed his hopes for financial salvation in the Park Theater. This new building, intended to replace the John Street Theater as the home of the American Company, was finally ready for occupancy in January of 1798. It could accommodate 2,000 customers; each night that it was filled, the company would take in 1,600 dollars.[74] According to Dunlap's calculations, the weekly expenses of the company, which included salaries for the players and orchestra, plus scenery, lighting, costumes, and rent, averaged approximately 1,200 dollars per week.[75] If the company put on three regular shows each week, as planned, the potential income was 4,800 dollars. It therefore followed that during the course of a 100-play season, which was what the contract for the building called for, the company would earn profits of almost 40,000 dollars even if the theater was filled to only half its capacity each evening. A share of those profits were owed to the proprietors of the building, but, theoretically at least, the economic prospects looked extremely encouraging.

Three unforseen factors played havoc with Dunlap's optimistic projections. First, the proprietors demanded free tickets for each performance. Each night Dunlap was required to reserve 113 choice boxes for the owners of the building free of charge. "This," he remembered, "was another step in the downhill road."[76] Second, the outbreak of yellow-fever epidemics in New York during the summer consistently delayed the opening of each theatrical season from 1798 to 1805. And this in turn meant that the total number of performances in a season was reduced, even though salaries and rent remained constant and winter weather struck just as the season started.[77] Third, and most important, attendance was disappointing. With a shortened season, it was imperative that the theater be half-filled for each performance. Each night that receipts fell below 800 dollars, the company lost money. During the first week the Park Theater was opened, however, receipts averaged 333 dollars for each performance of Shakespeare's *As You Like It*. When the company performed *André* in the spring of 1798, Dunlap took in 817 dollars the first night but only 387 and 329 dollars for subsequent performances. And the size of the audiences for *André* was typical. From February to March of 1799, receipts averaged about 600 dollars for each performance. Every evening, in effect, only one quarter of the seats in the theater were occupied. Those empty seats were Dunlap's major problem. In a city of approximately 60,000 residents, he had to find a way at attract 1,000 paying customers into the theater three times a week.[78]

Each device that Dunlap employed to increase attendance forced him to compromise his aesthetic standards and debase his idealistic hopes for the theater in America. One tactic involved the introduction of novelty acts during intermissions. Dunlap hired jugglers, acrobats, daredevils, and other circus performers and made them a featured part of the evening's entertainment. "To support the treasury," Dunlap explained, "the stage was degraded by the exhibitions of a man who could whirl around on his head with crackers and other fireworkers attached to his heels." (This man, who advertised himself as "the Antipodean Whirligig," was the same acrobat who performed at Peale's museum.) Newspaper advertisements for *Romeo and Juliet* announced that one Signor Manfredi would do his death-defying tightrope act as a prelude to the tragedy. Audiences were encouraged to come to the Park Theater in April of 1800 to watch "Signior Joseph Doctor, from Sadler's Wells" do his "Tumbling, Postures and Equilibriums" as he passed "through a Hoop with a Pyramid of Thirteen Glasses of Wine on his Forehead, to Conclude with the Italian Serpentine, on a Ladder 20 Feet High." Dunlap rationalized that spectators who came to view the circus stunts might inadvertently develop an appreciation for the plays and become regular patrons of the theater.[79]

Dunlap also increased the number of stridently patriotic plays, even though he considered them insults to the intelligence of the public. In 1798 he staged *The Federal Oath,* a play that glorified the American Revolution by contrasting it with events in revolutionary France. Dunlap described the drama, a mixture of pageantry and national propaganda, as "patch'd work [intended] to inculcate some grand and novel political truths, Such as, that, we ought to damn all Frenchmen, and that 'two yankee

boys can beat four mounseers'." In July of 1802 the American
Company put on *Bunker's Hill,* a glorification of American bravery that Dunlap called "vile trash"; he admitted, however, that
patriotism had box-office appeal and that "the receipts were the
greatest ever known at that time, 1245 dollars." The popularity
of patriotic extravaganzas even caused him to revise *André.* In
the revised version, entitled *The Glory of Columbia—her Yeomanry,* Dunlap replaced the intellectual drama of *André* with
battle scenes in which poorly equipped Americans beat off a
much larger group of British regulars. The play concluded with a
lavishly staged depiction of the battle of Yorktown, which had
nothing to do with André's death, followed by the crowning of
Washington with laurel. Advertisements for *The Glory of Columbia* reported that between acts a tightrope walker would traverse
a wire stretched from the gallery to the stage, "a feat never attempted by any but himself." Dunlap remarked caustically that
The Glory of Columbia was "amusements for holiday fools," but
he also noted that it earned 1287 dollars the first night, surpassing
Bunker's Hill as a moneymaker.[80]

Finally, he discovered the current rage of European and
English theater, a German playwright named Augustus F. F. von
Kotzebue, and presented his own translations and adaptations
of Kotzebue's highly popular pieces of sentimental melodrama
to American audiences. Kotzebue was the closest thing to guaranteed box-office success that Dunlap could find. London audiences had already turned out in droves to see the newest play of
"the German Shakespeare"; Americans could be expected to follow suit.

Kotzebue had perfected the formula for the melodrama. Although he wrote about a wide variety of subjects, ranging from
family discord in Prussia to pregnant vestal virgins in Peru,
Kotzebue invariably exalted the omnipotence of true love and the
supremacy of the passions. In the same way that religious revivals
generated enormous popular followings by making emotional conviction the core of the conversion experience and dispensing with
rational appeals to books and clerical wisdom, Kotzebue's plays
glorified the nobility of the ordinary heart, unfettered by learning or self-discipline. Federalist critics like Joseph Dennie warned
that Kotzebue wanted only to "villify greatness, to calumniate

clergymen and lawyers, to taint the imagination of youth, to 'loosen the rudder hands of society'. . . ." Dunlap thought that Kotzebue was vastly overrated as a dramatist and that pure-hearted heroes and heroines were not true to life, at least as he knew it. But there was no arguing with Kotzebue's popularity.[81]

From the 1798–99 season onward, Dunlap loaded the company's repertoire with Kotzebue; his *The Stranger* was performed twelve times that year. Although he regretted that *The Stranger* kept "*Hamlet* and *Macbeth* and all the glories of the drama" from the stage, he also realized that "the success of this piece alone enabled the author to open the theater." In fact, Kotzebue's plays made it possible for Dunlap to offer a Shakespearean classic now and then. In March of 1798, for instance, he recruited Thomas Cooper, the best young actor in America, to play Hamlet. Dunlap claimed it was "the best acting I ever saw," but the receipts were a pitiful 288 dollars. On the other hand, the critic for the *Commercial Advertiser* reported that *The Stranger* played to "a crouded audience at our Theatre, and [was] received with a most hearty welcome." The next season Kotzebue's *False Shame* replaced *The Stranger* as "the pillar on which all rested." In all, the American Company put on twenty Kotzebue plays during Dunlap's managerial career. In several seasons Dunlap devoted between 30 and 40 percent of the company's repertoire to Kotzebue, who was described as "Shakespeare without his quibbles. . . ."[82]

Even Kotzebue could carry the struggling company only so far. By 1803 the Kotzebue vogue began to wane and Dunlap's creditors began to close in. "It is much to be regretted," reported the *Morning Chronicle*, "that so little encouragement is given to our theatre by the fashionable world. Night after night exhibits nothing but a beggarly account of empty boxes." The reporter noted ominously that "the manager has been sinking money by every performance, for this some time past." Hodgkinson left the company in January of 1803, sensing disaster and eager to disassociate himself from a losing enterprise. Hallam had already surrendered his share of the company to Dunlap, now sole owner, which meant that he alone was responsible for the mounting debts. He survived a bout with the yellow fever, but his poor health combined with the financial pressures to produce constant depression. "Oppressed with disease and debt," he confided to his diary on January 1, 1805, "I commence another year of life with sentiments of gloom and self-approbation." Such sentiments were not misguided: the next month his creditors forced him to declare bankruptcy. He lost all his property in New York and Perth Amboy, the theater closed its doors, and his theatrical career came to an unhappy end.[83]

•

Twenty-seven years later, when Dunlap published his *History of the American Theatre*, most of his recommendations for the future were based on his personal experiences in the past. He called for the elimination of the star system and the cultivation of acting companies composed of virtuous rather than self-centered players. He bemoaned the tendency to construct large and lavish theaters, because this tendency focused attention on the theater itself rather than on the quality of the plays; moreover, the construction of large theaters invariably generated "a desire to fill them." And the need to fill the seats led to the creation of a circus atmosphere in which good plays were replaced by "shameful exhibitions of monsters, and beasts, and other vulgar shows."[84] Finally, he warned that economic pressure crushed the aesthetic judgment of the manager and transformed him from a moral guide into a businessman who followed rather than directed public opinion.

The manager . . . has but one object in view, and is as careless of the tendency of plays he adapts for his stage as the player. Money is his object. Both [manager and player] say "we must please the public." But their public becomes that public which is filled with glitter, parade, false sentiment, and all that lulls conscience or excites to evil. . . . Now all this would be, *must be, changed.* . . .

In the future, he urged, the direction of the American theater "should be wrested from the hands of any person whose sole aim is profit (either by making money or increasing his professional celebrity), and guided by the enlightened portion of society."[85] This, of course, was exactly the opposite of what eventually happened. Dunlap was warning against the commercialization of art and the creation of mass culture at precisely the moment they were becoming dominant.

At times Dunlap implied that the core of the problem was personal rather than social, that the source of the corruption was the greed or stupidity of individual managers or actors, as if American dramatic history were a melodrama with an overabundance of villains. By the time he wrote his *History of the American Theatre*, the melodrama had established itself as the dominant force in American drama. Although Dunlap lamented this development, and frequently blamed himself for encouraging the trend when he should have opposed it, his tendency to personalize the problem was itself a melodramatic device that distorted history by making success or failure solely a function of character; he was in part a prisoner of the very values he lamented.

In point of fact, Dunlap had done all that was humanly possible to make the theater a respected and influential institution in the new nation. His motives were noble: he was not greedy, only anxious about making the American Company solvent; he was not ignorant when it came to questions of dramatic quality, only mindful that Kotzebue and circus acts and patriotic drivel were absolutely essential to keep the theater opened; he was not driven by selfish or self-centered desires, only eager to play his role in the improvement of public morals and taste. Indeed, by the standards of postrevolutionary America, Dunlap had conducted himself as the epitome of the virtuous man, sacrificing his health and wealth in the interest of the community. His poverty was a clear sign of his disinterestedness.

Like Peale and Brackenridge, Dunlap attempted to serve two masters—the arts and the people—and presumed a high degree of compatibility between their mutual dictates. That presumption, a key article of the republican credo, was the source of his difficulty. To the end of his life he retained the conviction that all practitioners of the arts in America had social responsibilities and that the value of literature, painting, and drama derived from their uplifting influence on public attitudes. The theater, he continued to believe, had the greatest potential usefulness:

What engine is more powerful than the theatre? No arts can be made more effectual for the promotion of good than the dramatic and the histrionic. They unite music, poetry, painting, and eloquence. The engine is powerful for good or ill—it is for society to choose.[86]

But what was "society" if not the people, the same people who either preferred Kotzebue to Shakespeare or simply stayed away from the theater altogether? How could the theater nudge popular opinion in the right direction when the people exercised such massive influence over the choice of plays and over the very capacity of a theatrical company to survive?

These were not the kind of questions susceptible of answers that fixed the responsibility on "good" or "bad" managers. Moreover, the moralistic categories Dunlap employed after 1805 frequently masked a significant social distinction that had crept into his diagnosis of the arts in America and that was loaded with ideological implications. On the one hand, he claimed, there were "the wise and the good," whose attendance at plays guaranteed that "the lessons learned must be those of patriotism, virtue, morality, religion . . ."; on the other hand, there were "the uneducated, the idle, and the profligate," whose attendance encouraged the "bad" or "mercenary managers" to put on "such ribaldry or folly, or worse, as is attractive to such patrons, and productive of profit to themselves."[87] Dunlap's distinction between the enlightened and ignorant segments of the American population was a social as well as a moral and intellectual distinction. He was, in effect, abandoning the poor, the uneducated, the kind of people who sat in the gallery, because he had come to regard them as a corrupting influence. Throughout his *History of the American Theatre* Dunlap continued to insist that the stage was a moral training ground for the American people, at the same time that he warned that the stage must be rescued from the degenerate and unsophisticated, who presumably needed moral training the most, lest it become "a breeding ground for ignorance and depravity." A critical change in his thinking had taken place: he no longer regarded "the people" as an undifferentiated mass. The stage needed to be protected from one segment of "the people" in order to serve the remainder. In practice this meant that the stage should serve an upper- and middle-class constituency predisposed to appreciate dramatic presentations. If the theater was to replace the church as a shaping influence on public mores and attitudes, it should not attempt to convert the worst sinners. They were, at least temporarily, beyond salvation.

Dunlap also believed that the American theater had to be rescued from the marketplace as well as the masses. It had to be "supported by a power ... which will not look for profit from it, but rather, if any deficiency of money from the receipts occurs, is ready to make good. ..." In Dunlap's view, the only way to protect the stage from the cupidity and capriciousness of the market place was to "make the theatre an object of government patronage." If the city, state, or national government provided adequate subsidies, "then such a theatre will be truly a school of morality, of patriotism, and every virtue; the glory of the fine arts, and the delight of the wise and the good." He concluded his *History of the American Theatre* with a copy of the regulations governing the nationally endowed French theater.[88]

Dunlap had a knack for many different things, but consistency was not one of them. Two years after he had completed his account of the theater in America with an eloquent plea for government support, he published *A History of the Rise and Progress of the Arts of Design in the United States,* in which he opposed governmental interference of any sort with the fine arts. "There are individuals in America," he wrote,

who, without due reflection, or from residing too long in England, or, perhaps, being foreigners, and not understanding the nature of our institutions and the manner of thinking which these institutions induce, sometimes talk of patronage and protection. . . . The laws here are the only patrons. Industry, virtue, and talents, the only protectors. . . . [T]he artist—the man who possesses the genius, skill, and knowledge which entitles him to that name—will look to be honored and esteemed by his fellow citizens.[89]

Somehow, dramatists and actors needed protection from the demands of the people and the capriciousness of the marketplace, while artists could be expected to overcome these obstacles on the basis of their individual talents. The discrepancy between Dunlap's two recommendations did not reflect a belief that dramatists and artists confronted essentially different conditions in America; in fact, Dunlap frequently argued that all the arts were joined together in common cause in the new nation and would flourish or degenerate as one. He was simply of two minds. His recommendations for the theater drew upon his own bitter experience with the American Company; his recommendations for artists drew upon his undying optimism that the great mass of

Americans were potential members of "the wise and the good" and were capable of enlightened judgments about artistic quality. He never resolved his dual commitment to aesthetic standards, which he always described as absolute principles independent of public opinion, and to popular sovereignty, which he considered the keystone of republicanism.

This ambivalence never seemed to trouble him or to shake the bedrock optimism that he retained even during the difficult years after 1805. Like Peale, Dunlap continued to believe that history was on his side, that the disparity between the arts and the people, between aesthetic standards and public opinion, was a temporary phenomenon destined to disappear at some unspecified time in the future. Apparent discrepancies between the demands of audiences and the artistic convictions of serious dramatists were temporary abberations. He likened money-minded playwrights and clamorous supporters of melodramatic nonsense to recently emancipated slaves. Of course they behaved irresponsibly and were licentious; it was to be expected; it was only a phase. But his favorite analogy was drawn from his own life: most American theatergoers as well as many actors and dramatists were like children unaccustomed to freedom; they were as he had been as a young man; naturally they abused their liberty, because they lacked the maturity to recognize their long-range self-interest; just as naturally, he expected them to outgrow their immaturity. When they did, Americans would discover that their cultural and political ideals were identical; then harmony between the arts and the people would reign supreme.

In the meantime, Dunlap decided to live out his life in that space between aesthetic standards and popular opinion, trying to serve as an emissary between the various arts and the public. He published a biography of George Frederick Cooke, a prominent English actor and infamous alcoholic; Dunlap used Cooke as an example of how talent is wasted if it is not disciplined—the traditional republican message of self-control. He also wrote a biography of his old friend Charles Brockden Brown; this book, plus his histories of the theater and the arts in America, was designed to encourage public appreciation of America's cultural pioneers. He returned to painting, turned out miniatures that sold quite well, and then historical portraits, *Christ Rejected* and *Calvary,* which were sent on tours through towns and villages in the West. Friends did their best to provide him with salaried jobs and handouts disguised as assignments. He was appointed assistant postmaster general of the militia in New York. And members of the American Academy of Fine Arts named him librarian. But he remained impoverished, a cheery pauper who was frequently obliged to do hackwork in order to survive. When he finished several new plays which had been written for a fee, he described them as "poor commodities" done for "meager compensation." He was seldom bitter about his situation, however, and spent considerable time buoying up the spirits of struggling writers and artists. When he died in September of 1839, he had just completed a multivolume history of the State of New York. A lengthy obituary in the *Commercial Advertiser* commented upon his range of friends, his many-sided life, the vigorous quality of his conversation, and his animated expressions of hope for the future, even on his deathbed.[90]

Chapter Six

Noah Webster:
The Connecticut Yankee
as Nationalist

≫✦≪

*A constant increase of wealth is ever followed by a multi-
plication of vices. This seems to be the destiny of human
affairs; wisdom, therefore, directs us to retard, if possible,
and not to accelerate the progress of corruption.*

Noah Webster, *An American Selection* (1787)

When he was an old man, Noah Webster liked to sit on the front
porch of his home in New Haven and bemoan the policies of
Andrew Jackson and the fate of the nation. "Papa is sitting in his
rocking chair with a [news] paper in his hand," his wife reported
to their daughter. "Once in a while a deep groan escapes from
him at the critical state of the country.... Yesterday three hundred new freemen were qualified to vote."[1] Webster himself declared that "the true principles of republican government are
now abandoned by all parties ... and instead of expecting things
to grow *better*, I am confident they will grow *worse*." Members of
the Yale faculty and old Federalist friends would drop by for tea
and listen to the crusty New England patriarch deliver jeremiads
from the rocking chair. He denounced the extension of the
franchise, the belief that "the people can govern themselves,"

and the notion that "the rich capitalists are drones in society, living on the industry of the working bees. How can men utter such sentiments?"[2] In 1837, at the age of seventy-nine, he regretted his participation at the battle of Saratoga; he recalled that he had "shouldered the best musket he could find, marched up the Hudson in sight of the flames and smoking ruins . . . to lend his feeble aid in checking the enemy." If he had then been able to foresee "the popular outrages upon life, liberty and prosperity" that followed the winning of American independence, he claimed, he "would not have moved a step to oppose the enemy." He chose not to remember that he had arrived at Saratoga late, after the battle was over and General Burgoyne had surrendered, and had marched home without ever firing a shot.[3]

Although at times Webster could sound like a latter-day Cotton Mather, mourning the decline of standards and the ravages of progress, his disappointment had its roots in expectations generated during and immediately after the American Revolution. As a young man, Webster had burst on the scene with an elaborate and ambitious plan for the development of both American nationalism and his own reputation; from that point forward Webster's personal needs and ambitions and his nationalistic schemes were yoked together and evolved as a unit. His "Blue-Backed Speller," published in 1783, soon was selling over 200,000 copies a year and eventually became the most popular book ever written by an American.* During the 1780s and '90s Webster became the leading advocate of a new American way of spelling, writing, speaking, even thinking. On the basis of his travels through postrevolutionary America, combined with his reading of Rousseau, Richard Price, and Joseph Priestley, Webster fashioned a radical vision of national development that

* Sales figures for the speller lack the precision we have come to expect with our modern, computerized accounting methods. The best estimate is that the speller has sold approximately 100 million copies. In 1804 Webster reported annual sales of 241,000 copies. In 1880 the publisher of the speller, William H. Appleton, said that "Webster's speller . . . has the largest sale of any book in the world except the Bible. We sell a million copies a year. Yes, and we have been selling it at that rate for forty years. . . ." In the 1840s a special steam press was constructed expressly for printing Webster's speller at the rate of 525 copies an hour. Facsimile editions of the speller continue to sell a few thousand copies a year.[4]

called for the deliberate creation of indigenous American customs and habits. For twenty years he was the most prolific author in America, tossing off textbooks, political essays, and newspaper articles at such an unprecedented pace that a modern bibliography of his published works required 655 pages.[5] Along the way he moved through various careers as school teacher, lawyer, journalist, and scientist; became a personal acquaintance of almost every prominent leader of his generation; lobbied successfully for copyright laws to protect American authors; became one of the earliest and most zealous advocates of a strong federal government; insisted on the empirical study of diseases and the urban conditions in which diseases flourished; and began work on *An American Dictionary of the English Language* (1828).

The dictionary, of course, is his most enduring legacy and the achievement that allows his name to remain familiar in the twentieth century. We all continue to "look it up in Webster," even though we are not sure whether the author's first name is Noah or Daniel. But the renowned "man who made the dictionary" compiled his monumental piece of scholarship after he had retired from public life, repudiated his youthful ideals, and settled into his patriarchal pose. By then he had made himself into what one historian has called "a classic symbol of the lost cause of American Federalism" and a very different man from the young radical of the 1780s. The old sage frequently wrote marginal comments in his own books, denouncing his earlier views as a "Great Mistake," or "taken from Rousseau's *Social Contract* and therefore chimerical," or "the reverse of the truth." It seems fitting that the only word Webster claimed that he himself had coined was the verb "to demoralize."[6]

Even before his "demoralization," Webster was an irascible and stubborn character, difficult to know and even more difficult to like. In 1786 Timothy Pickering, one of his warmest supporters, admitted that when Webster addressed an audience "there was so much of egotism, especially in a young man . . . as to prevent his hearers [from] receiving the satisfaction which might otherwise have been derived from [his] many ingenious observations."[7] He had the capacity to advocate egalitarian reforms—such as the elimination of state support for all religions, the establishment of tuition-free schools for all children, and the redistribution of private property—in a style that smacked of aristocratic arrogance. Benjamin Franklin Bache called him a "self-exalted pedagogue" and "an incurable lunatic." William Cobbett, who disagreed with Bache on virtually all political questions of the day, concurred when it came to Webster; Cobbett called him "a spiteful viper" and a "prostitute wretch." Jeremy Belknap, mimicking Webster's unorthodox suggestions for spelling, referred to him as "No-ur Webster eskwier junier, critick and coxcomb general of the United States." Jefferson described him as "a mere pedagogue of very limited understanding."[8]

The opinions of his contemporaries, along with Webster's austere image as the ultimate arbiter of a word's meaning in America and his reputation as the last die-hard Federalist, all come together in the stereotype of the insufferable Yankee schoolmaster. Although this stereotype can be misleading and can impede an appreciation of the depth and range of Webster's historical significance, it is too well established to be ignored and too well founded to be explained away. In the most comprehensive biography of Webster, written in 1936, Harry Warfel attempted to turn the stereotype to Webster's advantage. He described Webster as "the typical schoolmaster, the man who is more concerned to have lessons well learned than to secure the adulation of shirking, fawning ignorance." Warfel's motives were admirable: he wished to rescue Webster from pundits and earlier biographers who accorded him only grudging admiration. But in fact Webster was far from a "typical schoolmaster," his critics were not always ignorant, and Webster himself cared deeply about his public reputation. Much like John Adams, Webster cannot be made to fit conventional American heroic molds without a distortion of his real character. He is not the stuff of American mythology.[9]

He is, however, an arresting example of the way the American Revolution, which began as a colonial war for independence, generated shock waves that destroyed much more than the political connection with England. Webster was one of the first Americans to understand that the Revolution initiated a long-range process of social change. "A fundamental mistake of the Americans," he wrote in 1787, "has been that they considered the revolution as completed when it was just begun...."[10] This insight

excited Webster at first—by 1800 it terrified him—because he saw
himself as a founding father with an unprecedented opportunity
to shape popular attitudes. To this awesome task he brought the
intellect of a *philosophe,* the cupidity of a capitalist, the bearing of
a natural aristocrat committed to public service, and the compul-
siveness of a young man on the make. In this sense Webster embodied the conflicting characteristics of the emerging nation he
strove to shape. And the trajectory of his life—from excited advocate of revolutionary change to heroic defender of old and
dying values—makes him the most dramatic illustration of the
disenchanted eighteenth-century republican, a man whose belief
in the benign potential of individual freedom dissipated as he
encountered its liberal consequences.

•

Webster always insisted that childhood was crucial. "The impressions received in early life usually form the character of individuals," he once observed, adding that the "period from twelve to
twenty is the most important" and that impressions made then
"*always* remain for many years, and generally thru life."[11] Unfortunately, we know very little about the first twenty years of
Webster's life. And most of that is the result of second- or third-
hand reminiscences tailored to fit his later accomplishments by
descendants or defenders of his reputation.

He was born in West Hartford, Connecticut, on October 16,
1758. His father, Noah Webster, Senior, was descended from a
family that had emigrated from England to Massachusetts in
the 1630s and joined Thomas Hooker's band of settlers to found
Hartford. His mother, Mercy Steele, was a great-granddaughter
of William Bradford, the founder and longtime governor of
Plymouth Colony. Both sides of his family, then, had roots that
reached back to the origins of New England. But by the middle
of the eighteenth century the Webster family had fallen on hard
times. Although Squire Webster held several offices in the local
church and government, he owned only an unpretentious house
and a few acres of farm land. The farm itself had to be mortgaged
when, at the age of sixteen, Noah requested permission to attend
Yale College. According to family lore, Webster's father often
found his son "stretched on the grass, forgetful of his tasks,"

studying a Latin-grammar book that he had obtained from Nathan Perkins, the local minister. In 1774 paternal wisdom led Squire Webster to indulge his son's "decided love for study and books." The father went into debt so that the son could go to Yale.[12]

It happened that Yale was in the doldrums. Under Thomas Clap's autocratic leadership the college had become a bastion of Congregational orthodoxy in the 1750s. For the next twenty years, while new colleges like Pennsylvania and Princeton liberalized their curricula and experimented with new ideas, Yale remained rock-ribbed and stultifying. "Ignorance wanders unmolested," wrote John Trumbull, a former student and tutor, and most of the students in Webster's class seemed to agree. In 1776 they called for the resignation of Naphtali Daggett, who had been serving as temporary president of the college since Clap's departure in 1766. The next year they petitioned to have their class tutor, Joseph Buckminster, replaced by Timothy Dwight, a charismatic young tutor who encouraged the student demands and advocated the overhaul of Yale's curriculum and leadership. Although Dwight was on the side of progress—he wanted to replace some of the courses in Latin with courses in English grammar and literature—he was also an ambitious young man with his eyes on the college presidency. He became a hero to Webster and to most Yale students, but his subversive tactics added to the confusion that paralyzed the operation of the college throughout Webster's stay. Only with the inauguration of Ezra Stiles as the new president in 1778 did Yale begin to recover. Stiles brought intellectual leadership and the Enlightenment to the college, much as Witherspoon had done at Princeton. But Stiles arrived at Yale just as Webster was leaving, too late to exercise much influence.[13]

Since Webster's college career coincided with the outbreak of the American Revolution, and since Webster went on to become a major spokesman for American cultural independence, it seems reasonable to conclude that he acquired some major ideas and much patriotic zeal during his student days at Yale. But this conclusion does not square with the evidence. True, most Yale students, including Webster, supported the Revolution. When Washington marched through New Haven in 1775 on his way to take command of the Continental Army, Webster played the flute in a student parade. And the following year Timothy Dwight told the assembled student body that their generation would be "concerned with laying the foundation of American greatness." But wartime Yale was in constant disarray. New Haven's coastal location made it vulnerable to British raiding parties, so classes were frequently dispersed to inland towns; food shortages and the currency inflation exacerbated problems of governance; tutors and professors squabbled with each other and with the moribund Yale board of governors (called the Corporation). As a result, although the war undoubtedly aroused excitement among the students, Yale was too disorganized to channel the excitement into productive activities.

In August of 1776, when he escorted his brother Abraham to a militia unit on Lake Champlain and had his first real look at army life, Webster belittled the glorified accounts of the war; his major impression was that over half the soldiers had dysentery and the mosquitoes were so thick that tents had to be filled with smoke at night to permit sleeping. Most significantly, after his graduation from Yale in September of 1778, Webster did not join the Continental Army or the Connecticut militia or attempt to find any job related to the war effort; capital rather than country was his chief obsession. His major concern was to establish himself in a profession that would provide a steady income.[14]

This should not surprise us. Webster was an ambitious but poor young man who graduated from college still owing Yale 120 pounds. When he returned home to West Hartford his father handed him an eight-dollar bill in Continental currency, then worth only a fraction of its face value. "Take this," he reportedly said; "you must now seek your living; I can do no more for you." Joel Barlow, one of Webster's Yale classmates, tried to sound an upbeat note. "You and I are not the first in the world to have broken loose from college without friends and without fortune," wrote Barlow. "Let us show the world a few more examples of men standing upon their own merit and rising in spite of obstacles." It was good advice, if for no other reason than that Webster had no other choice.[15]

But then Webster hardly needed Barlow to remind him to exert himself. In his diary Webster frequently made a one-word entry, "Do"; or, on other days, "Do (one would think me a steady man)." And the obstacles that Barlow had mentioned were, as young Webster saw them, divinely arranged opportunities to prove himself. "The author of the universe seems to have framed it," he confided to his diary, "with a view to give his creatures an opportunity to exert virtues, which would not exist without natural and moral evil." This was a way of interpreting hardships as old as New England. Webster, like so many New Englanders before him, regarded obstacles as tests of his will, fixed objects against which he could do the isometric exercises that would strengthen his character.[16]

Webster's problem was not lack of ambition or adversity, but lack of direction. For four years after his graduation he wandered about Connecticut in search of a respectable calling, teaching school, studying law, groping. He was admitted to the bar at Hartford in April of 1781 and began to append the word "Esquire" to his name as an advertisement of his new professional standing.[17] After only one month, Webster abandoned his legal aspirations and returned to schoolmastering. He moved from Hartford to Sharon, where he proposed "to open a school . . . in which Gentlemen and Ladies may be instructed in Reading, Writing, Mathematics, the English Language, and if desired, the Latin and Greek Languages . . . at the moderate price of Six Dollars and two thirds per quarter per Scholar."[18] Once ensconced in Sharon, he submitted an essay to *The Clio, A Literary Miscellany,* which was edited by a precocious young woman named Juliana Smith, who, it turns out, did not think much of Webster's prose or his personality:

Mr. Webster has not the excuse of youth, (I think he must be fully twenty-two or three), but . . . his reflections are as prosy as those of our horse . . . would be if they were written out. Perhaps more so, for I truly believe, judging from the way *Jack Horse* looks 'round at me sometimes, when I am on his back, that his thoughts of the human race and their conduct towards his own might be well worth reading. At least they would be all *his own,* and that is more than can be said of N.W.'s. In conversation he is even duller than in writing, if that is possible, but he is a painstaking man and a hard student. Papa says he will make his mark; but then you know that our Papa is always inclined to think the best of every one's abilities. . . .[19]

Here was a case in which "Papa" knew best.

When he appeared in New Haven to pick up his M.A. degree in September of 1781, Webster's prospects looked bleak. An aspiring lawyer who had never had a client, an itinerant schoolmaster who wandered from town to town in search of pupils, Webster remained what he had been at his graduation from college: an ambitious, earnest, but impoverished young man, still on the make, a bundle of ambitious energy searching frantically for the main chance. Barlow again tried to console him by sharing his sense of disappointment. "We are all a pack of dogs," he wrote, "and I have worn out my life in buffeting my destiny, and all I have got for it is the knack of keeping up my spirits, letting the world slide, and hoping for better days."[20]

During the autumn of 1781 events began to move Webster's way. First, Cornwallis surrendered to Washington at Yorktown in October. The end of the war meant that a whole range of questions that had been postponed or ignored during the conflict would now have to be faced, questions involving the social, political, and economic policies to be followed by the thirteen states that had banded together to defeat England; this, it turned out, was Webster's subject material. Second, while teaching in Sharon, Webster had encountered John Peter Tetard, a former Genevan minister who was well steeped in the literature of the French Enlightenment. Tetard became the tutor that Webster never had at Yale. Webster learned French and began to study Italian, German, and Spanish. Most importantly, Tetard introduced him to the political philosophy of Montesquieu, Abbé Raynal, Jean Jacques Rousseau and encouraged him to read Tom Paine's revolutionary writings. Rousseau's *Social Contract* and later his *Emile* became Webster's favorites. Just after the war ended, Webster began to develop a radical vision of what it had all been about.[21]

In a four-part essay entitled "Observations on the Revolution of America," originally published in the *New York Packet*, Webster made his first public statement about the new American nation. He denounced the idea then circulating among influential Whigs in New York and Philadelphia that America should sever its ties with France and reestablish political and economic ties with Great Britain. This idea, Webster claimed, was the work of "disappointed courtiers" and would only serve "to disunite the Americans and overturn our independence." He applauded Abbé Raynal's *The History of the Revolution in America* for its "very pathetic representation of the miserable state of Europeans; and its philanthropic sense of the felicity of America in its disconnected situation." He insisted that an independent America, founded on revolutionary principles, would have a "considerable influence in unfettering the shackles which are so generally rivetted on the human race." One of the most binding shackles that the Revolution had unfettered, wrote Webster, was the "idea of a system of religious principles and a mode of worship, prescribed and established, by human authority." This was "only a milder form of tyranny . . . an insult to humanity, a solemn mockery of all justice and common sense. . . ." He concluded with a message that became the centerpiece of his newfound nationalistic philosophy:

America sees the absurdities—she sees the kingdoms of Europe, disturbed by wrangling sectaries, or their commerce, population and improvements of every kind cramped and retarded, because the human mind like the body is fettered 'and bound fast by the chords [*sic*] of policy and superstition': She laughs at their folly and shuns their errors: She founds her empire upon the idea of universal toleration: She admits all religions into her bosom—She secures the sacred rights of every individual; and (astonishing absurdity to Europeans!) she sees a thousand discordant opinions live in the strictest harmony . . . it will finally raise her to a pitch of greatness and lustre, before which the glory of ancient Greece and Rome shall dwindle to a point, and the splendor of modern Empires fade into obscurity.[22]

Here, albeit in embryonic form, were all the ingredients that Webster would subsequently develop into a mature and distinctive vision of the American nation. He presumed, along with Berkeley and a host of eighteenth-century prophets, that America was destined to succeed Greece, Rome, and more recent European powers as the capital of civilization. He located the wellspring of inevitable American greatness in the absence of traditional constraints on human thought and action and the unprecedented degree of individual freedom possible in America. He insisted that the liberation from the shackles of the old world would lead to harmony rather than anarchy in the new world, although he did not yet explain how or why. He wrote in a buoyant, exclamatory style that conveyed an impression of absolute certitude. As we have seen, these assertions and expectations were widespread several years before the war for independence broke out. Now, at the end of the war, Webster embraced them with all the fervor of a new convert. They quickly became the vehicle for his personal independence and for his salvation from anonymity and poverty.

•

The first indication of the direction in which Webster's nationalistic thinking was moving appeared in an advertisement for his school in Sharon, published in April of 1782, in which he mentioned "the general inattention to the grammatical purity and elegance of our native language. . . ."[23] Only a few pupils responded to his advertisement, not enough to justify continuation of the school, so in May he left Sharon and moved to Goshen, New York. There he found employment as a teacher but devoted the bulk of his time and energy to his own writing. "I have been indefatigable this winter," he boasted to an old friend in Sharon. "I have sacrificed ease, pleasure, and health to the execution of it, and have nearly completed it." The "it" to which Webster referred was not, he said, a "folio upon some obtuse philosophical subject" which "would be read by only a few, and its utility seldom reach further than the philosopher's head. . . ." It was "a little fifteen-penny volume, which may convey much useful knowledge to the remote, obscure recesses of honest poverty" and shed its light "equally upon the peasant and the monarch."[24]

Even before he had finished the book, he wrote letters to the legislatures of Connecticut and New York, requesting passage of a copyright law that would guarantee him exclusive rights to the printing, publishing, and marketing of the book for the next thirteen years. In his first venture into lawmaking, Webster found himself arguing that books and the ideas they contained were a form of personal property. Unless the legislatures complied with his request, he vowed, he would "not pursue the plan any further."[25] The two legislatures did pass a copyright law, soon followed by similar laws in every New England state as well as

New Jersey and Pennsylvania, all drafted at the personal request of Webster. And in October of 1783 the Hartford firm of Hudson and Goodwin printed 5,000 copies of a 119-page book entitled *A Grammatical Institute, of the English Language, Comprising, An easy, concise and systematic Method of Education, Designed for the Use of English Schools in America. In Three Parts. Part I.* It sold for fourteen cents a copy. Known soon thereafter as *The American Spelling Book* or "the Blue-Black Speller," it was destined to become the best-selling book ever written by an American and one of the most profitable ventures in American publishing history.[26]

Part of the book's appeal to late-eighteenth-century Americans lay in Webster's bold and distinctive brand of patriotism. The introduction to the first edition of the speller—there would be 385 editions in Webster's lifetime—was a skillful polemic. He reminded Americans that before the recent Revolution "the king, the constitution, the laws, the commerce, the fashions, the books and even the sentiments of Englishmen were implicitly supposed to be the *best* on earth. Not only their virtues and improvements, but their prejudices, their errours, their vices, and their follies were adopted by us with avidity." Now, however, most Americans "stand astonished at their former delusion and enjoy the pleasure of a final separation from the insolent sovereigns. . . ." That separation had produced major reforms in American institutions, especially in "the very erroneous maxims in politics and religion" accepted during the colonial era. It remained to be seen, wrote Webster, whether there were not other "errours to be corrected, some defects to be supplied, and some improvements to be introduced into our systems of education, as well as those of our civil policy."[27]

The most important improvement, he claimed, involved the rescue of "our native tongue" from "the clamour of pedantry" that surrounded English grammar and pronunciation. He charged that the English language had been corrupted by two practices that Americans should avoid: first, the standard for proper spelling and pronunciation was set by the English aristocracy; second, it was presumed that the study of Greek and Latin must precede the study of English grammar. The appropriate standard for the American language, said Webster, was not the arbitrary practice of an aristocratic class or the rules of a dead language. The American language must be guided by "the same republican principles as American civil and ecclesiastical constitutions," which meant that the people-at-large must control the language; popular sovereignty in government must be accompanied by popular usage in language. "The truth is," wrote Webster, "general custom is the rule of speaking—and every deviation from this must be wrong." Americans who doubted whether it was possible to create a republican and an American language did not understand what the Revolution had accomplished:

To attack deep rooted prejudices and oppose the current of opinion, is a task of great difficulty. . . . But the present period is an aera of wonders. Greater changes have been wrought in the minds of men in the short compass of eight years past than are commonly expected in a century. . . . Europe is grown old in folly, corruption and tyranny. . . . For America in her infancy to adopt the present maxims of the old world would be to stamp the wrinkles of decrepid age upon the bloom of youth and to plant the seeds of decay in a vigorous constitution. American glory begins to dawn at a favourable period and under flattering circumstances.[28]

None of these ideas, it should be noted, originated with Webster. Benjamin Franklin had called for thoroughgoing reform of the English language in America in 1768.[29] At Yale Webster had heard Timothy Dwight criticize the primacy of Latin and Greek in the curriculum and demand closer study of "the mother tongue." The notion that political changes were only part of any genuine revolution, that they must be accompanied by more basic changes in customs and habits in order to produce lasting and meaningful social change, was a central argument in Rousseau's *Social Contract*.[30] The contrast between European decline and age on the one hand, and American ascendancy and youth on the other hand, was a widespread idea; Hugh Henry Brackenridge had said much the same thing in *The Rising Glory of America* in 1772. And a host of prominent Americans, including men as different as John Adams and Charles Willson Peale, had voiced the opinion that America was born at a particularly fortuitous moment in history when old values could be discarded with relative ease and newer, more enlightened policies could be designed to take their place. Indeed, the phenomenal popularity of Webster's first book was partly owing to the fact that it brought together in one place several ideas that had been circulating on their own for many years.

But the center of the book, and the core of its appeal, was the elegantly simple and orderly presentation of words and the rules specifying how they were to be spelled and pronounced. As a teacher, Webster had learned from experience that his pupils acquired knowledge most readily when he broke a complex problem into its component parts and then made certain that each pupil had mastered one part before proceeding any further. Webster anticipated some of the insights currently associated with Jean Piaget's theory of cognitive development; on the basis of observations in the classroom, Webster insisted that children pass through distinctive learning phases in which they master increasingly complex or abstract tasks. He argued, for example, that it was useless to try to teach a three-year-old how to read, because children were not capable of mastering that skill until they were about five. For the same reason a child ought not to begin learning arithmetic until he was ten. He organized the speller in accord with these pedagogic principles, beginning with the alphabet and moving systematically through the different sounds of vowels and consonants, then syllables, then simple words, then more complex words, then sentences.[31]

Despite the bold and chauvinistic claims of the introduction, this first edition of the speller made very few revisions in standard English spelling and pronunciation. Webster chose *s* over *c* in words like "defense"; he changed the *re* to *er* in words like "center"; he dropped one of the double consonants in "traveller"; but he explicitly rejected eliminating the *u* in words like "colour" or "favour." (In later editions of the speller this would be one of his most prominent revisions. For now, however, he said that only "some pedantic fondness for singularity" would justify writing "favor" for "favour." Anyway, if it were spelled as it was pronounced, wrote Webster, it should be "favur.") Webster inadvertently explained why the number of orthographic changes was so small when he admitted that "in spelling and accenting, I have generally made *Dr. Johnson's* dictionary my guide; as in point of orthography this seems to be the most approved authority in the language." So much for popular American usage.[32]

At the very end of the speller, however, Webster's nationalism surfaced again. For spelling practice with difficult words, he listed the names of the states and counties of the United States. The speller concluded with two pages of important dates in American history, beginning with Columbus's discovery and ending with the battle of Yorktown. This litany of national names and dates replaced any mention of God, the Bible, or sacred events. "Let *sacred things* be appropriated for *sacred purposes*," wrote Webster. In place of Christian myths, Webster began to construct a secular catechism to the nation-state. Here was the first appearance of "civics" in American schoolbooks. In this sense, Webster's speller was the secular successor to *The New England Primer* with its explicitly biblical injunctions.[33]

Webster was confident that his speller would rescue him from obscurity, but he had no way of knowing how massive its sales were to become. In the meanwhile, he remained poor, unemployed, and almost unnoticed. Timothy Pickering, then quartermaster general of the Continental Army, obtained a cópy of the speller soon after its publication and observed that "the author is ingenious, and writes from his own experience as a schoolmaster as well as the best authorities; and the time will come when no authority . . . will be superior to his own."[34] This judgment proved prophetic, but at the time Pickering wrote Webster was penniless and had moved back to Hartford and taken a room with John Trumbull, a friend from Yale days. He listened to debates in the state legislature and visited the courthouse in an effort to drum up law clients. In the evenings he often accompanied Barlow, Trumbull, and Oliver Wolcott, Jr., another Yale classmate, to dances and dinner parties. In his diary he noted that there was "a multitude of pretty faces" at the dances but added, "My heart is my own." "Divide my time between the Ladies and books," he recorded one day. A month later he lamented that "money is so scarce that I cannot borrow £30 for a few weeks."[35]

Three separate projects kept him busy and helped provide at least the appearance of a settled occupation. The first project involved him in the political squabbles riddling Connecticut after the Revolution. From August of 1783 to May of 1784 Webster, often using the pseudonym "Honorius," sent essays and letters to the *Connecticut Courant*, urging the inhabitants of the state to dispense with their local jealousies and provincial prejudices. He criticized the townsmen who had assembled in a convention at Middletown to oppose the recent decision by the federal Congress granting officers of the Continental Army full pay for five years. Webster called the opponents of full pay "knaves and hypocrites" and argued that "the securities given to the army, however they amount to great sums on paper, are scarcely an equivilant [*sic*] for their services." Here, in Webster's first personal exposure to the rough and tumble of public controversy, he discovered that he could out-argue his opponents. He urged, for example, the adoption of a national impost, insisting that the Connecticut economy would benefit much more from the duties on imported articles than it would lose in revenue. When critics disputed his claim, he gave them an extended lesson in economic theory. At the same time as he was discovering that public debates provided an outlet for his personal ambitions and that nationalism was his special message, he also discovered his natural posture toward his readers: he was the tecaher and they were students.[36]

His second project grew naturally out of the first. People who had tangled with Webster in the newspaper exchanges invariably suffered embarrassment and were hungry for revenge. Eventually some of them discovered that "Honorius" was Noah Webster, an unemployed schoolteacher who had written a textbook with the pompous title *A Grammatical Institute of the English Language.* Since they could not match Webster's polemical skill or his knowledge of political economy, they decided to ridicule his speller. In the introduction to the speller Webster had declared that his book would replace Thomas Dilworth's *A New Guide to English Tongue;* so, in the summer of 1784, a series of satirical articles signed "Mr. Dilworth's Ghost" appeared in the local papers. Webster responded in kind, suggesting that "some petty schoolmaster or bungling printer, who has a large number of Dilworth's books on hand and finds them less saleable than formerly, had called up the Ghost to defend the books and help the sale." Within a few weeks it dawned on Webster that he was not only getting the better part of the exchange but also effectively promoting the sale of his own speller. Long after "Dilworth's Ghost" retired from the contest, Webster continued to publish

extended defenses of his *Grammatical Institute,* despite charges
that his sole intention was to "excite public attention and increase
the sales of my books."[37]

Promotion became a full-time activity. In June of 1784, with
a second edition of the speller already guaranteed, Webster set
off on a month-long journey through New England to confer with
booksellers and teachers. He visited Providence, Newport, Boston, Cambridge, Newburyport, and Portsmouth, trumpeting the
superiority of Webster over Dilworth all the way. "I have just
called on some of the Booksellers & made a sale of about 200,"
he wrote his publishers. "But if I take any trouble in the business
I must have a small profit." He wrote to James Madison requesting the passage of a copyright law in Virginia, since it now
appeared that there might be a national market for his speller.
"I am determined," he informed his publishers, "to have nothing
to do with selling in small quantities."[38]

His third project went hand in hand with his promotional
efforts. He had always intended the speller to be the first part of
a three-part *Grammatical Institute* that, when completed, would
allow a student to learn the English language from one source—
Noah Webster. As the potential market for the speller grew larger
and larger, he worked hard to complete the remaining two thirds
of his original scheme.

In the spring of 1784 he completed and published part two
of his *Grammatical Institute,* a 139-page grammar text. The introduction repeated many of the claims made in the speller:
Americans should not regard England as the fountain of all wisdom; the notion that a student must first learn Latin grammar before mastering English was "a stupid opinion" that demonstrated
"the amazing influence of habit upon the human mind"; just as
the spelling of a word ought to be based on the way it was pronounced and spelled by most people, the grammatical principles
of the language should be a codification of the way common
people use words and should be presented in "a style and method
suited to the most ordinary capacities." But the main part of the
text, despite the claims of the introduction and Webster's denunciation of Dilworth's text as "the most defective and erroneous of
all the schoolbooks now in use," made no major revisions of
Dilworth's presentation of English grammar. Although he im-

proved the organization of the grammar lessons, Webster proposed no new rules based on American ways of speaking or writing.[39]

The same could not be said about part three of his *Grammatical Institute,* published early in 1785, a reader designed to "diffuse the principles of virtue and patriotism...." Webster did not try to disguise the nationalistic criteria that governed his selection of reading material. "In the choice of pieces," he observed, "I have not been inattentive to the political interests of America. Several of those masterly addresses of Congress, written at the commencement of the late Revolution, contain such noble, just, and independent sentiments of liberty and patriotism, that I cannot help wishing to transfuse them into the breasts of the rising generation."[40] Young readers were not only offered standard selections from such recognized masters as Plutarch, Shakespeare, Swift, Addison, and Johnson but were also provided with an equal complement of American authors. Webster printed selections from Joel Barlow's *Vision of Columbus,* Timothy Dwight's *Conquest of Canaan,* and John Trumbull's *M'Fingal,* none of which had been published previously. The explicitly political writings included an extract from Tom Paine's *The Crisis,* the Continental Congress's response to the passage of the Intolerable Acts, and a pamphlet by Thomas Day calling for the abolition of slavery in accord with the principles of the Declaration of Independence.[41] Homilies and epigrams exhibiting the Whiggish wisdom of an updated Poor Richard were also sprinkled liberally throughout the text:

Money, like manure, does no good till it is spread.
There is no real use of riches, except in the distribution; the rest is all conceit.
Deference is the most complicated, the most indirect, and the most elegant of all accomplishments.
Party is the madness of many, for the gain of a few.[42]

Echoing the statement he had already made in the speller, Webster claimed that his reader was designed to place the Bible as the book from which American children would be required to read aloud. The coming generation of Americans would be asked to emulate the eloquence of national statesmen and poets instead of the ancient prophets or Jesus or the apostles. Webster expressed confidence that, like the Bible, his selections would continue to "form the morals as well as improve the knowledge of youth." In addition to being the first anthology of Americana, the reader encouraged civic pride and a semireligious devotion to the accomplishments of the new nation. It became the prototype for the McGuffey's readers of the nineteenth century.[43]

•

Webster was not one to sit back and wait for the royalities to roll in. Even before the completion of his reader he began to make plans for a grand tour of the United States, an expanded version of the earlier promotional trip through New England, this time designed to publicize his *Grammatical Institute* throughout the nation. In addition, he hoped to promote the passage of copyright laws in all the states and become acquainted with political and intellectual leaders who shared his national vision.[44]

Just before the start of his lecture tour, Webster published a short pamphlet entitled *Sketches of American Policy* that he intended to distribute on his travels through the country and refer to in his lectures. In his old age Webster frequently noted the significance of this publication, primarily because he believed that it showed that he had been the first to propose a plan for the creation of a stronger federal government. Whether Webster was first is debatable—several new schemes for a more effective central government came into circulation about this time. But the pamphlet was the first attempt on Webster's part to lay out systematically his own political philosophy.[45] Webster's nationalistic ideology was a strange blend of radical analysis, heavily indebted to the reading he had done in the works of Montesquieu, Richard Price, and Rousseau, applied to America in a way that was both self-serving and conservative. The radical analysis consisted of Webster's identification of six conditions that prevailed in America as a result of its geographic isolation from Europe and its unique historical development.

First, America enjoyed a roughly equal distribution of property among its inhabitants. Webster insisted that was America's most critical asset. In Europe the feudal system had created massive inequities that placed "most of the human race in extreme servitude." These inequities had "grown venerable by time. . . . All that Europeans can do is to introduce gradual alterations, and from time to time make such amendments as circumstances will permit. . . ." America, in the meanwhile, already enjoyed a degree of property distribution that European reformers regarded as utopian.[46]

The next four observations followed naturally from the first: America had no hereditary aristocracy and no religious establishment but possessed a broad diffusion of knowledge and a widely distributed population. Webster was careful to point out that these conditions were the product of history and circumstance rather than wise planning. Nevertheless, the benefits were incalculable. While Europe was plagued by a proliferation of privileged classes, a vestige of "the dark ages of Europe," wealth in America "is revolving from person to person and entitles the possessor to no pre-eminence. . . ." In Europe the combination of priests and kings conspired "to take the business of the Deity out of his own hands" and to manipulate "imaginary prodigies, miracles, dreams, tricks of magic, and fabulous stories of demons" as "instruments of tyranny." America needed to make more progress here, Webster admitted, since some states, including his own Connecticut, still attempted to regulate religious opinions. But in America complete religious toleration was just a matter of years; in Europe it would be a matter of centuries. Next, while the vast majority of Europeans was illiterate and unschooled, in America "knowledge is diffused through all classes" and "it is rare to find a person who can not read and write." Finally, Europe was "a populous country" in which land was scarce and labor overabundant. The development of manufacturing had created divisions of labor, so that "a man who makes heads of pins or springs of watches, spends his days in the manufacture and never looks beyond it." But in America—and here Webster anticipated Frederick Jackson Turner's interpretation of the frontier—"every man is in some measure an artist. . . . This will always be the case in America, so long as there is a vast tract of fertile land to be cultivated, which will occasion emigrations from the states already settled."[47]

Webster's sixth observation was really a conclusion based

on his previous diagnosis of conditions in Europe and America: America was in an unprecedented historical situation that was "in every point of view, the reverse of what has been the infant situation of all other nations." Europeans could offer little in the way of advice to Americans, because social conditions in the new nation were so dramatically different. In the final section of his pamphlet Webster called for the creation of a more powerful federal government—the details of his scheme were hazy—in order to consolidate the unique advantages America currently enjoyed. He argued that the new central government "will not be corrupted or degenerated into tyranny" because, quite simply, the forces that had historically corrupted governments were not present in America. Webster claimed that America was the first nation in history in which "the sovereign power resides in the whole body of the people." Borrowing from Rousseau's doctrine of "the general will," Webster described how "the general voice" would guide government in America "because the same power which frames a law, suffers all its consequences, and no individual or collection of individualls will knowingly frame a law injurious to itself." In America, claimed Webster, "*patriotism* or *public spirit* is nothing but self-interest, acting in conjunction with other interests for its own sake." America was not only free from the traditional impediments that had previously corrupted European societies; it was also the one place where the interest of each individual and the interest of the nation as a whole were synonymous.[48]

It was a volatile ideological mixture. Some of the most radical ideas of the English and French Enlightenment were being cited with approval: support for property distribution and complete religious toleration were rubbing shoulders with Rousseau's murky doctrine of "the general voice" and with rapturous exaltations of popular sovereignty. Nevertheless, Webster's political philosophy also had fundamentally conservative implications, and the Federalist pronouncements of his later years were not so much reversals of judgment as they were workings out of these early conservative implications.

For although Webster appropriated the radical ideas and programs of European thinkers, he described them as plans of action that *already existed* in America. The major function of a stronger federal government, as he saw it, was to conserve the social and economic advantages that history, circumstance, and the Revolution had deposited on America's doorstep. Webster's nationalistic philosophy emphasized the influence of impersonal, long-range forces on social conditions in America; his work with language and his familiarity with the way words and meanings evolve over time probably contributed to Webster's historical perspective. But his own personal needs also shaped his public statements. Webster's argument that the impediments to freedom and progress that stifled individual initiative in Europe were not present in America encouraged a laissez-faire, free-enterprise philosophy by assuring Americans that their efforts at material advancement would be rewarded and by equating personal achievement and national development. This was a notion that fit perfectly into the emerging capitalistic mentality of postrevolutionary America. It was also a comforting doctrine for an ambitious young American striving for personal fame and fortune with a nationalistic message as his major asset, for it sanctioned Webster's unrestrained self-aggrandizement and self-promotion. The lobbying for copyright laws, for example, was an act of public service that only incidentally benefited its primary advocate; and the lecture tour of the United States might bring personal recognition, but fame would be won in a public cause. Ambition need not be restrained or worried over; it was a virtue rather than a vice.

From March of 1785 to October 1786 Webster carried his message to every major town and city from Boston to Charleston and made it his business to become acquainted with virtually every prominent leader of the time. After a swing through New England in the spring of 1785, he moved down through New Haven to New York, where he visited the family of Aaron Burr—he had taught the children at Sharon—then headed south toward Virginia. It was the first time the young nationalist had ever seen any part of the country outside New England.[49]

He was quite taken with the grandeur of the Virginia gentry. And Madison and Washington both seemed to be impressed with him. "Play whist with the Gen¹ and his Lady, who is very social," he recorded in his diary while spending two days at Mount Vernon. Webster then followed up the visit with a letter to Washington, requesting a public endorsement of the *Institute*, something the general could not bring himself to make. A few months later, when Webster passed through Alexandria on the way north again, Washington's nephew invited him to attend a ball and then lecture to the guests. But things did not go smoothly: "Gen¹['s] Nephew a young imprudent Lad; he prepares supper & liquors to the value of 18 pounds; no persons come & he cannot pay the bill. Virginia hospitality."[50]

Other features of southern life also failed to match Webster's expectations. "Gentlemen are obliged to send their children to the Northward for education. A shame to Virginia," he noted at Norfolk, adding, "I shall leave 3 dozens of the Institute with Mʳ Benn Pollard & Co. to be sold." Although he marveled at the warm climate—several times he jotted down, "Green peas are still plentiful"—the South kept suffering in comparison with New England. In South Carolina the size of the black population astonished him; even though the slaves in Charleston seemed "to behave with more decorum than I have seen in America," Webster noted the constant worry about slave insurrections and observed that the work habits and even the speech habits of the whites were sloppy and slovenly. Most Virginians, he wrote, "fix their churches as far as possible from town & their play houses in the center." He was disposed to believe a merchant in Alexandria, who told him "that of 50 planters in Virginia, who sold him Tobacco, [only] 4 or 5 could write their names. . . . O New England! how superior are thy inhabitants in morals, literature, civility and industry."[51]

After distributing free copies of his *Institute* among the leading citizens of Charleston, Webster returned to Baltimore for the summer, hoping to open a school there in order to earn some money. Not enough subscribers appeared, however, so Webster spent his time composing a series of lectures on language and education. "My criticisms are *new*," he wrote to Timothy Pickering, "and no person here is capable of disproving my remarks. I have begun a reformation of the language, and my plan is yet in embryo." Pickering had been one of the first and most enthusiastic supporters of the speller, and Webster felt free to confide in him as a friend and request his assistance. "As I am the first American who has entered on such important plans and a youth, as well as a Yankee," he observed, "I shall need the countenance of gentlemen of your established character." Here was the theme Webster repeated in most of the letters he wrote to prominent Americans during his travels: the request for a personal endorsement, mention of his inexperience and the importance of his work, capped off by the hope that "a few of the distinguished persons" or "the leading characters in the country" or "the major figures" would support his efforts.[52] The closer he got to the elite members of American society, and the more he began to see himself as one of them, the more he realized that they were indispensable.[53]

The lectures on language and education that he composed in Baltimore and began to deliver during his second swing through the South in October of 1786 reiterated the nationalistic themes he had first articulated in his textbook introductions: America was politically independent of Great Britain but had yet to declare cultural independence; Great Britain "should no longer be *our* standard" in speaking and writing, because "the taste of her writers is already corrupted, and her language on the decline"; the firmest foundation for an indigenous American language was popular usage, and "a critical investigation of the subject" verified that "common practice, even among the unlearned, is more defensible . . . than some Latin rule . . ."; the unprecedented social conditions of postrevolutionary America provided "the fairest opportunity of establishing a national language . . . that ever presented itself to mankind."[54]

This was Webster's old message, more a nationalistic polemic than a profound analysis of language. But the lectures also reflected Webster's increased understanding of the history of language. His textbook introductions had contained extravagant claims which the texts themselves then failed to justify. Now, however, his lectures evidenced considerable study. One lecture traced the English language back to its origins in Latin, Celtic, Saxon, and Norman words. The great Doctor Johnson, praised as the supreme lexicographer in the first edition of the speller, was now described as a misguided literary critic "whose pedantry has corrupted the purity of our language. . . ."[55] He began to discuss language in general, and the English language in particular, as an organic creation that came into existence as different cultures collided over extended periods of time. He suggested, for the first time, that Americans might one day speak and write in a way that no Englishman would find intelligible and that "in a course of time, a language in North America" would be as distinct from English "as the modern Dutch, Danish, and Swedish are from the German, or from one another." And he began to grapple with an incongruity that had always been inherent in his thinking about social change: if popular usage or common practice shaped language, if language was not made but evolved and grew like moss on a rock, how could anyone, including Noah Webster, influence its development? Webster's tentative answer was compatible with his newfound respect for America's natural leaders: American culture was in the condition of a newborn infant and highly susceptible to guidance from enlightened parents; these founding fathers could establish, at this opportune moment in history, a set of lingual as well as political precedents that would shape succeeding generations. One of the most practical actions to take, obviously, was to insist on the national adoption of Webster's textbooks.[56]

In the winter of 1785–86 Webster carried these ideas back into the South, where his affection for Washington and his apprehension at southern mores were confirmed. In February he began to wind his way back toward New England, lecturing and socializing as he traveled up the coast. Philadelphia was the high spot of the journey. There he met Benjamin Franklin, John Dickinson, Tom Paine, Timothy Pickering, and Benjamin Rush. On March 2 he noted in his diary: "Read my 2^d Lecture to a small audience, the weather is bad." Pickering tactfully suggested that the weather was not the major reason for the small crowd, that Webster's manner of presentation was offensive, especially his "*quantum sufficit* of vanity." (Charles Willson Peale was showing his "Moving Pictures" at the same time, another possible reason for the poor attendance.) Webster met with Peale and the famous American astronomer David Rittenhouse before he departed for New York. "You see I am moving on slowly to the eastward," he wrote his publishers. "I am just beginning to make a bustle." Princeton proved to be a disappointment; only sixteen students signed up for his lecture, so he refused to give it. In New York he met Alexander Hamilton and dined with several prominent families. "Take tea with Miss Ray—a ten thousand pounder," he remarked in his diary (presumably referring to wealth). After a short stop to renew old friendships at Hartford, he set out for Boston, where he lectured throughout the summer and met Samuel Adams, James Bowdoin, John Winthrop, and most of the people who mattered. He did not settle in again at Hartford until October.[57]

And he did not remain there for long. "I wish for business—it is my life—my pleasure as well as my support," Webster wrote to Franklin, "but I begin a vast design without a shilling. . . ." The lecture tour had confirmed Webster's hunch that his ideas about language, politics, and national development were original and important; prominent citizens of each state seemed interested and supportive; and he had begun to visualize himself as a national leader. But there was no immediate way to translate his intellectual assets and new friendships into a steady income. On Thanksgiving Day of 1786 he headed south for Philadelphia again. "I leave Hartford—perhaps for life—to seek a living," he jotted in his diary.[58]

He remained in Philadelphia for eleven months, earning his living as a teacher at the Episcopal Academy while he cultivated his friendships with the social and intellectual elite of the city and, in the spring of 1787, hobnobbed with the delegates arriving for the Constitutional Convention. He even managed to get himself included among the passengers on the trial run of John Fitch's experimental steamboat. But the discrepancy between his prominent acquaintances and his status as a schoolmaster rankled, especially when an anonymous contributor to the *Freeman's Journal* published a letter that focused attention on the uppity mannerisms and presumption of a "mere schoolteacher." Although Webster's published response was, strictly speaking, accurate, it strained the truth in a way that revealed his own defensiveness. He insisted that he, Noah Webster, Esquire, was

a descendent [*sic*] of the oldest and most respectable families in America, and that his ancestors governed provinces fifty years before Pennsylvania was settled; that he has received as good an education as America can afford, and improved it by a personal acquaintance with the greater part of the principal literary gentlemen in the United

States; that his grammatical publications are received into use in one half the States and are spreading in the others as fast as they can be published; that his *neglected* lectures have been, and still are, under the patronage of the first characters in America; that his political writings have been the acknowledged means of restoring federal measures of great consequence.[59]

By the spring of 1787 he had a particular need to impress, because he had fallen in love with an attractive and socially prominent young woman, just the kind of catch guaranteed to win Webster's deepest affection. Her name was Rebecca Greenleaf, and she came from a well-to-do Boston family. "I have been happy with you," he wrote after he returned to Boston, adding, "I could have been happier had it not been for some restraints which you judged prudent...." Letters to "my dear Becca" reiterated promises of trustworthiness: "I sometimes go to dances and other parties, where I see ladies," he later wrote, "and good girls too, they are. But there is not a Becca Greenleaf among them...." He even took her advice about his hairstyle: "I have turned it back," he reported, "and I think I look like a witch."

Eventually he decided to abandon his teaching job, leave Philadelphia, and cultivate his prospects in New York City. In January of 1788 he wrote Becca from New York, confessing that he was "in the dumps a little." He worried that he had "elevated my views too high, that I have mistaken my own character and ought to contract my wishes to a smaller compass." But one month later he was out of the doldrums and talking up a new scheme. He had formulated a plan to establish a national magazine, issued from New York, which would serve as a vehicle for his many ideas and as a source of income that would allow him to ask for Becca's hand. "The eyes of America are upon me," he confided to her, "and having made my appearance upon the stage, I must act my part well or lose both my reputation and my propects. I do not doubt of success...."[60]

•

Successes or failures are surely influenced by individual intelligence and energy, the kind of personal powers that Webster possessed in abundance. But long-range developments and impersonal forces of which the individual is usually unaware invariably

shape lives and attitudes and frequently define what constitutes
success or failure in particular historical situations. More than
most men of his time, Webster possessed an acute sense of the
options that history had opened up for himself and America. Not
even Webster, however, appreciated the degree to which his own
ideas, and their eventual success or failure, grew out of the sedi-
ment that had piled up over the preceding centuries.

First, Webster's efforts to codify and standardize language in
postrevolutionary America were part of a movement initiated
in Europe during the Renaissance with the discovery of print.
Prior to the spread of printing, language was generally regarded
as a spoken rather than as a written form of communication, and,
as a result, people used words without the precision and uniformity we have come to expect. Until the appearance of printed
dictionaries and grammars, there were no standard guidelines
for "correct" pronunciation or spelling, in fact no acceptance of
the principle that words ought to be pronounced or spelled uniformly. When the first American colonies were founded, William
Bradford—Webster's distinguished ancestor—spelled the same
word differently in the same sentence; his orthography and grammar were regarded as legitimate expressions of his personality.
It was not until the late seventeenth and early eighteenth centuries that uniform spelling and standard usage came to be established and language was regarded as a written rather than as
a spoken medium subject to rigorous rules. It was not until the
publication of Samuel Johnson's *Dictionary* in 1755 that writers
and printers possessed a standard which almost everyone accepted. When Webster compiled his speller and grammar and
initiated his personal crusade for a uniform American language,
he was in fact joining a centuries-old movement in Western
civilization just as it became dominant.[61]

Second, the language spoken and written by Americans of
the revolutionary generation was already a remarkably uniform
brand of English. Although travelers, including Webster, often
noticed differences in dialect and pronunciation between New
England and the South, the overwhelming impression of most
observers agreed with the evaluation of Jonathan Boucher: "in
North America, there prevails not only . . . the purest Pronunciation of the English Tongue that is anywhere to be met with," he

wrote, "but also a perfect Uniformity." Webster himself claimed, in 1789, that "the people in America speak the most pure English now known in the world." Exactly what Webster and his contemporaries meant by "pure" is not clear; at times it seems to have served as a synonym for "uniform." Webster seemed to mean that the American language was not riddled with class distinctions, that America possessed no lower class that spoke its own distinctive dialect as in England. There was no consensus as to how this situation had come about. John Witherspoon claimed there was "a very obvious reason, viz. that being much more unsettled, and moving frequently from place to place, they [Americans] are not liable to local peculiarities either in accent or phraseology." Webster argued that the American language was not differentiated by class because the class distinctions present in England and Europe existed in America only in muted form. Whether the uniformity of American English was primarily a product of geographic mobility or social mobility, or was a consequence of revolutionary America's high literacy rate (approximately 70 percent) and therefore another measure of the impact of print on language, the net result was the same: the vast majority of citizens in the new nation did not need Webster's textbooks to teach them how to speak and write the language. Much like the traditional Whig justification of the American Revolution, Webster's advocacy of standardized American orthography and pronunciation only required Americans to conserve something they already possessed; his textbooks merely codified and celebrated longstanding lingual habits that seemed self-evident to most Americans. While artists like Peale and authors like Dunlap and Brackenridge confronted a populace that was grossly ignorant of aesthetic or literary principles, Webster courted a mass audience that, in language at least, was already civilized.[62]

Fourth, although Webster described himself as a man with "an enterprising turn of mind," he was also an eighteenth-century man for whom the values of what we would call "capitalism" and what he and his contemporaries called "commerce" were profoundly disturbing. Here was a situation in which history closed off, or at least limited, his options and generated tensions rather than opportunities. Put simply, it was difficult for Webster to commit himself completely to any social philosophy that countenanced unbridled pursuit of his own pecuniary self-interest unless he was able to convince himself that it contributed to the public interest. From the very start of his career as a publicist, Webster had exalted the advantages of individual freedom and had claimed that, in America, the unrestricted pursuit of material wealth led inexorably to benefits for society-at-large. In his *Sketches of American Policy* he had claimed that patriotism and self-interest were synonymous. Similarly, Benjamin Franklin's essay "The Way to Wealth," which Webster reprinted in the 1787 edition of his reader, affirmed the legitimacy of such bourgeois values as acquisitiveness, cupidity, and self-advancement, especially as measured by increased material goods and wealth.[63]

But a belief in unrestrained individualism flew in the face of the traditional attitudes that Webster and most other eighteenth-century Americans inherited and that the Revolution had reinvigorated in the ideology of republicanism. From Machiavelli through Harrington to Montesquieu and Rousseau, the guiding assumption had been that each individual bore a responsibility to the commonweal. Men who acted in accord with that responsibility were virtuous and those who did not were selfish, weak, and corrupt. "Virtue," more than "reason," was the watchword of the eighteenth century, most especially in revolutionary America, where the entire debate surrounding the movement for independence had been couched in terms of the virtue of the American people and the venality and corruptibility of British officials. Not until the middle third of the nineteenth century, when the American economy became thoroughly commercialized, did a full-blooded individualistic, free-enterprise philosophy become dominant. By then the venerable ideal of virtue, the belief that the individual must constrain his private passions and subordinate his self-interest to the civic good, had lost its power. In the late eighteenth century, however, the ideal of virtue was far from dead. And it posed problems that gave an ambitious man like Webster a good deal of trouble.[64]

Webster's psychological predicament was a product of the shifting climate of opinion in late-eighteenth-century America, combined with his own intense commitment to mutually exclusive ideals. Like Adams, Hamilton, Jefferson, Washington, and other prominent leaders we have come to call founding fathers,

Webster lusted after fame. Hamilton called fame "the ruling power of the noblest minds"; Washington called it "an ambition of the laudable kind." Fame was generally regarded as a legitimate goal because it required men to channel their private ambitions into projects that benefited the public. And only such public-spirited actions would earn fame, because one's niche in history depended upon contributions to society-at-large and to subsequent generations. Personal success in one's individual calling would not suffice. The accumulation of massive amounts of material wealth was also inadequate; indeed it was considered mean-spirited and selfish if pursued too avidly.[65]

These values were slowly changing. In fact, Webster's insistence that the unrestrained pursuit of self-interest would ultimately generate public benefits shows how the change crept into postrevolutionary thought and how private ambition was being rationalized. But the belief in the superior standing of public-spiritedness, the commitment to the ideal of virtue, remained alive. And with it remained the lingering suspicion that the burden of proof rested with an intensely ambitious man like Webster to verify his ultimate loyalty to public rather than personal advancement. Webster tended to respond by proclaiming his nationalism with a stridency that only increased suspicions and exposed his own sensitivity and self-doubt. Moreover, nagging poverty forced him to become an entrepreneur of his publications. The prominent gentlemen Webster most admired formed unfavorable judgments of his character on the basis of his excessive avidity in the marketplace. A century later, such a dogged entrepreneur would be enshrined in the pantheon of Horatio Alger heroes. In the 1780s, however, he had to be denounced, or at least stigmatized as an enemy to virtue. If fame followed fortune, then a poor man in late-eighteenth-century America was trapped within a neat paradox: his efforts to acquire the prerequisite for fame disqualified him for the ultimate prize. By the late 1780s the competing demands of these contradictory ideals had not only shaped Webster's nationalistic ideology; they had also shaped the distinctive features of his neurotic personality.

This vicious cycle became more vicious when the *American Magazine,* his best hope for financial security, collapsed in November of 1788 after a year of publication. James Greenleaf began to send Webster letters reminding him that Becca was accustomed to material comfort and that an impoverished author without any prospects had best look elsewhere for a wife. Becca did not help; her brother gave Webster 1,000 dollars to outfit their prospective home and she promptly spent it all on chintz furniture and china just before they were married, leaving no money for household necessities. At the same time, the mortgage that Webster's father had taken out to finance his son's college education came due and he was forced to sell the family farm.[66]

So it is not surprising that Webster began to speak more frequently of his writings as assets, forms of property protected by copyright laws he had pioneered, his only marketable commodities. In 1789 he published his *Dissertations on the English Language,* a revised version of the lectures he had delivered on his tour. The following year he gathered together articles from the *American Magazine* and some of his lectures into *A Collection of Essays and Fugitiv Writings,* where he experimented with radical spellings. Instead of describing these works as virtuous contributions to the public debate over American culture and politics, Webster admitted that they were private investments. Predictably, they did not pay off. "Some of my essays found a sale," he wrote Pickering, "perhaps a third; the rest will be a dead loss." He announced that he was "done with making books" and returning to Hartford to pursue the law again. John Trumbull welcomed him home, but was not sanguine. "Webster has returned and brought with him a very pretty wife," Trumbull wrote to Oliver Wolcott. "I wish him success, but . . . I fear he will breakfast upon Institutes, dine upon Dissertations, and go to bed supperless."[67]

One way of understanding Webster's published thoughts during this frustrating phase of his career is to see them as rationalizations of these personal and financial problems. In a pamphlet urging the adoption of the federal Constitution, for instance, Webster asked rhetorically, "In what then does *real* power consist?" A survey of English history told him that "the power of the people has increased in an exact proportion to their acquisition of property." This led him to the unqualified conclusion that "*A general and tolerably equal distribution of landed property is the whole basis of national freedom.*" James Harring-

ton had said much the same thing in his *Oceana* (1656); political
philosophers as far back as Aristotle had identified the relationship between property distribution and political rights. And
Webster himself had said much same thing in his *Sketches of
American Policy*. Now, however, Webster launched an all-out
assault on the ideal of virtue. Like Madison in *Federalist 10,* he
couched his argument in terms of an attack on Montesquieu:

The system of the great Montesquieu will ever be erroneous, till the
words *property or lands in fee simple* are substituted for virtue
throughout his *Spirit of Laws*.

Virtue, patriotism, or love of country never was and never will be,
till men's natures are changed, a fixed permanent principle of government. But in an agricultural country [with an abundance of unoccupied land] a general possession of land in fee-simple may be
rendered perpetual, and the inequalities introduced by commerce are
too fluctuating to endanger government. An equality of property, with
a necessity of alienation constantly operating to destroy combinations
of powerful families, is the very *soul of a republic*.[68]

In 1787, at about the same time that Webster was writing
these words, Jefferson was writing Madison that the American
republic would remain stable "as long as agriculture is our principal object, which will be the case, while there remains vacant
lands in any part of America. When we get piled upon one other
in large cities, as in Europe, we shall become corrupt as in Europe."
Webster's vision of America, like Jefferson's, was fundamentally
agrarian: he thought of property as land; he regarded the equal
distribution of land as essential, indeed, as "the very *soul of a
republic*"; he worried about the establishment of commerce and
commercial forms of property because they are unlikely to be
shared equally, although he was willing to allow for some
commerce as long as America remained predominantly agricultural. In all these ways, Webster was a disciple of traditional
values.[69]

But Webster also endorsed the unrestrained pursuit of property and repudiated the classical ideal of the virtuous citizen.
Virtue was unnecessary in America, he suggested, because there
was so much unoccupied land that, in the uninhibited scramble
for property, everyone would receive a fair share. By rejecting

the desirability of virtue, Webster eliminated the centerpiece of eighteenth-century republican ideology and helped clear the way for the development of a liberal, individualistic mentality. And not incidentally, Webster's new formulation also legitimized his own quest for property. Here was the kind of seductive rationalization that would prove enormously attractive to other men on the make in a nation just beginning to tap its economic resources.

From the very start of his public career as a spokesman for American nationalism, Webster had shown himself adept at tailoring his political ideology to fit his psychological needs, most particularly his need to be liberated from constraints on his ambition. In the late 1780s, however, during the debates over the Constitution, Webster began to alter the emphasis of his political message.[70] The focus of his thinking tended to shift from the unprecedented freedom and latitude for action possible in America to the unalterable demographic conditions; the metaphors he chose shifted from images of release to images of preservation and consolidation.[71] He began to talk about "the sense of a nation," a phrase referring to the dominant attitudes that accompanied the growth of population and the filling up of the land. Unlike his earlier view of "the general voice," Webster's "sense of a nation" did not originate in popular opinion or the constitutional principle of "popular sovereignty."[72] People were only epiphenomena, he now insisted, and their attitudes were determined by prevailing demographic conditions. He became preoccupied with the inevitable limits imposed by time and circumstance. In short, his nationalistic ideology began to be affected by his personal frustration, his increasing fatalism, and the sense that his time was running out.

Once America's land gave out, he argued, commerce and manufacturing would replace farming as the foundation of the economy. America would then go to the way of Europe, becoming overcrowded and riddled with class distinctions that inevitably accompanied the unequal distribution of property. "Such a change would, az in Rome, be ascribed to bad men," wrote Webster, experimenting with a simplified but short-lived form of spelling, "but it is more rational to ascribe it to an imperceptible progress of corruption, or those insensible changes which steel into the best conditions of government." Webster insisted that the evolution from agrarianism to commerce and manufacturing was inevitable, but unlike Hamilton and most Federalists, he described this evolution as degeneration rather than progress. "A constant increase of wealth is ever followed with a multiplication of vices—this seems to be the destiny of human affairs," he observed, adding that "wisdom directs us to retard, if possible, and not to accelerate the progress of corruption." Webster tended to analogize the new nation to a person: it was born, grew up, became old, then died. And the establishment of an economy based on commerce and manufacturing was a clear sign of the nation's middle age. America's nearly boundless frontier, on the other hand, was a fountain of youth that preserved republican vitality.[73]

Instead of being a forward-looking nationalist who relished the advance of modernity, Webster now wanted to stop history or at least to slow it down. There was little one could do about economic development; that was inevitable and irreversible. But one could prevent Americans from accelerating the national aging process. Here was the source of Webster's hostility to the importation of European institutions and mores. "It is perhaps always true," he noted, "that an old civilized nation cannot, with propriety, be the model for an infant nation, either in manners or fashions, in literature, or in government." European countries were at a more advanced stage of national development and had corresponding mores and customs. "A dancing school among the Tuscaroras, is not a greater absurdity, than a masquerade in America," he warned. "A theatre under the best regulations is not essential to our public and private happiness." Most significantly, the establishment of European customs like masquerades and theatrical companies "carry us forward by hasty strides to the last stages of corruption; a period that every benevolent man will deprecate and endeavor to retard." European culture was "highly pernicious in this country," not because it was intrinsically evil, but because it sped up the natural historical processes and made America old before its time. "This circumstance— the difference in the stages of our political existence—should make us shun the vices which may be polite and even necessary in older states," Webster cautioned, "and endeavor to preserve our manners by being our own standards . . . [lest we] be hurried down the stream of corruption, with older nations. . . ."[74]

Webster's efforts to establish American ways of speaking and spelling, his efforts to generate respect for American authors and to institutionalize American practices in education, were all part of an attempt to inculcate habits during the most favorable phase of national development and thereby to deter the onrush of inevitable corruption. "*Now* is the time and *this* is the country in which we may expect success in attempting changes favorable to language, science, and government," he wrote in his *Dissertations on the English Language.* "Let us then seize the present moment and establish a national language as well as a national government."[75] If Brackenridge thought of optimum values geographically, as a middle ground between East and West, Webster now thought of them chronologically, as an ideal moment between infancy and old age. From this perspective the Constitution was not praiseworthy because it provided America was the federal power to propel the nation toward a bright, capitalistic future, but for precisely the opposite reason: it rooted the American government in traditional or "premodern" values and promised to make those values the standard against which national development would be measured; like a Peale portrait, it captured the best features of a youthful nation and held them up to posterity. In this scheme of things Webster was able to depict himself as a virtuous citizen whose various projects and publications were designed to serve the national interest by freezing time at the ideal moment of American history. His sense of urgency and impatience with his lack of recognition derived from the awareness that both he and America were growing old fast.

•

While the administration of President Washington established the new national government in New York, Webster remained in Hartford, suffering from the old and familiar frustrations. "I have lamented that in the general scramble for property, I had not a small capital to employ," he complained to James Greenleaf. "Had I more property, I should gratify some of the strongest desires of my heart in projecting and carrying into effect schemes of public utility, but ... I have not influence enough. *Money gives that influence.*" His chief complaints concerned the *Grammatical Institute.* He had surrendered ownership of the copyright to the publishers in return for a fixed amount of immediate cash. Now, as the royalties rose to "about 2000 dollars annually," he was disconsolate: "Could I have kept my copyright in my own hands till this time, I might now have rid in a chariot." Greenleaf cautioned against "a depression of spirits" and observed that "if you are not as rich as you wish to be or even as you are conscious of deserving, you have on the other hand such domestic happiness as falls to the lot of but a few."[76]

Webster did have Becca, who brought to the marriage a handsome dowry and the status of her Boston background. In February of 1790 the new couple was awarded a prominent pew in the Hartford Congregational Church which, along with their large new house in a fashionable neighborhood, served as visible signs of admission to the local elite. Webster was also admitted into the Friendly Club, a literary society comprised of old friends like Trumbull and Wolcott and former idol Timothy Dwight. He became a regular contributor to the *Connecticut Courant,* served as secretary for Hartford's antislavery society, and was elected to Hartford's city council.[77]

Although this was only local and not national recognition, it allowed Webster to enjoy a measure of respectability that he had never experienced before. But until he could, as he put it, "push off some of the old lawyers," his income was insufficient to support his family in the manner to which he wished to grow accustomed. In 1791 he published *The Prompter,* a collection of epigrams and pithy anecdotes modeled on Franklin's *Poor Richard's Almanac;* it sold well and provided Webster with much-needed cash. Neither *The Prompter,* nor the hastily compiled textbooks he published the preceding year to supplement his income, followed the simplified spelling rules he had urged on Americans in the latter chapters of his *Dissertations on the English Language.* There he had advocated spelling words as they sounded when spoken by ordinary Americans: "bread" became "bred"; "speak" became "speek"; "machine" became "masheen." English words like "know," "reign," and "laugh" were described as "faults which produce innumerable inconveniences"; the final *e*'s on most words were characterized as "unnecessary trappings." Webster insisted that "Ther iz no alternativ" to his proposed reforms. But none of the books or pamphlets Webster published after 1790 attempted to put the new orthography into practice. "I suspect," wrote Ezra Stiles, "you have put in the pruning knife too freely for general acceptance." Webster agreed that it was "doubtful whether the public mind is prepared." And since Webster was dependent on the sales of books like *The Prompter* for his livelihood, he abandoned the crusade rather than risk popular disapproval. Respectability required caution; but despite the caution, by July of 1793 Webster was 1,815 dollars in debt and on the verge of selling his law library for 300 dollars in cash.[78]

Then quite unexpectedly came an offer that promised to rescue him from debt and to thrust him into the very center of national affairs. Alexander Hamilton and Rufus King offered a loan of 1,500 dollars if he would move to New York and initiate publication of a newspaper that would support the policies of the Washington administration. Although there was little chance that Webster would pass up this opportunity, he nevertheless dickered with his Federalist backers for several months in order to obtain assurances that he would retain ultimate control over the editorial policy of the paper. On November 13, 1793, he arrived in New York City with his family. Less than a month later the first issue of the *American Minerva* appeared. In addition to several advertisements for his textbooks and readers, this first issue of the *Minerva* carried Webster's declaration of editorial independence; he claimed that his newspaper would "be chaste and impartial, it will avoid purely personal attacks and will support the Administration."[79]

Webster did not regard these claims as inherently inconsistent or contradictory. And on this issue he was a representative American of the postrevolutionary generation. For Webster entered the national arena at precisely the moment when our modern version of the two-party system was being born. It was not until the nineteenth century, however, that political parties became an accepted feature of American political life and the word "party" carried anything but negative connotations. In the 1790s there was as yet no tradition to support the notion of a loyal and legitimate opposition.[80] Men who gave themselves over to an opposition party or faction, it was thought, were disloyal creatures who placed their personal interests above the interests of the nation as a whole. This was an old and soon-to-be-outdated way of understanding politics, but in the 1790s it continued to dominate the thinking of most prominent Americans, including Webster. It allowed him to perceive the administration of President Washington as the only legitimate representative of the national interest; opponents of the established and duly elected government were an illegitimate cabal. Of course there would be disagreements among different members of the government; it was with this in mind that Webster had requested a guarantee that he be given editorial autonomy. But persistent or permanent opposition to the policies of the elected government was regarded as mean-spirited and potentially destructive of the republican experiment itself. Webster estimated that during the four years that he remained in personal charge of the *Minerva,* he wrote the equivalent of over twenty volumes in the form of articles and editorials; the constant refrain running through them all was his condemnation of "party spirit," which he usually contrasted with "the public interest." Even though he was funded by Federalist leaders and was generally regarded as a partisan supporter of Federalist policies, he insisted to the end that he was "independent of all influence whatever but that of my own judgment."[81]

Virtually every historian who has studied the political history of America in the 1790s has noted the frantic, crisis-ridden tone of the public debate that Webster was entering.[82] Americans accustomed to devotional descriptions of the era's leading statesmen must adjust their sensibilities when exposed to the newspaper exchanges and Congressional speeches of the 1790s. One finds Washington, the most revered of the founders, described as "treacherous in private friendship, and a hypocrite in public life" and the wellspring of "political iniquity and . . . legalized corruption." Adams, Hamilton, and Jefferson received the same treatment, or worse. Webster found himself labeled "Domine Syntox," "a pusillanimous, half-begotten, self-dubbed patriot," "an incurable lunatic," and "a deceitful newsmonger . . . Pedagogue and Quack." Marshall Smelser has dubbed the 1790s an "Age of Passion," and John Howe has observed that "the political battles of the 1790s were grounded upon a complete distrust of one's political opponents. . . . No real dialogue was possible for there no longer existed the toleration of differences that debate requires." The mutual suspicions, supercharged rhetoric, and exaggerated accusations are important to recognize, in part because they confounded Webster and eventually drove him out of public life, in part because they reflected the widespread apprehension about the stability of the infant republic and the future direction of the new nation. It was not only that each initiative of the administration established a precedent that was likely to mold subsequent American political history, or that the emergence of an opposition party disconcerted Federalist leaders, who looked upon an organized opposition as a subversive influence, or that national leaders were aware of the fragility and short-lived history of earlier republics. All these concerns came together in the 1790s, and the resulting welter of worries created an explosive situation that was touched off by the specific decisions facing the first federal government. As the smoke cleared after each of the successive explosions, two distinctive and contrasting visions of what the Revolution had meant and what the new nation should become came into sharper focus. And Webster insisted that both visions were myopic.[83]

As editor of the *Minerva*, Webster expressed an opinion on every controversial issue of the day. He opposed capital punishment, reviewed major books like Tom Paine's *Age of Reason*, proposed the gradual abolition of slavery, condemned the attacks of North African pirates on American ships, translated foreign pamphlets that narrated the progress of the French Revolution, endorsed legislation to provide compensation for workers injured on the job, and even advocated, in satire, the use of royal titles as names for local streets. (The satire backfired when the New York Corporation, which apparently thought that Webster was being serious, renamed four streets "King," "Queen," "Princess," and "Duke.") "How do you get thro'... translating, transcribing, composing (tho' the last I know you can do when asleep) correcting other peoples' blunders, answering other peoples' absurdities, in short finding brains for people who, when they've got them don't know what to do with them?" asked James Greenleaf. "Mercy on them (or rather on *you*) how do you produce so many columns in a week, and so many good ones? I don't believe you have kissed Beccy these six months." Becca worried about the way her husband was driving himself; twice he experienced physical breakdowns. A friend claimed that Webster's eyes were "permanently lined with red ferret." But John Francis, a local physician, observed that work on the *Minerva* was a tonic for Webster and that he walked to his office each day like a natural aristocrat strolling to an appointment with destiny.[84]

The most distinctive feature of Webster's writing during these years, apart from its sheer volume, was his capacity for detachment and his almost scholarly insistence on dispassionate analysis. Like most Americans, he applauded the outbreak of the French Revolution and described it as "a prelude to a general regeneration of Europe." After Louis XVI went to the guillotine and control of events passed into the hands of Jacobin societies in Paris, many American observers, especially Federalists, began to back away from their earlier endorsements. But Webster reminded his readers that the French revolutionaries, unlike their American predecessors, were confronted with a feudal society. Even the Reign of Terror was justifiable, he argued, to eliminate the deep-rooted inequities maintained by privileged classes for centuries; the Jacobins were obliged "to create some evils to correct enormous abuses."

Just as he warned that the extremism of French radicals ought not to be condemned, because the historical situation they faced was not analogous to the situation in America, he also warned Americans against emulating the French for exactly the same reason. Americans were not confronted with "the feudal despotism and tyrannical hierarchies of the 12th century." When Edmund Genêt, the French emissary to America, began to encourage the establishment of Jacobin societies here, Webster condemned him for meddling in American affairs and denounced the need for the violent tactics of French radicals in America. While many Federalist newspapers advocated military action against the Democratic-Republican clubs that patterned themselves after the French Jacobins, Webster wished that "editors would all agree to let the clubs alone—publish nothing for or against them. They are a plant of exotic and forced birth: the sunshine of peace will destroy them." What was essential in France was inappropriate in America, he observed, and he trusted that time would make his point more tellingly than federal troops could. He predicted that Danton and Robespierre would be swept to the guillotine and that order in France would only be restored if "some popular man, who can attract around him a military superiority" assumed arbitrary power. As his predictions came true, Webster began an essay "We told you so," and attributed his insight to "nothing more than an ordinary share of historical knowledge, united with a candid comparison of all the circumstances. . . ." To Count Volney, a French refugee living in Philadelphia, he confided that he had great faith in the good sense of the American citizenry, but that he had found it "a Herculean task, even in the United States, to keep the people from committing suicide. . . ."[85]

Although Webster consistently maintained that the excesses of the French Revolution were inevitable and justifiable responses to entrenched inequities, he lamented the confusion and the intellectual incoherence which French ideas produced when they were introduced into American discussions. The founding father of American lexicography usually couched his criticism of French political ideas in the form of a critique of the verbal imprecision that the French Revolution had made fashionable:

As the French Jacobins artfully brought into use two abstract terms, *Liberty & Equality,* to save the trouble of defining or understanding a true Republican Constitution of government, so with great address they gave themselves the name of *patriots,* and their opposers in general the name of *Aristocrats.* . . . The great Mass of people annex no clear ideas to these terms. Patriot is undoubtedly a friend to his country, but what kind of opinions such a man must have, or what kind of government he must advocate, is never subject of enquiry . . .[86]

He was most distressed by the insertion of terms like "the people," "democracy," and "equality" into the public debate, complaining that such words were "metaphysical abstractions that either have no meaning, or at least none that mere mortals can comprehend." From this time forward Webster argued that it was impossible to have a meaningful discussion about politics in America, because the language used by spokesmen on all sides of a controversy had become hopelessly convoluted. "It has been a prevailing opinion, even with some of our greatest men, that the *people* can govern themselves and that a *democracy* is of course a *free government*," he wrote. "The men who have preached these doctrines have never defined what they mean by *democracy*, nor how the *people* are to govern themselves." As far as Webster was concerned, "the word *people* denotes any collection of individuals, either in meetings legally assembled or in mobs collected suddenly, no matter how, for any purpose good or bad."[87]

His preference for clarity when using words like "the people" was not a sinister device that masked his lack of respect for popular opinion. He frequently reminded his Federalist colleagues that "our government stands on *popular opinion,* and if that should fail to support it, it must fail to be supported." He warned that "the leading gentlemen of the Washington School have uniformly erred" when they "attempted to resist the current popular opinion instead of falling into the current with a view to direct it." He told Pickering that Federalist obsession with government secrecy was misguided, asking "how else are those steady and intelligent men who constitute the yeomanry of our country and who are its *strength* and *defense* to know exactly the merits of the controversy?"[88]

Nevertheless, Webster's frustration at the imprecision of American political discourse in the 1790s, as much as his loathing for political parties, was a measure of the increasingly traditional cast of his thinking. He had no affinity for the clamorous, hurly-burly politics of democratic society. As a man only recently permitted to participate in public affairs at the national level, he imposed a rigorous standard of civility and integrity on himself and fully expected that others would do likewise. A newly arrived natural aristocrat, he was determined to show old enemies and himself that his blatant scramble for personal recognition throughout the 1780s had an honorable, public-spirited motive; he embraced the code of virtue and held it up for emulation just as it was becoming an anachronism. And despite the outspoken recognition of the power of popular opinion, he believed that his primary responsibility—now that he was a recognized public leader—was to lead rather than follow popular thinking. Webster saw himself as a custodian of the national interest, which was itself shaped by the long-range social, economic, and demographic forces that had molded nations throughout history. In this sense he did not think that popular opinion or "the people" were reser-

voirs of political wisdom at all; they were the products of impersonal agents of historical change. When Webster depicted himself
as a man who "stood above party," he meant that he gave his
ultimate allegiance to the rational pursuit of the national interest
as dictated by an understanding of history, even when it ran
counter to the opinion of various parties or factions, and even if
one of the factions happened to be a majority of the people.

The clearest example of Webster's commitment to a disinterested assessment of America's national interest came in his writings on foreign policy. Federalist leaders, especially the High
Federalists loyal to Hamilton, favored closer ties with England
and periodically urged war against France. The opposition party
regarded an alliance with England as a return to colonial status
and instead urged support for France, who had aided America
during her war for independence and now allegedly required our
assistance in her own revolutionary fight against England and the
European powers.

Webster claimed that strict neutrality was America's only
defensible posture. "We firmly believe that the question of peace
or war depends mostly on events in Europe," he wrote, "not on
the measures or mode of negociating adopted by the United
States. Our duty is within a narrow compass . . . to be united
among ourselves in whatever measures shall be pursued." He
based this advice on two considerations: first, that America's primary task for the next century was to consolidate its own national power on the North American continent; geographical fate
had made this task easier by placing an ocean between America
and Europe; this natural shield allowed the new nation to expand
inward into the continent without interference and effectively
separated American interests from Europe; second, the forces
that the French Revolution unleashed within Europe were destined to produce massive political and social changes that no
nation, certainly not the United States, could control. "Whatever
may be the ultimate result," Webster wrote, "certain it is that
during the struggle between the old and new systems, Europe
must be a continual scene of convulsions and misery." He condemned the invasion of France by the combined European powers and, in a series of articles, denounced the imperialistic policy
of the French, predicting that France would go the way of im-

perial Rome under the Caesars. During the bitter party fight over the Jay Treaty, Webster lamented the concessions the treaty made to England but ultimately recommended ratification on the grounds that it prevented war between England and America. Seven years later, in 1802, when he reviewed his record as editor of the *Minerva,* this was the one decision he regretted. "Amidst the angry passions of parties the writer has hitherto preserved that independence of mind without which man is no better than a machine," Webster boasted; then he cited his support for the Jay Treaty as the one occasion when he himself was blinded by party spirit and "a more careful investigation [would have] compelled him to change his opinion."[89]

Webster's ability to provide a more detached brand of analysis than other editors, and his almost compulsive insistence on his impartiality, derived from his experiences in the 1780s. It was then that he developed an ideological perspective that focused on the significance of social and demographic influences on national development. This perspective served him well in the 1790s, because it allowed him to concentrate on long-range issues rather than arguments about personalities and it caused him to draw attention to the common advantages all Americans possessed by virtue of America's unoccupied land and the absence of a feudal past. And since Webster had issued some of his most dire warnings against England's cultural imperialism, especially England's continued dominance over American language and literature, he could not share the Anglophilia of Federalists like Hamilton. He had distrusted England years before he came to distrust French ideas; by 1795 the two different apprehensions left him truly neutral. His constant reiteration of his disinterestedness also harked back to the 1780s, when he had promised himself, and anyone else who would listen, that his chief goal was public service and not personal advancement. His frequent announcements of editorial independence and his refusal to engage in name-calling were declarations of virtue from a man who had endured years of criticism and self-doubt because of his highly visible ambition. Now he wanted everyone, including himself, to notice that he was a disinterested patriot.

By the fall of 1797, however, he was beginning to conclude that his much prized independence of judgment had made him irrelevant rather than effective. The party fight between the Federalists and supporters of Jefferson had intensified; in addition, the Federalists themselves had split into pro-Adams and pro-Hamilton factions. During a debate over the size of the American navy, Webster recalled that "one member of congress said openly, that if our little navy was on fire, and he could extinguish the fire by spitting, he would not spit." William Cobbett began publication of *Porcupine's Gazette* that year; when Webster refused to support Cobbett's crusade for a war with France, Cobbett labeled him "a traitor to the cause of Federalism" and launched an assault on Webster's character, calling him "a toad in the service of sans-cullottism," "a prostitute wretch," "a great fool, and a barefaced liar," "a spiteful viper," and "a maniacal pedant." "In this condition of things," moaned Webster, "when the domineering spirit of party frowns on moderation as apostasy or cowardice, who are the men to listen to truth and impartial discussion?" The answer, of course, was "nobody."[90]

He devoted larger portions of his time to a study of the yellow fever, an infectious disease like party spirit and democracy, and a subject he believed that all Americans, regardless of party, could agree was an evil. His columns in the *Minerva* were now filled with statistical tabulations designed to show that yellow-fever epidemics were directly correlated with the density of population and sanitary conditions, especially the purity of the water, in urban areas. "We are now laying the foundation of cities," he wrote to Benjamin Rush, "and the question of pestilence or no pestilence in future depends much on the structure and arrangement of populous towns. I shall urge this point, that our posterity may not be doomed to the ravages which lay waste Cairo and Constantinople." His one-man crusade for public health allowed him to reiterate his opposition to European precedents in a style that smacked of the old Webster certitude: "In the United States everything that has been done hitherto in the construction of cities," he observed, "is an imitation of the old European and African mold, and of course is *wrong*." But it turned out that even the study of disease was not immune to party bickering. Hostile editors belittled his alleged dependence on "careful observation" and "the evidence of facts," charging that Webster's essays were biased because, they argued, outbreaks of yellow fever were imported from Europe or the West Indies; they simply could not originate on American soil; Benjamin Franklin Bache's *Aurora* noted that Webster was only using disease as he had used politics and education, "to furnish him a ladder to mount to fame and guineas." Ironically, Bache died during the yellow-fever epidemic that struck Philadelphia in 1798.[91]

Webster was not present to say "We told you so." He had quit the *Minerva* and retired to New Haven in April, chastising politicians, narrow-minded editors, and party spirit as he left. But even his removal from New York did not free him from what he called "scurrilous attacks on my character." Hamilton was so outraged at Webster's criticism of Federalist infighting that he set up a rival newspaper in order to cut into the *Minerva*'s sales and thereby reduce the size of Webster's monthly commission. "I have spent the best portion of my life without honor and with little pecuniary reward," Webster lamented, "and an attempt to deprive me and my family of subsistence at this period of life, too late to renew my profession, is proof of an unfeeling heart." He need not have worried; the copyright to the speller was about to return to him. With the annual royalties that it provided Webster was able to remain permanently retired from public life. In revealing language, he confided to his diary that he was relieved to escape "the bustl of commerce & the taste of people perpetually inquiring for news & making bargains." He voluntarily exchanged prominence for solitude and almost immediately began work on his dictionary.[92]

•

In the first edition of his reader Webster had observed that "the latter part of a wise man's life is taken up in curing the follies, prejudices, and false opinions of the former." Since "the latter part" of Webster's life lasted so long—he lived for forty-five years after his retirement—he had an extended opportunity to repudiate his former "follies" and play the role of wise man. "I have long observed," he wrote Rush, "that men who explode error seldom have credit for it during their lives. But when the men are dead who are jealous . . . a new generation who examine the doctrines without prejudice will do them justice. . . . So that you and I are to have our portion of fame when we are dead." Nevertheless, as he grew older he advocated passage of a federal law requiring that men be denied the vote until they are forty-five and prohibited from holding office until they are fifty. Otherwise, he announced to Rush, *"old* men [will be stripped] of their dignity and *wise* men of their influence, and long, long are we to feel the mischievous effects of our modern policy." The trouble with posthumous fame, of course, was that one was not around to enjoy it; the aging Webster's condemnation of youthful voters or legislators and his self-serving support for "the maxims of Moses, Lycurgus, and the patriarchs" suggest that the sage of New Haven wanted to have his fame and enjoy it too. This was one folly he never outlived.[93]

Nor did he ever stop worrying about money. Although the income from his textbooks averaged between two and four thousand dollars a year, his past debts, family expenses, and the cost of the rare books required to do research on the dictionary kept him on the edge of solvency. In 1809 he wrote President-elect Madison to ask if there might be a government position with a modest salary available for him. Then, in typical Webster fashion, he informed Madison that even if he were brought into the administration he would continue to oppose almost all of Madison's policies "on principle." The bulk of the letter offered Webster's unsolicited advice about what was in the best interest of the United States, including his strictures against *"office seekers"* who are *"flatterers."* He did not get the job. In 1812 he moved to Amherst, Massachusetts, where the lower cost of living allowed him to maintain his family on profits from his textbooks. He remained there for nine years, long enough to play a leading role in the founding of Amherst College. All the while he devoted several hours each day to research for his dictionary, which he came to regard as his major intellectual achievement and his best guarantee of financial security.[94]

In time *An American Dictionary of the English Language* would assure Webster's fame and make a fortune for his heirs; he lived long enough to hear a few accolades but not to watch the dictionary sell. When he died in 1843 at the age of eighty-five, unbound and unsold copies of his *magnum opus* remained in the warehouse. Only after the firm of G. & C. Merriam acquired the publishing rights did the Webster dictionary begin to sell in large quantities. Webster had been dead for over twenty years before the revised version of his work achieved recognition as the best dictionary of the English language in the world. By then the Merriam Company had begun to take legal action to retain the name "Webster" as their exclusive property and prevent rival publishers from cashing in on the reputation of the man famous as "America's Samuel Johnson."[95]

Although one can imagine Webster whispering "We told you so" from the grave, very few of his contemporaries would have believed it. Outside of his coterie of friends in New Haven he was generally regarded as an irascible old fool who regularly confused his prejudices with principles. Federalist critics were particularly severe, seldom missing an opportunity to dismiss his proposed dictionary of American English as "wigwam words by one who has [not] the memory of his ancestors in his heart, or a spark of English spirit glowing in his veins. . . ." David Daggett suggested that Webster's ideas about language led inevitably to communication by means of grunts and groans. John Pickering— the son whom Timothy Pickering reared on Webster's speller— ridiculed Webster's effort to surpass Johnson's dictionary and to study "the American language," which Pickering claimed did not exist. Characteristically, Webster responded to all his critics in lengthy diatribes that usually provided more ammunition for his detractors. "I believe I must touch up brother Noah," wrote one critic; "no that won't do either, [for] if he should get angry, he'll oppose my favorite scheme of augmenting the number of judges of the superior court, and come into the house and spend three days on the word 'augmentation.'" Jeffersonian Republicans considered him a stodgy former Federalist; Federalists considered him a joke.[96]

We should be able to see him more clearly and fairly. He was a complex man whose ideas defied the rules of simple logic and who was extremely adroit at linking his personal needs with nationalistic goals. But he is justifiably famous, despite his other inconsistencies, as the most articulate and consistent advocate of what we would call "cultural nationalism" in postrevolutionary America.[97] The young man who wrote the speller and the old man who compiled the dictionary, though different in many other ways, shared a commitment to the cultivation of native American mores and values. And at the center of Webster's commitment lay something more profound than patriotic zeal or love of country. His celebration of things American grew out of a truly modern understanding of what American culture was. It was not, he kept insisting, a body of literature or art that could or should be judged against European standards; it was an expression of indigenous American customs that should, indeed must, be judged on their own terms. His ringing declarations of cultural independence, which he uttered over fifty years before Ralph Waldo Emerson delivered much the same message in his "American Scholar" address at Harvard, insisted that Americans had to develop their own cultural standards, which would necessarily reflect the early stage of America's national development and the unique social and economic conditions of the infant republic. The same man who came to suspect, eventually to loathe, Jeffersonian or Jacksonian appeals to "the people" never abandoned his contention that the folkways, patterns of speech, and day-by-day habits of ordinary Americans were the undeniable sources and final arbiters of republican culture. His polemical assaults against those foreigners and Federalists who were determined to see "the young Hercules of genius in America chained to his Cradle" often sounded like blind patriotic propaganda, but Webster's nationalism derived from the relativistic perspective now associated with cultural anthropology: namely, that cultures cannot be rated on some hypothetical scale, because no such scale exists; all cultures are inevitably expressions of particular social, economic, and historical conditions. Webster's insistence on this perspective marks him as one of the most farsighted social theorists of his time.

In most respects, however, Webster was a "premodern" man, which is to say that his thought and character were shaped by competing personal and social ideals. On the one hand, he drew the original inspiration for his nationalism from the liberal values popularized during the Revolution. Webster initially emphasized the unprecedented opportunities Americans enjoyed; his nationalistic message was based on an endorsement of individual freedom; his dominant metaphor was "escape from shackles," release from the constrictions that kings, priests, limited land and feudal custom had imposed on Europeans. And during this early phase of his career Webster's craving for personal independence and his need to justify the release of his own ambitious energies helped to sanction this liberal ideology.

On the other hand, Webster always harbored doubts about the destructive potential of unmitigated individualism and unbridled freedom. From the beginning he emphasized that only America's special environment, most especially the large expanse of unoccupied land, rendered the doctrine of national and personal liberation safe. By the mid-1780s, when he achieved national prominence, he began to deny the efficacy and tractability of liberal doctrines that had served him so well. By the late 1780s he began to talk about limiting freedom, slowing down history, preserving the unique advantages of the new nation, using the federal government to consolidate and control national development. His imagery changed from a vision of release or liberation to a vision of conservation or prolongation. By the 1790s he was wholly committed to the supremacy of self-control and the old ideal of virtue, which he insisted was the bedrock of national politics.

Webster's dictionary, so often cited as an example of the flowering of American nationalism during the age of Jackson, should be understood as the most dramatic example of Webster's conservative brand of nationalism, a nostalgic, backward-looking philosophy committed to the preservation of traditional values. *An American Dictionary of the English Language* is not an impartial listing of American words and their definitions; it is the life statement of a disillusioned republican who hoped to shape the language and therefore the values of subsequent generations in ways that countered the emerging belief in social equality, individual autonomy, and personal freedom.

Webster had convinced himself that all languages originated at a common source—he called it Chaldee—that, once discovered, allowed a lexicographer to identify the root meaning of all words. Modern scholars agree that this assumption was misguided and that most of Webster's etymologies are fictitious creations. But Webster used etymology to justify the biased definitions he wanted Americans to adopt. Thus, the word "people," he claimed, originally meant "babe and pupil, and perhaps originally signified the children of a family, like *gens*." And this root meaning allowed him to define "people" as "The body of persons who form a community.... The vulgar; the mass of illiterate persons. The commonality, as distinct from men of rank." Similarly, the verb "to educate" was defined so as to reinforce the commitment to duty and deference and to belittle the active powers of the learner: "To bring up, as a child.... To educate children well is one of the most important duties of parents and guardians." He defined duty as "That which a person owes to another ... obedience to princes, magistrates and the laws is the duty of every citizen and subject." His definition of "liberty" established the same distinction that John Winthrop had made in 1645: on the one hand there was "natural liberty," which was "the power of acting as one thinks fit, without any restraint or control, except from the laws of nature.... This liberty is abridged by the establishment of government"; on the other hand there was "Civil liberty," which was "an exemption from the arbitrary will of others, which exemption is secured by established laws...." One of the meanings of "freedom" was "license," which Webster then defined as "Excess of liberty"; at the end of the entry for "freedom" came the injunction "Beware of what are called innocent freedoms."[98]

Such definitions, he hoped, would go marching on long after he was in the grave, pulling the thoughts of nineteenth-century Americans back to the uncorrupted origins of the nation. In his final years he seemed to derive his deepest satisfaction from knowing that he was regarded as irrelevant. A "republic," he had decreed in the dictionary, was a word referring to "Common interest; the public." Then, in brackets, he observed, *Not in use.* And "virtue" was "Strength.... Bravery; valor." Again in brackets he noted, "Meaning obsolete." He liked to refer to himself as an "Old Whig" and never ceased explaining how painful it was to live in the world that Tocqueville described and Jackson symbolized. All his nobility grew out of despair about the future of democracy. Sitting on his front porch in New Haven, he was a one-man museum of the old, increasingly anachronistic attitudes, a die-hard republican whose flight from the implications of his youthful liberation had reached its final destination.

Epilogue

New Critics: Toward Emerson

By the early years of the nineteenth century the dreams of an American Athens had faded. A few die-hard chauvinists could still be heard trumpeting the imminent arrival of the muses, but they were anachronistic reminders of earlier and more hopeful days who looked more and more foolish as the decades passed and American Rembrandts, Miltons, and Shakespeares failed to materialize. The vast majority of commentators became defensive, apologetic about America's cultural accomplishments in a way that was reminiscent of the provincial mentality of the prerevolutionary era. And a few critics became preoccupied with the task of explaining what had gone wrong.

The most trenchant critics tended to be Federalists. After 1800, when Jefferson assumed the presidency, the Federalist Party was in a state of steady decline, a fact not lost on the Federalists themselves and not conducive to an uplifting or unbiased analysis of the American scene. The Federalists were the first group of Americans since the Loyalists to find themselves outsiders in their own country. This uncomfortable and unwanted position had some critical advantages, however, for it gave them a unique perspective on the political, social, and cultural developments in the new nation. Because of their alienation, the Federalists were well equipped to challenge conventional assumptions about the rising glory of America.[1]

The thrust of the Federalist argument was to question the

presumed connection between the arts and the liberal values of the emerging democratic, capitalistic society. Contributors to Federalist literary magazines, especially the *Portfolio* and *Monthly Anthology,* consistently juxtaposed the social and economic "progress" America had made with its acknowledged cultural poverty. "We may say that we have spice ships at the Philippines," wrote Arthur Walter in 1806, "and that our cannon has echoed among ice islands at either pole.... For myself, I think we ought to have produced a few scholars...."[2] The preceding year Edmund Dana lamented that "the times of inspiration are departed; and nature, the only muse of the poet, is unfeelingly forgotten. We have substituted rhetoric in her room and degenerated to a race of manufacturers."[3] In that same year Winthrop Sargent reviewed the extravagant expectations Americans had once held for themselves in the arts, then listed the familiar litany of literary embarrassments. He concluded with a letter allegedly from a European observer, who attributed the failure of American writers to their cupidity: "They [Americans] have a national maxim which the infant is taught to lisp in its nurse's arms; it is very long, and I do not recollect it; but I know it is equivalent to 'get money.' "[4]

In one sense, the Federalists were harking back to the republican ideology of the revolutionary years. They looked back nostalgically, and often romantically, to the days when stability was more valued than growth, self-denial was preferable to individual freedom, deference rather than social equality was the accepted ideal, and democracy was still an epithet. From this hallowed but dying republican tradition they tried to preserve whatever lingering suspicions Americans still had toward the values of the marketplace.

But unlike the former advocates of republicanism, most Federalist critics endorsed the cultivation of the fine arts; they described artists and authors not as symptoms of degeneration but instead as potential redeemers of a money mad and mindlessly materialistic society; they envisioned high culture as a cure for the ills of the marketplace rather than one of its products. "We are becoming familiar with wealth," wrote John Kirkland in 1807. "Out of wealth grows luxury. If those enjoyments that flow from literature and taste are not emulated, we shall be exposed to that enervating and debasing luxury, the object of which is sensual indulgence, its immediate effect, vice, and its ultimate issue, public degradation and ruin."⁵ Federalist critics generated the first body of sustained commentary on American culture that emphasized the redemptive role of poetry, literature, and the other fine arts, as well as the need for artists and writers who would steer clear of the clatter and corruption of the marketplace. Federalists refused to abandon the traditional belief that artists had social responsibilities, but they counseled artists to discharge these responsibilities in "a separate sphere," where aesthetic insights could be cultivated rather than compromised.

Another outsider, a French traveler who journeyed through the country for nine months in 1831–32, published his impressions in a two-volume work entitled *Democracy in America*. Like most foreigners, Alexis de Tocqueville described America as a cultural desert. "When I arrived for the first time at New York, by that part of the Atlantic Ocean which is called the East River," he wrote,

I was surprised to perceive along the shore, at some distance from the city, a number of little palaces of white marble, several of which were of classic architecture. When I went the next day to inspect more closely one which had particularly attracted my notice, I found that its walls were of whitewashed brick, and its columns painted wood. All the edifices that I had admired the night before were of the same kind.⁶

This experience proved symbolic. During his journey of over seven thousand miles through the United States and Canada, Tocqueville confirmed his impression that American culture was a mirage; at their best, American writers and artists were capable of work that was superficial and shallow. "America has hitherto produced few writers of distinction," he reported, "it possesses no great historians and not a single great poet . . . ; there are towns of second-rate importance in Europe in which more literary works are annually published than in the twenty-four states of the union put together."⁷ He had begun *Democracy in America* by warning his readers that "Whoever should imagine that I have intended to write a panegyric would be strangely mistaken," adding later that "there are certain truths which the Americans can only learn from strangers. . . ."⁸ Some of his most critical comments and most bitter truths concerned the impoverished condition of American culture.

What raised Tocqueville's account several notches above the critical reports of other European travelers in America, and gave it an enduring reputation as the classic study of America in the making, was his diagnosis of the social origins of national mores. Like the Federalists, Tocqueville distinguished between the attitudes generated in a burgeoning capitalistic society and the attitudes essential for the creation or appreciation of the arts. The arts and sciences demanded meditation, he noted, "and nothing is less suited to meditation than the structure of democratic society."⁹ By "democracy" Tocqueville meant much more than the political institutions of the new nation; he used the terms "democracy" or "democratic society" to refer to the broad range of attitudes and institutions that had come to dominate early-nineteenth-century America, most especially the liberal values of the marketplace. "How can the mind dwell upon any single point when everything whirls around it," he asked, "and man himself is swept and beaten onwards by the heady current that rolls all things in its course."¹⁰ All the incentives in this hectic world were materialistic and selfish and therefore incapable of motivating Americans to pursue higher, more refined truths. "If Pascal had had nothing in view but some large gain, or even if he had been stimulated by the love of fame alone," Tocqueville observed, "I cannot conceive that he would ever have been able to rally all the powers of his mind, as he did, for the better discoveries of the most hidden things of the Creator."¹¹ From Tocqueville's perspective, the arts and sciences were not like the other commodities that flourished in the marketplace; they required special cultivation. Here was the crucial point at which so many Americans of the revolutionary generation had gone wrong. They had failed to recognize the inherent antagonism between the bourgeois values of the marketplace and the sensibilities essential to the life of artists and intellectuals. By leaping into the marketplace, they had in effect, and quite unknowingly, committed cultural suicide.

Tocqueville also exposed another illusion that had lured the preceding generation of Americans into false optimism about the future of the arts; namely, the presumption that the people, once released from communal bonds and traditional constraints, would remain a malleable and educable mass ready to support the best efforts of aspiring writers and artists. There was no doubt, said Tocqueville, that in America "the people reign in the political world as the Deity does in the universe. They are the cause and aim of all things; everything comes from them, and everything is absorbed in them."[12] Tocqueville took great pains to show that the principle of popular sovereignty had several genuine attractions, the chief of which being that it eliminated the artificial and arbitrary tyranny of kings, lords, and outdated customs. But in its place the people substituted a subtle tyranny of their own by imposing the ordinary preferences of the average citizen on everyone else. "The majority lives in the perpetual utterance of self-applause," he warned. "If America has not yet had any great writers, the reason is given in these facts; there can be no literary genius without freedom of opinion, and freedom of opinion does not exist in America."[13] Eighteenth-century Americans had tended to look upon the market and the people-at-large as two new and dynamic allies for the arts. Tocqueville agreed that they were new and dynamic forces that would shape the character of modern society, but he considered them the mortal enemies of any high culture worthy of the name.

The whole thrust of Tocqueville's work was analytical rather than prescriptive. He was most interested in showing the way things were in America, because he was convinced that European society was about to be engulfed by the same democratic tidal wave. America was Europe's crystal ball; and Tocqueville confessed that what he saw filled him "full of apprehensions and hopes." Unlike the Federalists, he did not believe that it was possible to roll back time or insulate artists, authors, or anyone else from the pressures of popular opinion or the ravages of the marketplace. "I find that a great number of my contemporaries undertake to make a selection from among the institutions, the opinions, and the ideas . . . of society as it was; a portion of these elements they would relinquish, but they would keep the remainder and transplant them into the new world," he wrote at the end of *Democracy in America*. "I fear," he concluded in evocative language, "that such men are wasting their time and their strength in virtuous but unprofitable efforts."[14] If Federalist critics urged American cultural leaders to become dissenters who isolated themselves from the onrushing corruptions, Tocqueville implied that there could be no effective dissent from popular opinion or safe haven from the market; American artists had best adapt themselves and their work to the new conditions.

It was the genius of Ralph Waldo Emerson to embody and preach a version of both doctrines at the same time, and to do so in a serene way that captured the imagination of the rising generation. Henry James, Sr., once observed that Emerson's celebrated serenity appeared to be constitutional; it did not emerge from experience; it was like a beautiful woman's beauty; it was simply there.[15] This does not appear to be correct. Throughout most of the 1820s and '30s Emerson lacked direction, conviction or serenity and spent the bulk of his time filling up his mind and his journal—which he called "my Savings Bank"—with impressions that only gradually congealed to form the special self on which he would later rely. It was only after eleven years of study at Harvard, a ministerial career that ended with his voluntary resignation, the death of his first wife and both brothers, a ten-month trip to Europe, a second marriage, and several thousand entries in his journal that Emerson was prepared to offer his personal disposition as a model to aspiring men of letters in America.[16]

Although he has since become notorious as the most hopelessly unsystematic major thinker in American history, the need to abandon all systems and to become what he called "a faithful reporter of particular impressions" was central to his message. In 1837, soon after the critical success of *Nature* (1836), he began to report on his impressions in public lectures in and around Boston. "The present age is marked . . . by the immense creation of property," he told an audience at the Masonic Temple. "The first effect of this is everywhere to unlock the chains of caste . . . which had pinioned men's arms to their sides, and now to enable each to use what cunning lay in his hand or arm for his own profit."[17] Emerson expressed only distaste for the values of capitalistic society or, as he called it, "the Era of Trade." On the other hand, he marveled at the raw power released in the marketplace. "It is incredible," he noted, "what amounts of strength and wit that once slept inactive and went to the grave unknown, are now strained to their utmost."[18] Unfortunately, he concluded, this newly tapped human potential was being channeled into business rather than into the arts. "The first effect of external freedom in America," he lamented, "is to foster trade, to open a market." And in the market Americans' higher faculties were dulled "by seeing power and law at auction and the conscience of the citizen seared."[19]

In August of 1837, when he delivered an address entitled "The American Scholar" to the Phi Beta Kappa Society at Cambridge, Emerson reiterated his hostility toward the materialistic values of the marketplace and their corroding effect on prospective poets and writers. "Public and private avarice make the air we breathe thick and fat," he observed. "Young men of the fairest promise . . . are hindered from action by the disgust which the principles on which business is managed inspire, and turn drudges, or die of disgust, some of them suicides."[20] Emerson's cure for this sickness was perfectly in keeping with the liberal ideals of the revolutionary generation: recognize that the marketplace had become a new obstacle to the development of American potential, a new form of tyranny that must be overthrown if the full promise of the American Revolution were ever to be realized. "You will hear that the first duty is to get land and money, place and name," he told a Dartmouth audience. But while "the success of the market is in the reward, true success is the doing."[21] Each individual needed to liberate himself from material and monetary enslavement and cultivate "private obedience to his mind." The time was already approaching when "the sluggard intellect of this continent will look from under its iron lids and fill the postponed expectation of the world with something better than mechanical skill."[22] How was this monumental change to be effected? Emerson was sure of the answer even if it was somewhat vague: "This revolution is to be wrought by the gradual domestication of the idea of Culture."[23]

In a series of lectures delivered at the Masonic Temple during the winter of 1837–38, then again in "The Divinity School Address" delivered at Harvard the following summer, Emerson struggled to explain what he meant by "culture." If the explanations were often blurry, and if he frequently lapsed into rhapsodic nonsense, one must remember that Emerson was trying to say something new and was searching for the language to express it. At one point he talked not about "culture" but about "Cultus," which he defined as "the established worship of the civilized world."[24] Then he dropped "Cultus" and began to refer to "Human Culture," which he said was achieved "by listening to the voice of the Eternal in the heart of the Individual."[25] Culture, it eventually became clear, was the undeveloped creative potential inside every human being, the pent-up intellectual power which the founding fathers had tried to release in 1776, but which had gotten bottled up again when Americans became enamored with material prosperity. "Culture in the high sense," he explained, "does not consist in polishing or varnishing" but in breaking free of acquired habits so that "the slumbering attributes of man may burst their iron sleep and rush full-grown into the day."[26] Culture, in short, was a word referring to the "true" or "real" values, as opposed to the "false" or "fictitious" values of the marketplace; its development was the original goal of the revolutionary generation, since sidetracked, but now ready to be reclaimed by the current generation of American Scholars.

How was this final phase of the Revolution to be waged? Emerson made himself quite clear: each prospective man of letters in America must become a sovereign, self-reliant individual wholly unconcerned with the interests or opinions of others; he must, in effect, create a marketplace of the mind, transferring the laissez-faire mentality from material to spiritual pursuits. "The modern mind teaches," he maintained, "that the nation exists for the individual; for the guardianship and education of every man.... The object of Education should be to remove all obstructions and let this natural force have free play and exhibit its cultural product."[27] Over and over again, Emerson preached that serious American artists must abandon all sense of social responsibility and allow themselves to be seized by what he called "the highest Instinct." "The main thing we can do for it is to stand out of the way," he claimed, "to trust its divine force.... All general rules respecting intellectual culture must be based on this negative principle."[28] Each person, he assured his listeners, possesses untapped creative energy which is "present to all and like electricity in every part. It is always unconscious. And Culture teaches not to master it, but to be mastered by it."[29] Culture was something to be discovered, not created: "The dark walls of your mind are scrawled all over with facts, with thoughts. Bring a lanthorn and read the inscriptions."[30]

Emerson was one of the seminal minds in nineteenth-century America. Several streams of thought converged in him and then either disappeared altogether or flowed forward again in new directions. After Emerson the word "culture" in the modern sense became a permanent fixture in the American vocabulary. Artists and writers began to conceive of themselves as refugees from the American mainstream, the specially endowed inhabitants of a transcendent region sealed off from the hurly-burly of the marketplace, the banality of popular opinion, and the grime of industrialized society. Alienation became the customary and most comfortable posture for American intellectuals; criticism rather than celebration of the dominant American institutions and attitudes became the accepted norm. While the segregation of culture and artists had a distinctive history of its own, the origins of which can be glimpsed in the lives of men like Peale, Brackenridge, Dunlap, and Webster, it was also part of a larger process of differentiation that accompanied the emergence of modern society: families were more isolated from the community; schools, prisons, and asylums separated particular groups from the rest of society; children came to have special identities that separated them from adults; middle-class women became encased in a domestic world isolated from men; work and play became more distinguishable activities that went on in separate environments; academic disciplines diverged from each other and came to be understood as separate pools of knowledge.[31] From this perspective the voluntary withdrawal of American artists and intellectuals into a separate sphere was not peculiar; it was merely part of a major fragmentation that occurred as American society modernized; Emerson was its herald but hardly its cause.

But heralds are important, for they announce and dramatize significant shifts in attitude; like trees in the wind, they reveal the force and direction of prevailing currents. Emerson heralded the continuation and extension of the American Revolution as a liberation movement. His euphoria about the prospects for American culture depended on his boundless faith in the unexplored catharsis, the gush of creativity produced by what he called "internal freedom." By extending the liberal vision and applying it to the individual psyche, he recaptured the optimism of eighteenth-century enthusiasts.

Yet Emerson heralded an end as well as a new beginning. Culture was now considered a discrete region of sensibility and not an integral part of everyday life. And the eighteenth-century conception of virtue, which had been in the process of expiring ever since the 1780s, was finally given its coup de grace, for Emerson successfully cultivated an intentional obliviousness of the social dimension of human existence and counseled others to do likewise. He was the supreme individualist. When asked to lend his support to the Brook Farm project, he refused on the grounds that "to join this body would be to traverse all my long trumpeted theory . . . that one man is a counterpoise to a city . . . , that his solitude is more prevalent and beneficent than the concert of crowds."[32] Emerson simply presumed that if each artist steadfastly pursued his own insights without regard for others, the world would be a better place. Following his advice, aloof and alone, the rising generation created the first body of imaginative literature in America to endure. The aesthetic quality of this literature, it might be argued, was history's compensation for the social values that had been lost.

Notes

PREFACE

1. David Ramsay, *The History of the American Revolution* (Philadelphia, 1789), II, 316.
2. Quoted in Durand Echeverria, *Mirage in the West: A History of the French Image of American Society to 1815* (Princeton, 1957), 31.
3. This much repeated denunciation of American culture was originally published in the *Edinburgh Review*, XXXIII (1820), 69–80.
4. Frances Trollope, *Domestic Manners of the Americans* (rev. ed., New York, 1927), 267–68.
5. Alexis de Tocqueville, *Democracy in America*, Phillips Bradley, ed. (2 vols., New York, 1945), II, 36; see also *ibid.*, I, 326–27.
6. Edward Waldo Emerson, ed., *The Complete Works of Ralph Waldo Emerson* (12 vols., Boston and New York, 1903), I, 156–57.
7. Isaiah Berlin, *The Hedgehog and the Fox: An Essay on Tolstoy's View of History* (New York, 1953).
8. Noah Webster, *An American Dictionary of the English Language* (2 vols., New York, 1828). The first edition is unpaginated. Words, of course, are listed in alphabetical order.
9. Raymond Williams, *Culture and Society 1780–1950* (London, 1958); see also, by the same author, *The Long Revolution* (London, 1961) and *Keywords: A Vocabulary of Culture and Society* (New York, 1976).

CHAPTER ONE

1. Martha Brewster, *Poems on Divers Subjects* (New London, 1758), 3–4, 34.
2. *The New American Magazine*, January, 1759; see also Samuel Neville, *The History of North America from the First Discovery Thereof* (Woodbridge, New Jersey, 1761) for a reprint of the magazine essays.
3. Jonathan Mayhew, *Two Discourses* (Boston, 1759), 13, 57.
4. Quoted in Edmund S. Morgan, *The Gentle Puritan: A Life of Ezra Stiles, 1727–1795* (New Haven, 1962), 214.
5. Francis Hopkinson, *Science, A Poem* (Philadelphia, 1762), 6, 16.
6. Nathaniel Evans, *Ode, on the Late Glorious Successes of His Majesty's Arms, and Present Greatness of the English Nation* (Philadelphia, 1762), 12.
7. Leonard Labaree et al., eds., *The Papers of Benjamin Franklin* (20 vols., New Haven, 1960–), X, 232–3.

8. An unpublished manuscript by William D. Andrews, entitled "The Rising Glory of America: Early Sources of a National Myth," traces the history of this theme in both Europe and early America. I thank Mr. Andrews for making his study available while I was researching this chapter.

9. Alexander C. Fraser, ed., *The Works of George Berkeley*, D.D. (4 vols., Oxford, 1901), IV, 264–5, for the poem. For a discussion of Berkeley's vision of America and his influence see R. C. Cochrane, "Bishop Berkeley and the Progress of the Arts and Learning: Notes on a Literary Convention," *Huntington Library Quarterly*, XVII (1954), 229–49, and Kenneth Silverman, *A Cultural History of the American Revolution* (New York, 1976), 9–11, 288–9.

10. Andrew Burnaby, *Travels through the Middle Settlements in North America* (Ithaca, 1960), 110. Adams to Benjamin Rush, May 21, 1807, in Charles Francis Adams, ed., *The Life and Works of John Adams* (10 vols., Boston, 1856), IX, 600.

11. F. J. Hinkhouse, *The Preliminaries of the American Revolution as Seen in the English Press, 1763–1775* (New York, 1926), 106–7, for the newspaper account; Silverman, *Cultural History*, 288–9, for the Walpole quotation.

12. John Trumbull, *An Essay on the Use and Advantages of the Fine Arts* (New Haven, 1770), 5–7, 11, 13–15.

13. Hugh Henry Brackenridge and Philip Freneau, *A Poem on the Rising Glory of America* (Philadelphia, 1772), 21, 25.

14. *Ibid.*, 3, 16–17; see also William Smith, *An Oration . . . before . . . the American Philosophical Society* (Philadelphia, 1773) for the similiar claim that thoughtful colonists "anticipate the rising Grandeur of America . . . [and] trace the Progress of the Arts, like that of the Sun, from East to West. . . . THAT *Day* hath even now more than dawned upon us."

15. For a recent analysis of American provincialism and cultural defensiveness, see Jack P. Greene, "Search for Identity: An Interpretation of Selected Patterns of Social Response in Eighteenth-Century America," *Journal of Social History*, III (1970), 189–224; John Clive and Bernard Bailyn, "England's Cultural Provinces: Scotland and America," *William and Mary Quarterly*, 3rd ser., IX (1954), 200–13; Kenneth S. Lynn, *Mark Twain and Southwestern Humor* (Boston, 1959), 3–22, for scrutiny of William Byrd; Vincent Buranelli, "Colonial Philosophy," *William and Mary Quarterly*, 3rd ser., XVI (1959), 343–62, for Edwards's philosophical legacy.

16. Quoted in Constance Rourke, *The Roots of American Culture* (New York, 1942), 1.

17. Abbé Raynal, *A Philosophical and Political History of the Settlements and Trade of Europeans in the Two Indies* (London, 1770), 22.

18. Henry Steele Commager and Elmo Giordanetti, *Was America a Mistake? An Eighteenth-Century Controversy* (Columbia, South Carolina, 1967), 49–102; Durand Echeverria, *Mirage in the West: A History of the French Image of American Society to 1815* (Princeton, 1957), 8–14; Gilbert Chinard, "Eighteenth-Century Theories of America as a Human Habitat,"

Proclamations of the American Philosophical Society, XCI (1947), 27–57.

19. For an incisive analysis of this literature, see J. M. Bumsted, " 'Things in the Womb of Time': Ideals of American Independence, 1633–1763," *William and Mary Quarterly*, 3rd ser., XXXI (1974), 533–64; see also Edwin G. Burrows and Michael Wallace, "The American Revolution: The Ideology and Psychology of National Liberation," *Perspectives in American History*, VI (1972), 167–306.

20. Labaree, ed., *Franklin Papers*, IV, 225–34.

21. Stiles, *The Christian Union*, 97–113, 123; James H. Cassedy, *Demography in Early America: Beginnings of the Statistical Mind, 1600–1800* (Cambridge, Mass., 1969), 111–16. See also Edward Wigglesworth, *Calculations on American Population . . .* (Boston, 1775), 7.

22. Robert V. Wells, *The Population of the British Colonies in America before 1776: A Survey of Census Data* (Princeton, 1975), 69–171; Daniel A. Smith, "The Demographic History of Colonial New England," *Journal of Economic History*, XXXII (1972), 165–83; D. V. Glass and D.E.C. Eversley, ed., *Population in History* (London, 1965), especially the essay by J. Potter, "The Growth of Population in America, 1700–1860"; James Henretta, *The Evolution of American Society, 1700–1815* (Lexington, Mass., 1973), 5–39.

23. Marc Egnal, "The Economic Development of the Thirteen Colonies," *William and Mary Quarterly*, 3rd ser., XXXII (1975), 191–222; Alice Hanson Jones, "Wealth Estimates of the American Middle Colonies, 1774," *Economic Development and Cultural Change*, XVIII (1970), part two, 118–19, 130; George R. Taylor, "American Economic Development before 1840," *Journal of Economic History*, XXIV (1964), 427–44; Simon Kuznets, "Notes on the Pattern of United States Economic Growth," Robert Fogel and Stanley Engerman, eds., *The Reinterpretation of American Economic History* (New York, 1971), 17–24; Henretta, *Evolution of American Society*, 41–8, 103–06.

24. Phyllis Deane and W. A. Cole, *British Economic Growth 1688–1959: Trends and Structure* (Cambridge, Mass., 1962), 33–4, 86.

25. Bumsted, " 'Things in the Womb of Time,' " 556–7.

26. Labaree, ed., *Franklin Papers*, IX, 72–3.

27. *Ibid.*, 94–5.

28. *Ibid.*, 78–9.

29. Bernard Bailyn, *The Ideological Origins of the American Revolution* (Cambridge, Mass., 1967), remains the most succinct and probing analysis of this phase of colonial resistance.

30. [John Adams and Daniel Leonard], *Novanglus and Massachusettensis* (Boston, 1819), 80–82; Sam Adams to Arthur Lee, April 4, 1774, in H. A. Cushing, ed., *The Writings of Sam Adams* (New York, 1904), III, 101–02; Camden quoted in Burrows and Wallace, "The American Revolution," 238; Jeffrey Hart, ed., *Speech of Edmund Burke . . . March 22, 1775* (Chicago, 1964), 17.

31. Philip S. Foner, ed., *The Complete Writings of Thomas Paine* (2 vols., New York, 1945), I, 23–5, 31, 36.

32. The major community studies are Philip J. Greven, Jr., *Four Generations: Population, Land, and Family in Colonial Andover, Massachusetts* (Ithaca, 1970); Kenneth A. Lockridge, *A New England Town: The First Hundred Years* (New York, 1970); Michael Zuckerman, *Peaceable Kingdoms: New England Towns in the Eighteenth Century* (New York, 1970); Paul Boyer and Stephen Nissenbaum, *Salem Possessed: The Social Origins of Witchcraft* (Cambridge, Mass., 1974); Robert A. Gross, *The Minutemen and Their World* (New York, 1976). The best study of one colony is Richard Bushman's *From Puritan to Yankee: Character and the Social Order in Connecticut, 1690–1765* (Cambridge, Mass., 1965). Of the several excellent review essays analyzing this literature, I found John Murrin, "Review Essay," *History and Theory*, XI (1972), 236–75 and Rhys Isaac, "Order and Growth, Authority and Meaning in Colonial New England," *American Historical Review*, 76 (June, 1971), 728–37, most helpful. Robert Gross also allowed me to read an unpublished paper, "Communities in Colonial New England: An Historiographic Review," which I found quite insightful.

CHAPTER TWO

1. T. H. Green and T. H. Grose, eds., *Essays: Moral, Political and Literary by David Hume* (2 vols., London, 1898), I, 177, 195.

2. Quoted in Silverman, *Cultural History*, 219.

3. James M. Robertson, ed., *Shaftesbury's Characteristics of Men, Manners, Opinions, Times, Etc.* (2 vols., New York, 1900), I, 141–3.

4. Stiles, *The Christian Union*, 51–4; Gilbert Tennent, *A Persuasive to the Right Use of the Passions in Religion* (Philadelphia, 1760), *passim;* John Brown, *An Address to the Principal Inhabitants of North America* (Philadelphia, 1763), 13–15. See also Richard Bushman, *From Puritan to Yankee: Character and the Social Order in Connecticut, 1690–1765* (Cambridge, Mass., 1965), 267–90; Sidney E. Mead, *The Lively Experiment: The Shaping of Christianity in America* (New York, 1963), 16–37.

5. Milton M. Klein, ed., *The Independent Reflector . . . By William Livingston* (Cambridge, Mass., 1963), 195–6; Labaree, ed., *Franklin Papers*, IX, 61; James Lovell, *Freedom, the First of Blessings* (Boston, 1754), *passim.*

6. Joyce Appleby, "Ideology and Theory: The Tension Between Political and Economic Liberalism in Seventeenth-Century England," *American Historical Review*, LXXXI (1976), 499–515; Duncan Forbes, " 'Scientific' Whiggism: Adam Smith and John Millar," *Cambridge Journal*, VII (1954), 643–70; David M. Potter, *People of Plenty: Economic Abundance and the American Character* (Chicago, 1954), *passim.* A book by Albert O. Hirschman, *The Passions and the Interests: Political Arguments for Capitalism before its Triumph* (Princeton, 1977), provides a compelling explanation for the seductive power of free-market rationales in the seventeenth and eighteenth centuries. For an overview of colonial attitudes toward work,

freedom, and prosperity that emphasizes the staying power of traditional, pre-capitalistic values, see J. E. Crowley, *This Sheba, Self: The Conceptualization of Economic Life in Eighteenth-Century America* (Baltimore, 1974).

7. Marquis de Chastellux, "The Progress of the Arts and Sciences in America," in Howard Rice, ed., *Travels in North America in the Years 1780, 1781 and 1782* (2 vols., Chapel Hill, 1963), II, 545.

8. Silverman, *Cultural History*, xv.

9. Chastellux in Rice, ed., *Travels in North America*, II, 532.

10. The pioneering study of attitudes toward artists during the late eighteenth century is Neil Harris's *The Artist in American Society: The Formative Years 1790–1860* (New York, 1966), 27–53.

11. F. M. Cornford, ed. and trans., *The Republic of Plato* (New York, 1963), 321–40; see also C. L. Brownson, *Plato's Studies and Criticisms of the Poets* (Boston, 1920). For Rousseau's critique of the arts, see G.D.H. Cole, ed. and trans., *The Social Contract and Discourses* (London, 1973), 3–26. An abridged version of Rollin's thirteen volumes is available as Rollin, *The Ancient History* (2 vols., Boston, 1827); see also William Gribbin, "Rollin's Histories and Republicanism," *William and Mary Quarterly*, 3rd ser., XXIX (1972), 611–22. Edward W. Montagu, *Reflections on the Rise and Fall of the Ancient Republicks* (London, 1760), 125.

12. William Smith, *Discourses on Several Public Occasions During the War in America* (London, 1759), 76–7.

13. Richard Jackson to Benjamin Franklin, June 17, 1755, Labaree, ed., *Franklin Papers*, VI, 76–82.

14. The best treatments of this much discussed topic are Edmund S. Morgan, "The Puritan Ethic and the American Revolution," *William and Mary Quarterly*, 3rd ser., XXIV (1967), 3–42, and Michael Walzer, "Puritanism as a Revolutionary Ideology," *History and Theory*, III (1963), 59–90. For the clearest example of these attitudes in the revolutionary era, see Wendell Garrett, "John Adams and the Limited Role of the Fine Arts," *Winterthur Portfolio* (1964), I, 243–55.

15. The analysis of republican ideology has dominated the recent scholarship on the American Revolution. The seminal works are H. Trevor Colbourn, *The Lamp of Experience: Whig History and the Intellectual Origins of the American Revolution* (Chapel Hill, 1965); Bailyn, *Ideological Origins*; Gordon Wood, *The Creation of the American Republic, 1776–1787* (Chapel Hill, 1969). For a review of the literature on republicanism, see Robert E. Shalhope, "Toward a Republican Synthesis: The Emergence of an Understanding of Republicanism in American Historiography," *William and Mary Quarterly*, 3rd ser., XXIX (1972), 49–80.

16. Three recent scholarly articles have addressed the problems posed by the coexistence of "traditional" and "modern" attitudes in revolutionary America: Joyce Appleby, "Liberalism and the American Revolution," *New England Quarterly*, XLIX (1976), 3–26; Michael Zuckerman, "The Fabrication of Identity in Early America," *William and Mary Quarterly*, 3rd ser., XXXIV (1977), 183–212; James Henretta, "Families and Farms: *Mentalité* in Pre-Industrial America," *ibid.*, 3rd Ser., XXXV (1978), 3–32.

17. Henretta, *ibid.*, 19. For a different view of the same evidence, see Joyce Appleby, "The Social Origins of American Revolutionary Ideology," *Journal of American History*, LXIV (1978), 935–58. For the most comprehensive statement of the view that the attitudes and values of the revolutionary generation were decidedly not "modern," see J.G.A. Pocock, *The Machiavellian Moment: Florentine Political Thought and the Atlantic Republican Tradition* (Princeton, 1975).

18. The debate is reported in the *New Haven Gazette*, October 5, 12, 1786.

19. John Adams to John Marshall, August 11, 1800, in Adams, ed., *Works*, IX, 73.

20. John Adams to Thomas Jefferson, December 21, 1819, in Lester J. Cappen, ed., *The Adams-Jefferson Letters* (2 vols., Chapel Hill, 1959), II, 551; John Adams to Benjamin Waterhouse, February 16, 1817, in Koch and Pedens, eds., *The Selected Writings of John and John Quincy Adams* (New York, 1946), 200.

21. On this point see Raymond Williams, *Culture and Society, 1780–1950* and his *The Long Revolution, passim.*

CHAPTER THREE

1. Charles Willson Peale to Rembrandt Peale, August 28, 1823, Peale-Sellers Papers, Library of the American Philosophical Society. Unless otherwise specified, all references to Peale's letters, diaries, or autobiography are taken from this collection, here designated APS.

2. Sellers's biography appeared in 1947 as Volume 23, Parts 1 and 2, of the *Memoirs* of the American Philosophical Society. I have used the revised version, which contains new material and is available more readily as Charles Coleman Sellers, *Charles Willson Peale* (New York, 1969).

3. John Neal, as quoted in Sellers, *Peale*, 419.

4. James Thomas Flexner has an intelligent sketch of Peale's life in *America's Old Masters: First Artists of the New World* (New York, 1939). Oliver W. Larkin, *Art and Life in America* (New York, 1960), and Edgar P. Richardson, *Painting in America; The Story of 450 Years* (New York, 1956) help place Peale in the context of American art history. Neil Harris, *The Artist in American Society: The Formative Years 1790–1860* (New York, 1966), is a superb study of the social and intellectual history of early American art and artists.

5. The seminal book on the ideology of the revolutionary crisis is Gordon Wood's *The Creation of the American Republic, 1776–1787* (Chapel Hill, 1969). For an incisive discussion of the tension between the values of capitalism and the republican ideology of late-eighteenth-century America, see J.G.A. Pocock, "Virtue and Commerce in the Eighteenth Century," *Journal of Interdisciplinary History* (1972–73), III, 119–34, and the more extensive account in Pocock's *The Machiavellian Moment*. Finally, Kenneth Silverman's comprehensive survey of the subject, *A Cultural History of the*

American Revolution, appeared after this essay was drafted, but its account of Peale's career assisted my revisions.

6. Sellers, *Peale,* 3–51. Peale's *Autobiography,* 1–31, provides his version of these early years and is available in typescript among the Peale-Sellers Papers.

7. Copley to Captain Bruce, 1767, quoted in Jules Prown, *John Singleton Copley* (2 vols., Cambridge, Mass., 1966), I, 51. Quoted in Sellers, *Peale,* 82.

8. See Walter Jackson Bate, *From Classic to Romantic: Premises of Taste in Eighteenth-Century England* (Cambridge, Mass., 1949); Grose Evans, *Benjamin West and the Taste of His Times* (Carbondale, 1959); Ellis Waterhouse, *Painting in Britain, 1530–1790* (London, 1962).

9. Charles Carroll to Peale, October 29, 1767, quoted in Sellers, *Peale,* 62.

10. See Silverman, *Cultural History,* 24–25, for a superb discussion of portraiture and history painting. .

11. Peale to William Pearce, September 4, 1775, APS.

12. George Washington to Jonathan Boucher, May 21, 1772, quoted in Sellers, *Peale,* 99.

13. Peale to Beale Bordley, November, 1772, APS.

14. Peale to Beale Bordley, August 15, 1771, APS.

15. *Ibid.*

16. Peale to Beale Bordley, July 29, 1772, and November 1772, APS.

17. Notice in *Maryland Gazette,* September 1774, quoted in Sellers, *Peale,* 112.

18. Silverman, *Cultural History,* 176–78.

19. Peale to Beale Bordley, November 1772, APS.

20. Quoted in Sellers, *Peale,* 183–84.

21. Peale to Edmund Jenings, December 10, 1783, APS.

22. Copley to Benjamin West, November 24, 1770, quoted in Prown, *Copley,* I, 78.

23. Charles Merrill Mount, *Gilbert Stuart: A Biography* (New York, 1964), 80–81.

24. Theodore Sizer, ed., *The Autobiography of John Trumbull: Patriot-Artist, 1756–1843* (New Haven, 1953), 257–71. The authoritative account of patronage in early America is Lillian B. Miller's *Patrons and Patriotism: The Encouragement of the Fine Arts in the United States 1790–1860* (Chicago, 1966).

25. Peale to Benjamin West, August 31, 1775, APS.

26. Peale to Thomas Allwood, August 30, 1775, APS.

27. *Ibid.*

28. *Ibid.*

29. Peale to Edmund Jenings, August 25, 1775, APS.

30. The diary extract is reproduced in the Autobiography, 40a, APS.

31. Peale to Edmund Jenings, August 29, 1775, APS.

32. The estimate of the number of paintings is taken directly from Sellers, *Peale,* 138. For the commission from the Continental Congress see

Charles Coleman Sellers, "Portraits and Miniatures by Charles Willson Peale," *Transactions by the American Philosophical Society,* XLII (1952), 221.

33. Autobiography, 47, APS.

34. *Ibid.,* 63, APS.

35. Peale to Benjamin West, December 10, 1783, APS. This is not the same scene Leutze made so familiar, but Peale's sense of what history will regard as a dramatic and memorable event seems uncanny. Peale did a portrait of this scene in 1820.

36. Peale to Thomas Jefferson, August 21, 1819, APS.

37. Peale to Benjamin West, August 25, 1783, APS.

38. Autobiography, 40, APS.

39. The mezzotint is reproduced in Sellers, *Peale,* 68.

40. Peale to John Dixon, 1774, APS.

41. See James A Leith, *The Idea of Art as Propaganda in France, 1750–1799: A Study in the History of Ideas* (Toronto, 1965), 3–46, for the precedents provided in classical and medieval history; Joseph Burke, *Hogarth and Reynolds: A Contrast in English Art Theory* (London, 1943), for the English view of art's uses; and Peter Gay, *The Enlightenment: An Interpretation,* 2 vols. (New York, 1966–69), II. 216–381, for a stimulating discussion of eighteenth-century aesthetic theory.

42. Davis L. Dowd, *Pageant-Master of the Republic, Jacques-Louis David and the French Revolution* (Lincoln, Nebraska, 1948); Leith, *The Idea of Art as Propaganda,* 96–128; Harris, *The Artist in America,* 39.

43. For additional scholarship on art and propaganda in Europe, see Stanley J. Idzerda, "Iconoclasm during the French Revolution," *American Historical Review,* LX (October 1954), 13–26; Joseph Billiet, "The French Revolution in the Fine Arts" in J. A. Jackson, ed., *Essays on the French Revolution* (New York, 1945); T. J. Clark, *Image of the People: Gustave Courbet and the Second French Republic, 1848–51* (Greenwich, 1973); Leon Trotsky, *Literature and Revolution* (Ann Arbor, 1971).

44. Autobiography, 51–52, APS.

45. Peale to William Dunlap, no date, APS.

46. Autobiography, 52–55, APS.

47. *Ibid.,* 51a.

48. Sellers, *Peale,* 138–80. For more extensive analysis of wartime Philadelphia, see David Hawke, *In the Midst of a Revolution* (Philadelphia, 1961); Eric Foner, *Tom Paine and Revolutionary America* (New York, 1976); and Wood, *Creation of the American Republic,* 83–91.

49. Peale to Samuel Chase, November 23, 1784, APS.

50. Autobiography, 78a, APS.

51. Peale to Edmund Jenings [1780?], APS.

52. Autobiography, 78a–79, APS.

53. Quoted in Harris, *The Artist in America,* 12.

54. Critical estimates of Peale's portraits can be found in Flexner, *America's Old Masters,* 190, and Silverman, *Cultural History,* 168–70. Peale's own evaluation of his talent is contained in Peale to Joel Barlow, February 21, 1808, APS.

55. Ernest H. Gombrich, "Imagery and Art in the Romantic Period," in Fred Licht, ed., *Goya in Perspective* (Englewood Cliffs, 1973), 161.

56. August L. Mayer, *Francisco de Goya* (London, 1924); F. D. Klingender, *Goya in the Democratic Tradition* (New York, 1968); Licht, ed., *Goya in Perspective.* For a suggestive analysis of French artists who attempted to combine their allegiance to revolutionary politics with aesthetic principles, see the Marxist work of T. J. Clark, *The Absolute Bourgeois: Artists and Politics in France 1848–1851* (Greenwich, Conn., 1973).

57. Autobiography, 63; Peale to David Ramsey, October 15, 1786; Peale to Mr. Parkinson, December 30, 1800, all in APS.

58. For the hostility toward art and artists in the new nation, see the brilliant second chapter in Harris, *The Artist in American Society*, 28–53.

59. Jean Jacques Rousseau, "A Discourse on the Arts and Sciences," in G.D.H. Cole, ed., *The Social Contract and Discourses* (London, 1973), 1–26. For a discussion of the social context of these attitudes in eighteenth-century America, see above, chapter 2.

60. John Adams to John Trumbull, January 1817, quoted in Sizer, ed., *Trumbull*, 311.

61. Peale to Beale Bordley, June 14, 1783, APS.

62. Peale to George Walton, January 15, 1792, APS.

63. Peale to George Washington, July 22, 1780; Peale to John Hancock, July 25, 1780; Peale to Samuel Mifflin, July 25, 1780; Peale to Henry Laurens, February 20, 1787, all in APS.

64. Peale to Major Thompson, October 20, 1782, APS.

65. Peale to Benjamin Rush, December 13, 1782, APS.

66. Peale to Benjamin West, November 17, 1788, APS.

67. Peale to Mrs. Crawford, November 28, 1786, APS.

68. Peale to Benjamin Franklin, July 22, 1787; Peale to George Washington, December 27, 1790, APS.

69. From the *Freeman's Journal*, October 31, 1781, reprinted in Autobiography, 85a, APS.

70. See Sellers, *Peale*, 194–95, for a description and sketch of the arch.

71. Peale to General Weedon [?], February 10, 1784, APS. See also the account in the Autobiography, 85–87.

72. Autobiography, 90, APS. Peale to American Philosophical Society, March 7, 1797, APS. Here Peale was referring specifically to the museum, although he cited past failures of the government as well.

73. Sellers, *Peale*, 200–11, provides material from the newspapers as well as an excellent description of the scenes Peale tried to create. Sellers notes that a similar scheme had been tried in London in 1781. It is probable that Peale got the idea from exiled American Loyalists who returned to Philadelphia after the war.

74. Autobiography, 80–88, APS, for Peale's description of the pictures and audience reaction.

75. *Ibid.*, 91; Peale to General Weedon, July 13, 1785, APS.

76. Peale to Andrew Elicott, February 28, 1802, APS.

77. Peale to General Weedon, July 13, 1785, APS.

78. Peale to Mr. George, February 22, 1787, APS.

79. Peale to Mr. Brown [?], March 17, 1787; Peale to George Washington, May 16, 1787, May 27, 1787, August 6, 1787, all in APS.

80. Sellers, *Peale*, 227–29, 234.

81. Peale to Thomas Jefferson, May 2, 1815, APS.

82. Peale to Edmund Jenings, December 28, 1800, APS.

83. "The First American Art Academy," *Lippincott's*, IX (February 1872), 145.

84. Peale to Andrew Elicott, February 28, 1802; Peale to Timothy Matlack, March 9, 1800, both in APS: Sellers, *Peale*, 334–35.

85. Sellers, *Peale*, 285–86, 262–63, 406–10; Peale to Thomas Jefferson, Januray 29, 1808, and Peale to Rembrandt Peale, April 6, 1823, APS.

86. Allen Guttmann, "Copley, Peale, Trumbull: A Note on Loyalty," *American Quarterly*, XI (Summer 1959), 178–83.

87. See Peale to Henry Moore, April 6, 1819; Peale to Rembrandt Peale, June 25, 1781; Autobiography, 227, all in APS.

CHAPTER FOUR

1. Hugh Henry Brackenridge, *Gazette Publications* (Carlisle, Pa., 1806), 3–5.

2. Quoted in Claude M. Newlin, *The Life and Writings of Hugh Henry Brackenridge* (Princeton, 1932), 190–91.

3. Vernon Parrington, *Main Currents in American Thought: The Colonial Mind 1620–1800* (New York, 1927), 395–400; Newlin, *Life and Writings*, and editor of *Modern Chivalry* (American Book Company, 1937), which contains a short biographical essay and reproduces all six installments of the novel. Among the anthologies, Henri Potter's *The Early American Novel* (Columbus, Ohio, 1971), 126–36, is most comprehensive. See also Fred Lewis Pattee, *The First Century of American Literature 1770–1870* (New York, 1935), 154–65; Alexander Cowie, *The Rise of the American Novel* (American Book Company, 1948), 43–60; Herbert Ross Brown, *The Sentimental Novel in America 1789–1860* (Durham, 1940), 49, 158–60. Among the historians, Gordon Wood's *The Creation of the American Republic*, 480–82, pays most attention to Brackenridge. The final quotation is from Lewis Leary, ed., *Modern Chivalry* (New Haven, 1965), 7. The Leary edition contains a short essay on Brackenridge's life and reprints the first four installments of *Modern Chivalry*. Daniel Marder has edited *A Hugh Henry Brackenridge Reader, 1770–1815* (Pittsburgh, 1970); Marder's *Hugh Henry Brackenridge* (New York, 1967) is the most recent biography, and John R. Hendrickson's "The Influence of *Don Quixote* on *Modern Chivalry*" (Ph.D. dissertation, Florida State University, 1959) provides the most extensive literary analysis of the novel.

4. Quoted in Newlin, *Brackenridge*, 277–78.

5. Henry Marie Brackenridge, *Recollections of Persons and Places in the West* (Philadelphia, 1868), 43–54.

6. *Pittsburgh Gazette* (December 21, 1799), quoted in Newlin, *Brackenridge,* 213.

7. *Tree of Liberty* (September 13, 1800).

8. Erasmus Wilson, ed., *Standard History of Pittsburgh, Pennsylvania* (Chicago, 1898), 389; also Leland D. Baldwin, *Whiskey Rebels: The Story of a Frontier Uprising* (Pittsburgh, 1939), 43–4.

9. Newlin, ed., *Modern Chivalry,* 36–7.

10. *National Gazette* (April 20, 1793); Newlin, ed., *Modern Chivalry,* 471. Bergson quotation in Constance Rourke, *American Humor: A Study of the National Character* (New York, 1953), 22.

11. The best accounts of Brackenridge's early years are Newlin, *Brackenridge,* 1–7, and Henry Marie Brackenridge's recollection of his father's life in *The Southern Literary Messenger,* VIII (January, 1842), 1–19. See also Newlin, ed., *Modern Chivalry,* 799, for Brackenridge's recollection of his grandfather.

12. Newlin, *Brackenridge,* 8–24. The best analysis of early Princeton under Witherspoon is Lawrence A. Cremin, *American Education: The Colonial Experience 1607–1783* (New York, 1970), 465–66, 565. The best book on Witherspoon's influence is Lyman Butterfield's *John Witherspoon Comes to America* (Princeton, 1953). The most incisive study of Witherspoon's intellectual impact on his students is Douglass Adair's "James Madison" in William Thorp, ed., *The Lives of Eighteen from Princeton* (Princeton, 1946), 137–57.

13. V. L. Collins, ed., *Lectures on Moral Philosophy* (Princeton, 1912), gathers together the lectures Witherspoon delivered to his students.

14. Lewis Leary, *That Rascal Freneau: A Study in Literary Failure* (New Brunswick, 1941), 18–36, provides the best survey of Brackenridge's role in the Whig Society.

15. Newlin, *Brackenridge,* 15–24, reproduces the text of "Father Bombo's Pilgrimage" and most of Brackenridge's student poems.

16. *Ibid.,* 22–24. J.F.S. Smeall, "The Roles of Brackenridge and Freneau in Composing 'The Rising Glory of America,'" *Papers of the Bibliographical Society of America,* 67 (1973), 263–82, which identifies the last third of *Rising Glory* as the work of Brackenridge.

17. *United States Magazine* (Philadelphia, 1779), 53.

18. Kenneth Lockridge, *Literacy in Colonial New England: An Enquiry into the Social Context of Literacy in the Early Modern West* (New York, 1974), 5–6, 72–101; Lawrence Stone, "Literacy and Education in England, 1640–1900," *Past and Present,* 42 (1969), 69–139.

19. See the tables reproduced in James Henretta, *The Evolution of American Society,* 104–106, for a succinct summary of the distribution of wealth in the middle colonies. See also James T. Lemon, *The Best Poor Man's Country: A Geographical Study of Early Southeastern Pennsylvania* (Baltimore, 1972), and the more general study by Jackson Turner Main, *The Social Structure of Revolutionary America* (Princeton, 1965).

20. Ian Watt, *The Rise of the Novel: Studies in Defoe, Richardson and Fielding* (London, 1957), 35–59. Still useful is Q. D. Leavis, *Fiction and*

the *Reading Public* (New York, 1965), and Levin Schucking, *The Sociology of Literary Taste* (Chicago, 1966).

21. William Charvat, *Literary Publishing in America, 1790–1830* (Philadelphia, 1959), 17–37; Matthew J. Bruccoli, ed., *The Profession of Authorship in America: The Papers of William Charvat* (Columbus, Ohio, 1968), 5–28.

22. Van Wyck Brooks, *The World of Washington Irving* (New York, 1944), and John Allen Krout and Dixon Ryan Fox, *The Completion of Independence 1790–1830*, are two old but useful studies of early American culture and literature. Russel B. Nye, *The Cultural Life of the New Nation, 1776–1830* (New York, 1963), 235–67, interprets the period as a quest for a national literature. Lewis Leary, *Soundings: Some Early American Writers* (Athens, Georgia, 1975), surveys the lives of several aspiring authors. Although virtually all historians and literary critics who have studied this era agree that American writers produced little distinguished work, only Leary has begun to grapple with the problem in a systematic way. There is nothing like Watt's study of the rise of the English novel, for example, in part because data on American literacy rates and income levels is only now emerging, and in part because literary scholars have not made a serious effort to understand the social and intellectual history of the postrevolutionary era.

23. *United States Magazine*, 311–13.

24. Bruccoli, ed., *Profession of Authorship*, 5–28.

25. *United States Magazine*, 3, 4, 10, 11. All the quotations are from the first issue, which appeared in January 1779.

26. Wood, *Creation of the American Republic*, 48.

27. Newlin, *Brackenridge*, 29–30.

28. From "The Battle of Bunkers Hill," reprinted Montrose J. Moses, *Representative Plays by American Dramatists, 1765–1819* (New York, 1918), 258.

29. *The Death of General Montgomery at the Siege of Quebec: A Tragedy* (Philadelphia, 1777), 19.

30. Hugh Henry Brackenridge, *Six Political Discourses Founded on the Scripture* (Lancaster, 1778), 5.

31. Newlin, ed., *Modern Chivalry*, 621.

32. Brackenridge, *Six Political Discourses*, 28, 85; Hugh Henry Brackenridge, *An Eulogium of the Brave Men* (Philadelphia, 1779), 8.

33. *United States Magazine*, 6, 11–14.

34. *Ibid.*, 429–31, 28–30, 72–80, 14–15, 61–63.

35. Edmund Wilson, *Patriotic Gore: Studies in the Literature of the American Civil War* (New York, 1966), xxxii.

36. Lewis Leary, *That Rascal Freneau*, is still the best study of the influence of patriotic convictions on an American author of the revolutionary generation. See also Leary's *Soundings*, 131–60, for his reassessment of Freneau, who himself wrote, "an age employ'd in edging steel,/can no poetic raptures fell." Russel Nye suggests this same theme in his *American Literary History, 1607–1830* (New York, 1972), 101–73. Moses Coit Tyler's old book *The Literary History of the American Revolution* (New York, 1897) also

makes the connection between patriotic propaganda and "literary delinquency."

37. *United States Magazine,* 311–13.

38. Quoted in John Pope, *A Tour through the Southern and Western Territories of the United States* (New York, 1888), 17.

39. Hugh Henry Brackenridge, *Gazette Publications* (Carlisle, 1806), 7; Baldwin, *Whiskey Rebels,* 29–30; Newlin, *Brackenridge,* 58–69.

40. Brackenridge, *Gazette Publications,* 93–107.

41. Newlin, *Brackenridge,* 71–86; Baldwin, *Whiskey Rebels,* 38–44.

42. *Pittsburgh Gazette* (April 21, 1787), reprinted in Newlin, *Brackenridge,* 83–4.

43. Brackenridge, *Gazette Publications,* 53–57, 76–79, 80–86. For Brackenridge's recollection of the popular disfavor he aroused during the debate over the Constitution, see his *Incidents of the Insurrection in the Western Parts of Pennsylvania, in the Year 1794* (Philadelphia, 1795), III, 13.

44. *The Miscellaneous Works of Mr. Philip Freneau* (Philadelphia, 1788), I, 255–56.

45. *United States Magazine* (April 1794), I, 17–18. For similarly extreme endorsements of American writers, see *American Museum* (March 1787), I, 235, and *American Magazine* (May 1788), I, 370.

46. The phrase is the title of William Tudor's essay in the *North American Review* (1815–16), II, 33.

47. *Monthly Anthology* (November 1806), III, 579; *ibid,* 529; Freneau's comment from *Time Piece* (October 1797), II, n.p.; *Critical Review* (July 1817), IV, 54; *Intellectual Regale* (November 1814), I, 7. For a comprehensive review of the magazines of the period, see Anne L. Heene, "American Opinion Concerning Cultural Nationalism, as Reflected in American Magazines, 1790–1830" (M.A. thesis, Columbia University, 1944). Superb selections are also gathered in Lewis P. Simpson, ed., *The Federalist Literary Mind: Selections from the Monthly Anthology and Boston Review, 1803–1811* (Baton Rouge, 1962). Linda Kerber's *Federalists in Dissent: Imagery and Ideology in Jeffersonian America* (Ithaca, 1970) is the fairest and best study of Federalist thought.

48. Witherspoon quotation from *United States Magazine* (June 1794), I, 244; Paul L. Ford, ed., *The Writings of Thomas Jefferson* (New York, 1892–99), X, 104; Samuel Miller, *Retrospect of the Eighteenth Century* (New York, 1803), II, 173–76; Samuel Parker Jarvis lecture reprinted in *Port Folio* (April 1807), III, 263–64; *Weekly Magazine* (March 1798), 37; for novelists' denunciation of novels, see Tabitha Tenney, *Female Quixotism* (Newburyport, 1808), 211, and Mercy Otis Warren, *The Gamesters* (Boston, 1805), preface. The best review of the magazines is G. Harrison Orians, "Censure of Fiction in American Romances and Magazines 1789–1810," *Publications of the Modern Language Association,* LII (1937), 195–224.

49. Noah Webster, *A Collection of Fugitiv Writings . . .* (Boston, 1790), 29; *Port Folio* (April 1807), II, 107; *Massachusetts Magazine* (Novem-

ber 1791), III, 662; Timothy Dwight, *Travels in New England and New York* (2 vols., New Haven, 1821), I, 515–17; *Port Folio* (March 1810), IV, 85.

50. In his study of English circulating libraries, Paul Kaufman found that women did not constitute the majority of readers. See his "In Defense of Fair Readers," *A Review of English Literature* (1967), 68–75.

51. Newlin, ed., *Modern Chivalry*, 3–5, 643, 669–70, 727, 449.

52. Part one of *Modern Chivalry* was comprised of four volumes. Volume one and two appeared in 1792, volume three in 1793, and volume four in 1797. Part two was comprised of three volumes, which appeared in 1804, 1805, and 1815, although the last volume was mistakenly published as volume four. Versions of the entire work were reprinted in 1825 and 1846. The definitive edition by Claude Newlin appeared in 1937, and the Lewis Leary edition of part one appeared in 1965. The description of Farrago is from Newlin, ed., *Modern Chivalry*, 53; the challenge to government officials is in *ibid.*, 250.

53. *Ibid.*, 52.

54. *Ibid.*, 271.

55. *Ibid.*, 116.

56. *Ibid.*, 756, 405.

57. *Ibid.*, 479, 7, 21–22.

58. *Ibid.*, 476, 536, 560, 348, 120, 21.

59. Chase, *The American Novel*, 2; Newlin, ed., *Modern Chivalry*, 576.

60. Baldwin, *Whiskey Rebels,* is an old but dependable guide through the issues. More recent scholarship on the Whiskey Rebellion that further clarifies the problems faced by western farmers and Federalist officials include William D. Barber, " 'Among the Most *Techy Articles of Civil Police*': Federal Taxation and the Adoption of the Whiskey Excise," *William and Mary Quarterly*, 3rd ser., XXV (1968), 58–84; Richard Buel, *Securing the Revolution: Ideology in American Politics, 1789–1815* (Ithaca, 1972), 127–29; Jacob E. Cooke, "The Whiskey Insurrection: A Re-Evaluation," *Pennsylvania History*, XXX (1963), 316–46; Richard H. Kohn, *Eagle and Sword: The Beginnings of the Military Establishment in America* (New York, 1975), 157–73.

61. Brackenridge, *Incidents of the Insurrection*, III, 22. For an understanding of the implications of the issues raised by the insurrection, see John R. Howe, Jr., "Republican Thought and the Political Violence of the 1790s," *American Quarterly*, XIX (1967), 147–65; E. P. Link, *Democratic-Republican Societies, 1790–1800* (New York, 1942), is the best book on the societies; Marshall Smelser, "The Federalist Period as an Age of Passion," *American Quarterly*, X (1958), 391–419, is also a good review.

62. Brackenridge, *Incidents of the Insurrection*, III, 51.

63. *Ibid.*, I, 32–41.

64. *Ibid.*, I, 46–71.

65. *Ibid.*, I, 91–113. The letter from Brackenridge to Coxe is reprinted in Koch, *Eagle and Sword*, 166–67.

66. *Ibid.*, II, 72–77.

67. *Ibid.*, II, 82, III, 30–39.

68. Henry Marie Brackenridge, "Biographical Notice of H. H. Brackenridge," *Southern Literary Messenger*, VIII (1842), 4.

69. Newlin, ed., *Modern Chivalry*, 807.

CHAPTER FIVE

1. Dunlap's characterization of Webster is taken from his play "Cuttgrisingwoldes," which is included in *Diary of William Dunlap*, I, 22. The three-volume *Diary* is printed in *Collections of The New-York Historical Society*, LXII–LXIV (1929–31). Hereafter cited as *Diary*.

2. The anecdote and the attendance figures for the benefit are available in Oral S. Coad, *William Dunlap* (New York, 1917), 113–16. Dunlap reprints the story in his *History of the Rise and Progress of the Arts of Design in the United States* (3 vols., New York, 1834), I, 363. Hereafter cited as *Arts*.

3. *Diary*, I, 96–8.

4. *Ibid.*, 207, 264, for the remarks on Dwight; for the novel *Ante-Jacobin*, see *ibid.*, 152–55, 157–59, 163–65.

5. For Dunlap's career as an artist as seen by art historians, see Virgil Barker, *American Painting* (New York, 1950), 333–34; E. P. Richardson, *Painting in America* (New York, 1965), 79–80; Winslow Ames, *William Dunlap, Painter and Critic* (Andover, Mass., 1939); Harold E. Dickson, *Arts of the Young Republic: The Age of William Dunlap* (Chapel Hill, 1968). For Dunlap's influence on theater, see Arthur H. Quinn, *A History of the American Drama* (New York, 1923), 74–112; George O. Seilhammer, *History of the American Theatre* (3 vols., Philadelphia, 1888–91), III, 387; George C. D. Odell, *Annals of the New York Stage* (15 vols., New York, 1927–49), II, 219–26; and the introductory chapters in Arthur Hornblow, *A History of the Theatre in America* (2 vols., Philadelphia, 1919) and Oral S. Coad and Edward Mims, *The American Stage* (New Haven, 1929). Dunlap's own *A History of the American Theatre* (2 vols., London, 1833) is available in a one-volume reprint (New York, 1963), which is hereafter cited as *Theatre*.

6. Coad, *Dunlap;* Robert Canary, *William Dunlap* (New York, 1970); Lewis Leary, "The Education of William Dunlap," in *Soundings: Some Early American Writers* (Athens, Georgia, 1975), 208–28.

7. *Theatre*, II, 360.

8. *New York Magazine and Literary Repository*, V (November 1794), 654.

9. David Grimsted, *Melodrama Unveiled: American Theater and Culture 1800–1850* (Chicago, 1968), 1–21, contains a brief but brilliant discussion of Dunlap as a transitional figure in American dramatic history who tried to combine the classical values of eighteenth-century America with the emerging vogue of the melodrama. The quotation referring to Dunlap's financial incompetence is from Coad, *Dunlap*, 270.

10. Dunlap's autobiographical recollections are in *Theatre*, II, 38–69 and *Arts*, I, 288–317.

11. *Theatre*, II, 40–41; *Arts*, I, 288–89.

12. *Theatre*, II, 42–43; *Arts*, I, 290–91.

13. See Sigmund Freud, *A General Introduction to Psychoanalysis* (New York, 1952), 333–46; also Erik Erikson, *Childhood and Society* (New York, 1950), 247–58.

14. *Arts*, I, 304, 308–9.

15. For the most comprehensive and persuasive attempt to link psychological syndromes with early American history, see Philip Greven, *The Protestant Temperament: Patterns of Child Rearing, Religious Experience, and the Self in Early America* (New York, 1977).

16. *Theatre*, II, 43–47, *Arts*, I, 291–92.

17. *Arts*, I, 293–94.

18. *Theatre*, II, 78–103.

19. *Arts*, II, 297–98.

20. *Ibid.*, 298–301.

21. *Ibid.*, 310, 304.

22. *Ibid.*, 304–8; *Theatre*, II, 53–9; *Diary*, I, 51.

23. *Diary*, I, 1–10, for the firsthand account of the walking tour; *Theatre*, II, 60–67, for his recollection of the last days in England.

24. *Theatre*, II, 67.

25. *Arts*, I, 316–317; Coad, *Dunlap*, 16, for an account of Elizabeth Woolsey's family background.

26. *Theatre*, I, 147–48.

27. *Ibid.*, 12. In his biography of Dunlap, Coad described the time of Dunlap's commitment to the theater as a "propitious period." See Coad, *Dunlap*, 39.

28. Robert Treat Paine, "A Prize Prologue," written in 1794 and quoted in Grimsted, *Melodrama Unveiled*, 139. For similar affirmations, see the *New York Magazine and Literary Repository* (November, 1794), V, 654; see also *Theatre*, I, 126.

29. The best history of the stage during this period is Hugh Rankin's *The Theatre in Colonial America* (Chapel Hill, 1960). Dunlap's account in *Theatre*, I, 6–49, contains some significant errors.

30. *Theatre*, I, 104–24, covers the years from the Revolution to the late 1780s. Quinn, *A History of the Drama*, 33–73, is the best short treatment. In *Theatre*, I, 242–59, Dunlap provides extensive quotations from the debates in state legislatures and from petitions to the assemblies in Massachusetts and Pennsylvania.

31. *Ibid.*, 137–39 for Dunlap's recollection of the impression made by Tyler's play and for the quotation from *The Contrast*. The entire play is reprinted in Montrose J. Moses, ed., *Representative Plays by American Dramatists 1765–1819* (New York, 1918), 431–98.

32. Two early expressions of this viewpoint were James Fordyce, *The Folly, Infamy and Misery of Unlawful Pleasure* (Boston, 1761), and John Chater, *Another High Road to Hell* (Boston, 1768). Another early

critic of the stage, who was frequently cited during the 1780s and 1790s, was John Witherspoon, especially his *A Serious Enquiry into the Nature and Effects of the Stage* (London, 1765). The quotation about "states . . . on the decline" is from the debate in the Pennsylvania legislature in 1785, quoted in *Theatre*, I, 107.

33. Witherspoon, *A Serious Inquiry*, 13; Timothy Dwight, *An Essay on the Stage* (Middletown, Connecticut, 1824), 52, provides the Harvard regulation; Lindley Murray, *Extracts from the Writings of Diverse Eminent Authors . . . Representing the Evils and Pernicious Effects of Stage Plays and Other Vain Amusements* (Philadelphia, 1789), 3, 21; Samuel Miller, *Theatrical Exhibitions: Their Influence on the Character of Individuals and the Community* (New York, 1812), 15, 18–19; Rousseau's observation is from *A Letter to D'Alembert on the Theatre*, which was widely cited in America and is most readily available as Jean Jacques Rousseau, *Politics and the Arts* (Glencoe, 1960), 47.

34. Noah Webster, *Letters to a Young Gentleman Concerning His Education* (Hartford, 1823), 27.

35. For the design of theaters in America at the very end of the eighteenth century, see Grimsted, *Melodrama Unveiled*, 46–75; Murray, *Extracts*, 16–20, reprints criticism of theatrical audiences and the effect of theaters on a community. Rousseau claimed the theatrical audiences allowed individuals to lose their identity and become anonymous. See Rousseau, *Politics and the Arts*, 16–17. Dunlap reprints Washington Irving's comments on life in the pit in *Theatre*, II, 172–83. Dunlap's own comments on the gallery are in *Ibid.*, 127.

36. Miller, *Theatrical Exhibitions*, 83–4; Murray, *Extracts*, 17, which is a representation of Montague's arguments against the theater. In *Theatre*, II, 185–86, Dunlap reprints a letter he sent to Lindley Murray in 1803, in which he told Murray that his choice of authorities to cite against the theater could be improved if he would only select more passages from Witherspoon and Rousseau.

37. *Theatre*, I, 365, 145–6; Samuel Miller, *A Sermon [to] a Number of Young Gentlemen of the City of New-York* (New York, 1812), 20; Rousseau, *Politics and the Arts*, 79, 16; Murray, *Extracts*, 17, on ancient Greek and Roman precedents; Webster, *Dissertations on the English Language*, 178–79.

38. *Theatre*, I, 36–37, for prerevolutionary plays; also William W. Clapp, *A Record of the Boston Stage* (Boston, 1853), 7–16; *American Museum* (Philadelphia, 1789), V, 185–90. See also Herbert Brown, "Sensibility in Eighteenth Century Drama," *American Literature*, IV (1932), 47–60.

39. William Haliburton, *Effects of the Stage on the Manners of the People; and the Propriety of Encouraging and Establishing a Virtuous Theatre* (Boston, 1792), 29; *American Magazine* (October 1788), I, 793; *The New York Commercial Advertiser*, December 17, 1798; Judith Sargent Murray, *The Gleaner* (Boston, 1798), I, 228. Grimsted, *Melodrama Unveiled*, 171–203, provides a superb survey of the dramatic effort to exhibit moralistic concern. Edmund S. Morgan, "Puritan Hostility to the Theatre," *Proceedings of the American Philosophical Society* (1966), CX, 340–47,

locates the source of clerical opposition to the stage in the fear that actors and theaters usurped the function of ministers and churches.

40. *Theatre*, I, 150–53.

41. William Dunlap, *The Father, or American Shandyism* (New York, 1789), reprinted by The Dunlap Society (New York, 1887), 3–4.

42. *Ibid.*, 68.

43. *Theatre*, I, 153–60, contains reviews of *The Father*. The play has been studied by all Dunlap biographers; see Coad, *Dunlap*, 137–41, and Canary, *Dunlap*, 60–67. Daniel Havens, *The Columbian Muse of Comedy: The Development of a Native Tradition in Early American Social Comedy, 1787–1845* (Carbondale, 1973), 52–62, compares and contrasts the play with the work of English dramatists, especially Richard Sheridan.

44. Dunlap, *The Father*, 13, 36, 19, 55, 27, 64, 56–60.

45. *Theatre*, I, 220–21.

46. *Arts*, I, 316–17, for the fullest autobiographical account of these years.

47. *Diary*, I, 142.

48. *Ibid.*, 43; see also *Theatre*, II, 226, for Dunlap's description of a Boston merchant who symbolized all that Dunlap found despicable.

49. For Dunlap's role at the abolitionist convention in 1797, see *Theatre*, I, 323–29.

50. *Diary*, I, 54–110, 169–175, 311, for Dunlap's reading. For the Friendly Club, see *ibid.*, 324–36 and *Theatre*, II, 78–80; see also James E. Cronin, "Elihu Hubbard Smith and the New York Friendly Club," *Publications of the Modern Language Association*, LXIV (1949), 468–79. For Dunlap's journalistic work during this period, see Mary Rives Bowman, "Dunlap and the 'Theatrical Register' of the *New York Magazine*," *Studies in Philology*, XXIV (1924), 413–25, and Fred Moramarco, "The Early Drama Criticism of William Dunlap," *American Literature*, XL (1968), 9–14, which mistakenly attributes several anonymous articles to Dunlap.

51. *Diary*, I, 324.

52. *New York Magazine and Weekly Repository*, VI (January 1795), 1–6, and *ibid.*, new series, II (October 1797), 518.

53. Thomas Holcroft to Dunlap, December 10, 1796, *Theatre*, I, 310–11.

54. *Diary*, I, 13, 70, 126–27.

55. The best bibliography of Dunlap's plays is in Coad, *Dunlap*, 284–93; for Dunlap's own references to the plays composed during these years, see *Theatre*, I, 218–19, 264, 284–85, 305.

56. Montrose, ed., *Representative Plays by American Dramatists*, 510. *André; A Tragedy, in Five Acts* was first published in New York in 1798. The Montrose edition is faithful to the original and much more available to modern readers.

57. *Ibid.*, 508.

58. *Ibid.*, 513.

59. *Ibid.*, 524, 525.

60. *Ibid.*, 535.

61. *Ibid.*, 535.

62. *Ibid.*, 545, 546, 564.

63. *Ibid.*, 521–22.

64. *Ibid.*, 522.

65. Previous evaluations of *André* include Quinn, *A History of the American Drama*, 109–10; Coad, *Dunlap*, 166–67; Canary, *Dunlap*, 91–101; Grimsted, *Melodrama Unveiled*, 17–18.

66. *Theatre*, I, 287–88.

67. *Ibid.*, I, 181, 184, 190, 306, 317–22.

68. *Ibid.*, II, 149.

69. *Ibid.*, I, 206.

70. *Ibid.*, I, 391–401.

71. *Ibid.*, I, 302.

72. *Diary*, I, 54–55.

73. *Theatre*, I, 384–85, 390, 407–08; *ibid.*, II, 3–4; *Diary*, I, 67, 69, 143, for references to receipts.

74. Odell, *Annals of the New York Stage*, II, 6–8, reprints descriptions of the size and appearance of the theater from the newspapers of the day.

75. *Theatre*, II, 70–71.

76. *Ibid.*, II, 10.

77. *Ibid.*, II, 77.

78. *Ibid.*, II, 12, 19, 92; *Diary*, I, 236–37. The advertisements for *André* included a note that offered a fifty-dollar reward to anyone providing information about the identity of persons who had thrown objects at the players and the orchestra the previous week.

79. *Ibid.*, II, 151; Odell, *Annals of the New York Stage*, II, 88; Coad, *Dunlap*, 76–77.

80. *Diary*, I, 304; *Theatre*, II, 163, 198; *ibid.*, I, 21; Odell, *Annals of the New York Stage*, II, 181–82.

81. On the Kotzebue vogue, see Quinn, *A History of the American Drama*, 90–91; Coad, *Dunlap*, 205–10; for Dunlap's opinion of Kotzebue, see *Theatre*, II, 88. The Dennie quotations are from the *Port Folio* (September, 1801), I, 283, and (May 1802), II, 166.

82. Odell, *Annals of the New York Stage*, II, 42–45, 71; *Diary*, I, 231; *Theatre*, II, 118, 131.

83. The quotation from the *Morning Chronicle* is reproduced in Odell, *Annals of the New York Stage*, II, 169–70; *Theatre*, II, 213–14. For Hodgkinson's account of his relationship with Dunlap and the company, see John Hodgkinson, *A Narrative of His Connection With the Old American Company* (New York, 1797).

84. *Theatre*, II, 411–12.

85. *Ibid.*, I, 133–34.

86. *Ibid.*, I, 130.

87. *Ibid.*, I, 129.

88. *Ibid.*, I, 130, 125; for the appendix on the French theater, *ibid.*, II, 365–80.

89. *Arts*, I, 10.

90. The obituary is from the *Commercial Advertiser*, October 2, 1839.

CHAPTER SIX

1. Rebecca Webster to Harriet Webster Fowler, Emily E. Ford, *Notes on the Life of Noah Webster* (2 vols., privately printed, 1912), II, 317–18. Hereafter cited as *Notes*.

2. Noah Webster to Harriet Webster Fowler, April 6, 1835, in Harry R. Warfel, ed., *Letters of Noah Webster* (New York, 1953), 449. Hereafter cited as *Letters;* Noah Webster to Daniel Webster 1837, *ibid.*, 493.

3. Noah Webster to William Leete Stone, December 21, 1837, *ibid.*, 511–12 for the quotation. Webster provides the accurate account of his role at Saratoga in *Notes*, I, 27–8.

4. For lengthier discussions of its sales, see H. L. Mencken, *The American Language* (New York, 1936), 385, and Homer D. Babbidge, Jr., ed., *Noah Webster: On Being American* (New York, 1967), 177–78.

5. Emily Ellsworth Ford Skeel and Edwin H. Carpenter, eds., *A Bibliography of the Writings of Noah Webster* (New York, 1958). Hereafter cited as *Bibliography*.

6. See the marginal notes in Webster's hand, written on his personal copy of *Sketches of American Policy* in the Webster Papers, New York Public Library. See also *Bibliography*, 306, for more Webster marginalia. The word "demoralize" first appeared in Webster's *The Revolution in France Considered in Respect to Its Progress and Effects* (New York, 1794), 32.

7. Timothy Pickering to John Gardner, July 4, 1786, *Notes*, I, 102–03.

8. H. L. Mencken, *The American Language . . . Supplement One* (New York, 1945), 22, offers a convenient summary of the critical assessments offered by Webster's contemporaries. The Jefferson quotation is from *Notes*, II, 469.

9. Harry R. Warfel, *Noah Webster: Schoolmaster to America* (New York, 1936), is still the best full-scale biography. It replaced Horace Scudder, *Noah Webster* (Boston, 1882). Ervin C. Shoemaker's *Noah Webster: Pioneer of Learning* (New York, 1936) is not so much a biography as a study of Webster's writings interlaced with references to his life. Shoemaker is more critical of Webster than Warfel is, but his criticisms are often presentist (i.e., Webster was not a good statistician), and the book lacks Warfel's flair for the revealing anecdote. Babbidge's *Noah Webster: On Being American* is a judicious selection of Webster's writings on American culture that also contains succinct introductions by Babbidge. It is the only book that makes accessible Webster's major statements of the 1780s and 1790s. Finally, John S. Morgan's *Noah Webster* (New York, 1975) appeared while this essay was being written. It offers a more concise overview of Webster's life than does Warfel, but generally follows Warfel's interpretation, which verges on filio-pietism.

10. Noah Webster, *An American Selection of Lessions in Reading and Speaking . . .* (Philadelphia, 1787), 214.

11. Noah Webster, *A Collection of Essays and Fugitiv Writings* (Hartford, 1790), 31.

12. The primary sources of Webster's early life are collected in *Notes*, I, 15–21.

13. *Ibid.*, 21–31; Warfel, *Webster*, 22–32, is helpful but should be supplemented by Edmund Morgan, *The Gentle Puritan: A Life of Ezra Stiles 1727–1795* (New Haven, 1962), 308–59, for the best analysis of Yale during Webster's student days.

14. *Notes*, 18, for Webster's role in the parade; *ibid.*, 27–8, for the military expedition to Lake Champlain; Noah Webster to Thomas Dawes, December 29, 1808, *Letters*, 309–15, for Webster's reminiscences.

15. *Notes*, I, 38–9; the Barlow quotation is from Warfel, *Webster*, 35–6.

16. Webster's diary is reprinted in installments throughout *Notes*. The quotations are from February 14 and March 13, 1784, *ibid.*, 71, 72.

17. *Ibid.*, 39–41; Warfel, *Webster*, 35–50.

18. *Connecticut Courant*, June 5, 1781.

19. Quoted in Warfel, *Webster*, 42.

20. Joel Barlow to Noah Webster, August 31, 1782, *Notes*, 1, 55.

21. *Ibid.*, 41–6.

22. *New York Packet*, January 17, 31, February 7, 1782.

23. *Ibid.*, April 16, 1782; *Notes*, I, 42.

24. Noah Webster to John Canfield, January 6, 1783, *Letters*, 3–4.

25. *Ibid.*, 1–3, 5–7, for Webster's letters to the legislatures of Connecticut and New York.

26. *Bibliography*, 5–140, provides a complete listing of the editions of the speller along with an exhaustive description of details surrounding each new issue.

27. *A Grammatical Institute of the English Language . . . Part I* (Hartford, 1783), 4–5.

28. *Ibid.*, 1–3, 14.

29. Benjamin Franklin, *A Scheme for a New Alphabet and Reformed Mode of Spelling* (London, 1768); George P. Krapp, *The English Language in America* (2 vols., 1945), I, 329.

30. The most recent analysis of Rousseau's political thought, which emphasizes Rousseau's repudiation of political reforms that are not accompanied by changes in public attitudes and established customs, is Stephen Ellenburg's *Rousseau's Political Philosophy: An Interpretation from Within* (Ithaca, 1976).

31. *A Grammatical Institute . . . Part I*, 19–118; Barry Wadsworth, *Piaget's Theory of Cognitive Development* (New York, 1971), 101; Noah Webster, *A Collection of Papers on Political, Literary and Moral Subjects* (Boston, 1843), 307, for the clearest statement of Webster's pedagogy; Shoemaker, *Webster*, 60–69, 101, provides a good summary of the speller's format.

32. *Ibid.*, 11, for the comment on "favur" and the reference to Johnson's dictionary.

33. *Ibid.*, 12, 118–19.

34. Timothy Pickering to Mrs. Pickering, October 31, 1783, *Notes*, I, 96–7.

35. *Ibid.*, 64–5, 82, 84.

36. *Connecticut Courant,* January 12, 19, May 18, 25, 1784.

37. The exchange between Webster and "Dilworth's Ghost" is reprinted in *Letters,* 9–36.

38. *Notes,* I, 77–9, provides the diary entries during his trip; Noah Webster to Isaiah Thomas, February 23, 1784, reprinted in *Bibliography,* 142; Noah Webster to Hudson and Goodwin, July 10, 1784, Webster Papers, New York Public Library; Noah Webster to James Madison, July 5, 1784, *Letters,* 8–9.

39. *A Grammatical Institute of the English Language . . . Part II* (Hartford, 1784), preface. The various editions of the grammar are described in *Bibliography,* 141–60.

40. *A Grammatical Institute of the English Language . . . Part III* (Hartford, 1785), 5.

41. *Ibid.,* 94–113, 153–86.

42. *Ibid.,* 12, 23, 21.

43. *Ibid.,* 3–4; Shoemaker, *Webster,* 152, makes the comparison with the McGuffey readers.

44. Noah Webster to James Greenleaf, April 17, 1791, *Notes,* II, 419–20.

45. In his diary for January of 1785, Webster mentions that he was reading "Dr. Price's excellent remarks on the American Revolution." In February he reminds himself to "write politics." His *Sketches of American Policy* was finished on February 25, 1785, and given to the printers on the same day. *Notes,* I, 124.

46. Noah Webster, *Sketches of American Policy* (Hartford, 1785), 20–1.

47. *Ibid.,* 11–12, 13–18, 26–9. Webster's comments on the division of labor in manufacturing countries is lifted, almost word for word, from Adam Smith's *An Inquiry into the Wealth of Nations,* Book I, Chapter V.

48. *Ibid.,* 30–39, 3–5. Some of Webster's comments on political economy here foreshadow his later published views. He reviews the impact of commerce on European societies and claims that commerce is a "culprit" that creates an unequal division of property. In the United States, however, Webster argues that the economic inequality generated by commerce "is revolving from person to person and entitles the possessor to no pre-eminence in legislation. . . ." (18). He also recommends the abolition of slavery on capitalistic grounds: "Were the plantations leased for small rents or the fee of the soil vested in free men, who have the prospect of gain by their own labour, they would be better cultivated and yield more produce to their owners." (46)

49. *Notes,* I, 125–29, for his diary from March to May, 1785.

50. *Ibid.,* 132, 133, 145; Noah Webster to George Washington, July 18, 1785, *Letters,* 36–7.

51. *Ibid.,* 136, 142, 146.

52. *Ibid.,* 137–41; Noah Webster to Timothy Pickering, October 28, 1785, *Letters,* 38–9. See also Noah Webster to Benjamin Franklin, May 24, 1786, *Letters,* 50–1.

53. Noah Webster to George Washington, December 18, 1785, Noah Webster to Timothy Pickering, August 10, 1786, *Letters*, 41–2, 53–4.

54. Noah Webster, *Dissertations on the English Language* (Boston, 1789), viii, 20, 36.

55. *Ibid.*, ix, 41. Krapp, *The English Language in America*, I, 9, for the view that Webster's ideas demonstrated an awareness of some of the best scholarship of the day.

56. *Ibid.*, 397–99, 140–53, 11.

57. *Notes*, I, 149–67, for diary entries from February to October, 1786; Noah Webster to Hudson & Goodwin, March 22, 1786, *Letters*, 45.

58. Noah Webster to Benjamin Franklin, October 8, 1786, *Letters*, 55–6; *Notes*, I, 169–70.

59. *Freeman's Journal*, April 18, 25, 1787; Webster's letter is also reprinted in *Letters*, 59–62.

60. Noah Webster to Rebecca Greenleaf, June 20 and October 11, 1787, January 27 and February 10, 1788, *Letters*, 68–78.

61. Krapp, *The English Language in America*, I, ix, 328; Walter J. Ong, *The Presence of the Word* (New Haven, 1967); Harry S. Stout, "Religion, Communications, and the Ideological Origins of the American Revolution," *William and Mary Quarterly*, 3rd ser., XXIV (1977), 519–41, provides a fascinating analysis of the differences between oral and literary traditions in eighteenth-century America.

62. Jonathan Boucher, "Glossary of Archaic and Provincial Words," quoted in Daniel Boorstin, *The Americans: The Colonial Experience* (New York, 1958), 274. Boorstin's discussion of language in colonial America, *ibid.*, 267–90, is both an incisive and a brilliant investigation of American speech and writing, and I say this despite my reservations about the interpretive framework he imposes on American culture. Witherspoon's "The Druid" was initially published in the *Pennsylvania Journal and Weekly Advertiser*, May 9, 16, 23, 30, 1781. The Webster quotation is from his *Dissertations*, 36. See also William Eddis, *Letters from America . . . from 1769 to 1777* (London, 1792), 59–61, for additional remarks on the uniformity of English in colonial America. Krapp, *The English Language in America*, I, 3–67, and Mencken, *The American Language . . . Supplement I*, 1–20, discuss the travel literature and the initial appearance of American words and pronunciation.

63. *Notes*, I, 246, for diary entry from which the initial quotation is taken; for Webster's views of Adam Smith, see his essay "The Injustice, Absurdity, and Bad Policy of Laws Against Usury," *An American Selection of Lessons in Reading and Speaking* (Philadelphia, 1787), 304–16; *ibid.*, 85–92, for the selection from Franklin. J.G.A. Pocock, "Virtue and Commerce in the Eighteenth Century," *Journal of Interdisciplinary History* (1972–73), III, 119–34, analyzes the tension between the values associated with commerce or capitalism and the values associated with classical republicanism.

64. Pocock, *The Machiavellian Moment*, 462–552.

65. Douglass Adair, "Fame and the Founding Fathers," in Trevor Colbourn, ed., *Fame and the Founding Fathers: Essays by Douglass Adair*

(New York, 1974), 3–26; Edmund Morgan, *The Meaning of Independence: Adams, Washington and Jefferson* (Charlottesville, 1976); see also Peter Shaw, *The Character of John Adams* (Chapel Hill, 1976), Gerald Stourz, *Alexander Hamilton and the Idea of Republican Government* (Stanford, 1970), and Richard D. Brown, "Modernization and the Modern Personality in Early America," *Journal of Interdisciplinary History* (1971–72), II, 201–28.

66. The *American Magazine* ran from December 1787 to November 1788. It cost $2.50 a year or 25 cents a copy; see *Bibliography*, 396–97, for more information on individual issues; *Notes*, I, 208–48, provides the diary from 1787 through 1789; for Webster's correspondence with James Greenleaf in 1789, see *Letters*, 83–5, and *Notes*, II, 411–12, 417–18.

67. Noah Webster to Timothy Pickering, December 18, 1791, Webster Papers, New York Public Library; Noah Webster to James Greenleaf, February 1, 1789, *Letters*, 81–3; John Trumbull to Oliver Wolcott, December 9, 1789, *Notes*, I, 269. In 1787 Webster had revised the entire *Grammatical Institute* with an eye toward sales. This was the year the speller became *The American Spelling Book*, the reader became *An American Selection . . .*, and woodcuts were introduced to illustrate anecdotes. In 1789, however, Webster was pessimistic about the public response to his publications: "But an author's brats are doomed to be the sport of a mad world; I have treated others as I thought they deserved, and probably mine will fare as well." Noah Webster to Mason F. Cogswell, January 31, 1789, *Letters*, 81.

68. Noah Webster, *An Examination of the Leading Principles of the Federal Constitution* (Philadelphia, 1787), 43, 46, 47, 55.

69. Thomas Jefferson to James Madison, December 20, 1787, A. Koch and W. Peden, eds., *The Life and Selected Writings of Thomas Jefferson* (New York, 1944), 441. Webster repeated his view of property distribution several times between 1787 and 1790, most forcefully in *A Collection of Essays and Fugitiv Writings* (Boston, 1790), 326–27.

70. See also Alexander Hamilton as "The Continentalist," written in 1782, Harold Syrett, ed., *The Papers of Alexander Hamilton* (22 vols., New York, 1961–), III, 103; Stourz, *Hamilton*, 71–73; Wood, *The Creation of the American Republic*, 391–467, for the most comprehensive discussion of the debate about the reliability and durability of virtue during the 1780s.

71. Webster, *An American Selection*, 220–21; Webster, *A Collection of Essays*, 74. The entire essay, "Remarks on the Manners, Government, Laws, and Domestic Debt of America", deals with the question of national sovereignty and was published in *An American Selection*, 214–27, as well as *A Collection of Essays*, 81–118.

72. Although Webster tended to avoid discussions of the powers of different branches of government, by 1788 he had explicitly identified the legislatures, as opposed to the people-at-large, as the best arbiters of what he called "the collective sense of the state." *A Collection of Essays*, 45–71.

73. Webster, *A Collection of Essays*, 329–32, 85–86. For the analogy between personal and national development, see *ibid.*, 2–4.

74. Webster, *An American Selection*, 214–16, 218–19.

75. Webster, *Dissertations on the English Language*, 401–02.

76. Noah Webster to James Greenleaf, October 21, 1791, *Letters*, 103–05; Noah Webster to James Greenleaf, April 17, 1791, *Notes*, II, 419–20; James Greenleaf to Noah Webster, January 18, 1792, *ibid.*, 310.

77. *Notes*, I, 329–63, provides the diary from 1790 to 1792.

78. *The Prompter; or a Commentary on Common Sayings and Subjects . . .* (Hartford, 1791) sold well; it went through fifty editions during Webster's lifetime. In addition he published *Rudiments of English Grammar* (1790) and *The Little Reader's Assistant* (1790) in the hopes of making money. For the radical spelling proposals, see *Dissertations on the English Language*, 394–97, and *A Collection of Essays*, preface; the Stiles quotation is from Warfel, *Webster*, 203; Krapp, *The English Language in America*, 331–35, analyzes Webster's radical orthography. The account of Webster's finances is from Noah Webster to James Greenleaf, July 8, 1793, *Notes*, II, 426–27.

79. Noah Webster to Oliver Wolcott, October 10, 1793, *Letters*, 114–16; *Notes*, I, 438–43; *American Minerva*, December 9, 1793.

80. Richard Hofstadter, *The Idea of a Party System: The Rise of Legitimate Opposition in the United States, 1780–1840* (Berkeley, 1969).

81. Noah Webster to The Public, May 1, 1796, *Letters*, 134.

82. The best secondary accounts of the political history of the United States in the 1790s are John C. Miller, *The Federalist Era, 1789–1801* (New York, 1960); Joseph Charles, *The Origins of the American Party System* (New York, 1956); Richard Buel, *Securing the Revolution: Ideology in American Politics, 1789–1815* (Ithaca, 1972).

83. John R. Howe, "Republican Thought and the Political Violence of the 1790s," *American Quarterly*, XIX (1967), 147–65; the description of Washington is by Tom Paine and is quoted in *ibid.*, 149; Warfel, *Webster*, 234, offers a convenient summary of the slanders against Webster in the opposition press; Martin Smelser, "The Federalist Period as an Age of Passion," *American Quarterly*, X (1958), 391–419.

84. *American Minerva*, February 11, 1794; the newspaper went through several variations of its original name, which are described in *Bibliography*, 398–429; James Greenleaf to Noah Webster, February 9, 1795, *Notes*, I, 396; John Francis observation in *ibid.*, 378–9.

85. *American Minerva*, December 26, 1793; June 5, 1794; October 20, 21, 28, 30 and November 3, 4, 8, 15, 21, 24, 1794. Webster reviewed his reporting on the French Revolution in Noah Webster to The Public, March 4, 1797, *Letters*, 145–7; see also Noah Webster to C. F. Volney, July 10, 1796, *ibid.*, 136–38.

86. *American Minerva*, November 4, 1794.

87. Noah Webster to William Leete Stone, August 29, 1837, *Letters*, 504–5; see also Webster's *The Revolution in France Considered in Respect to its Progress and Effects* (New York, 1794).

88. Noah Webster to Oliver Wolcott, June 23, 1800, *Letters*, 217–18; Noah Webster to Rufus King, July 6, 1807, ibid., 277; Noah Webster to Timothy Pickering, December 8, 1796, *ibid.*, 143–4.

89. The quotations are from the *American Minerva*, July 7, 1797; Noah Webster to Rufus King, November 1, 1798, Letters, 185–6; Webster, *Miscellaneous Papers on Political and Commercial Subjects* (New York, 1802), 128. Webster's views on the Jay Treaty are in the *American Minerva*, July 18, 20, 22, 30 and August 1, 4, 5, 1795. Summations of his foreign-policy advice, in which he reiterates his belief in strict neutrality, are in *ibid.*, July 7 and August 2, 1797.

90. The remark about the navy is a recollection of Webster's reprinted in *Notes*, 1, 495; *Porcupine's Gazette*, December 15, 1797, January 31, August 3, 1798; Webster, *Miscellaneous Papers*, 124.

91. See the *American Minerva*, October 1797 through January 1798, for frequent articles on epidemics; Noah Webster to Benjamin Rush, December 2, 1797, Letters, 172; Noah Webster to William Currie, October 26 to December 20, 1797, ibid., 167; Noah Webster to Benjamin Rush, December 4, 1798, ibid., 194–6. Webster published *A Brief History of Epidemic and Pestilential Diseases* (Hartford, 1799) after his retirement. See also Aldred S. Warthen, "Noah Webster as Epidemiologist," *The Journal of the American Medical Association*, LXXX (1923), 755–64, and Martin S. Pernick, "Politics, Parties, and Pestilence: Epidemic Yellow Fever in Philadelphia and the Rise of the First Party System," *William and Mary Quarterly*, 3rd ser., XXIX (1972), 559–86.

92. Noah Webster to Timothy Pickering, April 3, 1798, *Notes*, 1, 434; Noah Webster to Timothy Pickering, July 17, 1798, Letters, 181–4; Noah Webster to Oliver Wolcott, October 13, 1801, *ibid.*, 239; *Notes*, 1, 485.

93. *A Grammatical Institute . . . Part III*, 21; Noah Webster to Benjamin Rush, September 11, 1801, Letters, 237; Noah Webster to Benjamin Rush, December 15, 1800, *ibid.*, 227–8.

94. Noah Webster to James Madison, February 20, 1809, Letters, 315–18; Noah Webster to John Jay, May 19, 1813, *ibid.*, 334–5, for motives behind the move to Amherst; Noah Webster to George Goodwin & Sons, November 20, 1815, *ibid.*, 337–9, for Webster's discussion of his finances and his effort to renegotiate the sale of the copyright for the speller.

95. Warfel, *Webster*, 287–323, 345–77, tells the story of Webster's work on the dictionary; Krapp, *The English Language in America*, 356–70, provides a balanced assessment of Webster's work. Webster believed that his greatest contribution was in the area of etymology, a belief that depended upon his conviction that all languages originated at a single source and that all contemporary languages contained vestiges of this primal language. He had converted to orthodox Congregationalism in 1808 and his belief in a single source for all languages represented, in part, his acceptance of the Biblical myth of the Tower of Babel. In 1833 he published a revised version of the King James Bible in which "offensive" or "obscene" words were expurgated. To the end of his life, he insisted that the revised version of the Bible was his most important work. Robert K. Leavitt, *Noah's Ark, New England Yankees, and the Endless Quest* (Springfield, Mass., 1947), provides the fullest account of the publication history of the Webster dictionaries.

96. *Port Folio* (August, 1801), 247; David Daggett, *Sun Beams May be Extracted from Cucumbers, but the Process is Tedius* (New Haven, 1799); John Pickering, *A Vocabulary or Collection of Words and Phrases...* (Boston, 1816); Webster's response to Pickering is reprinted in *Letters*, 341–94; the final quotation is taken from a pamphlet written by Leonard Chester in 1802, cited in Babbidge, ed., *On Being American*, 130. Federalist critics were reacting to work done for or publication of *A Compendius Dictionary of the English Language* (Hartford, 1806), a shorter dictionary that Webster compiled as a preliminary effort for the longer *magnum opus*. For additional criticism from Federalists, see the *Monthly Anthology* (December, 1807), 670–5, and *ibid.* (October, 1809), 246–64.

97. Webster would not have understood our contemporary use of the word "culture" to mean either the appreciation of excellence in the arts, letters, music, and theater or the sum total of the norms and folkways of a particular society. He defined "culture" as "the act of tilling and preparing the earth for crops; cultivation; the application of labor or other means of improvement...." See *An American Dictionary of the English Language* (2 vols., New York, 1828). The original edition of the dictionary is unpaginated. Subsequent references to definitions from this work may be found in alphabetical order.

98. See Richard M. Rollins, "Words as Social Control: Noah Webster and the Creation of the *American Dictionary*," *American Quarterly*, XXVIII (1976), 415–30, which appeared after this chapter had been written but in time to influence my revisions. My analysis of Webster's ideological motives agrees with Rollins's, except that Rollins argues that the dictionary represents Webster's repudiation of nationalism. I see it as a reinforcement of a backward-looking brand of nationalism.

EPILOGUE

1. The best book on the Federalists as critics of the emerging American society is Linda K. Kerber's *Federalists in Dissent: Imagery and Ideology in Jeffersonian America* (Ithaca, 1970); see also David Hackett Fischer, *The Revolution of American Conservatism: The Federalist Party in the Era of Jeffersonian Democracy* (New York, 1965); Lewis P. Simpson, ed., *The Federalist Literary Mind: Selections from the Monthly Anthology and Boston Review, 1803–1811* (Baton Rouge, 1962), is the best collection of documents.

2. *Monthly Anthology* (November, 1806), 579.

3. *Ibid.* (October, 1805), 531–32.

4. *Ibid.* (January, 1805), 15–16.

5. *Ibid.* (January, 1807), 27.

6. Alexis de Tocqueville, *Democracy in America*, Phillips Bradley, ed. (2 vols., New York, 1945), II, 54.

7. *Ibid.*, I, 326–27.

8. *Ibid.*, I, 14, 275.

9. *Ibid.*, II, 43.

10. *Ibid.*, II, 43–4.

11. *Ibid.*, II, 45.

12. *Ibid.*, I, 60.

13. *Ibid.*, I, 275.

14. *Ibid.*, II, 351–52.

15. The James observation is taken from F. O. Matthiessen, *American Renaissance: Art and Expression in the Age of Emerson and Whitman* (New York, 1941), 10.

16. The definitive modern biography is by Ralph L. Rusk, *The Life of Ralph Waldo Emerson* (New York, 1949). The secondary literature on Emerson is enormous. Of the many studies of his life and work, I found the following most helpful: Howard Mumford Jones, *Emerson Once More* (Cambridge, Mass., 1953); Regis Michaud, *Emerson, The Enraptured Yankee* (New York, 1936); Edward C. Wagenknecht, *Ralph Waldo Emerson: Portrait of a Balanced Soul* (New York, 1974); Stephen E. Whicher, *Freedom and Fate: An Inner Life of Ralph Waldo Emerson* (Philadelphia, 1953). For the journal of Emerson, see *The Journals and Miscellaneous Notebooks of Ralph Waldo Emerson* (12 vols., Cambridge, Mass., 1960–), which is being edited by a shifting board of scholars. For an abridged version of the journal entries, see Bliss Perry, ed., *The Heart of Emerson's Journals* (Boston, 1926).

17. Stephen Whicher, Robert Spiller, Wallace Williams, eds., *The Early Lectures of Ralph Waldo Emerson* (2 vols., Cambridge, Mass., 1964), II, 160.

18. *Ibid.*, II, 161.

19. *Ibid.*, II, 160–61.

20. Edward Waldo Emerson, ed., *The Complete Works of Ralph Waldo Emerson* (12 vols., Boston and New York, 1903–05), I, 114.

21. *Ibid.*, I, 185, 181.

22. *Ibid.*, I, 81.

23. *Ibid.*, I, 107.

24. *Ibid.*, I, 128.

25. Whicher, *et. al., Early Lectures*, II, 310.

26. *Ibid.*, II, 216.

27. *Ibid.*, II, 209.

28. *Ibid.*, II, 255.

29. *Ibid.*, II, 281.

30. *Ibid.*, II, 251.

31. The most concise interpretation of "modernization" as a process of "unhinging" is by Michael Zuckerman, "The Fabrication of Identity in Early America," *William and Mary Quarterly*, 3rd ser., XXXIV (1977), 183–212. Richard D. Brown, *Modernization: The Transformation of American Life* (New York, 1976) touches on this theme. Nancy Cott, The *Bonds of Womanhood: 'Woman's Sphere' in New England, 1780–1835* (New Haven, 1977), and Ann Douglas, *The Feminization of American Culture* (New

York, 1977), explore the segregation of women in the early nineteenth century. Edward N. Shorter, *The Making of the Modern Family* (New York, 1975), discusses the impact of industrialization on family structure. David Hackett Fischer, *Growing Old in America* (New York, 1978), analyzes the shifting attitudes toward youth and old age in a provocative book that makes a powerful case for the significance of the early nineteenth century. Daniel T. Rogers, *The Work Ethic in Industrial America, 1850–1920* (Chicago, 1978), offers an elegant treatment of the separation of work and play in the middle and late nineteenth century.

32. Entry in Emerson's Journal, October 17, 1840, Perry, ed., *The Heart of Emerson's Journals*, 157.

Index